South Florida
Folklife

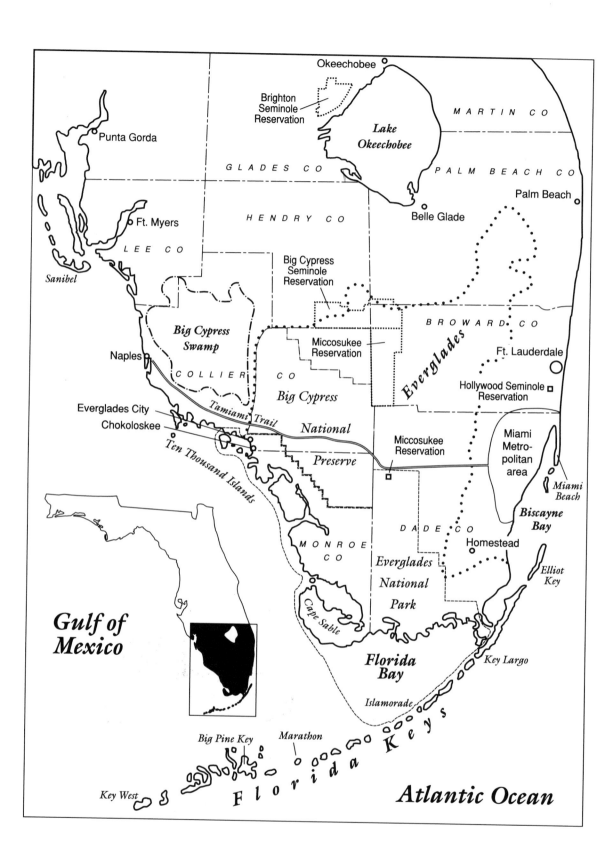

William Lynwood Montell, General Editor

FOLKLIFE IN THE SOUTH SERIES

South Florida Folklife

Tina Bucuvalas, Peggy A. Bulger,
and Stetson Kennedy

University Press of Mississippi   Jackson

Library of Congress Cataloging-in-Publication Data

Bucuvalas, Tina.

    South Florida folklife / Tina Bucuvalas, Peggy A. Bulger, and
Stetson Kennedy.

       p.   cm. — (Folklife in the South series)

    Includes bibliographical references and index.

    ISBN 0-87805-659-9 (alk. paper). — ISBN 0-87805-660-2 (pbk. :
alk. paper)

    1. Florida—Social life and customs. 2. Folklore—Florida.

I. Bulger, Peggy A. II. Kennedy, Stetson. III. Title. IV. Series.

F316.2.B78 1994

975.9'06—dc20

                            93-29928

                              CIP

British Library Cataloging-in-Publication data available

Contents

Folklife, a familiar concept in European scholarship for over a century, is the sum of a community's traditional forms of expression and behavior. It has claimed the attention of American folklorists since the 1950s. Each volume in the Folklife in the South Series focuses on the shared traditions that link people with their past and provide meaning and continuity for them in the present, and sets the traditions in the social contexts in which they flourish. Prepared by recognized scholars in the various academic disciplines, these volumes are designed to be read separately. Each contains a vivid description of the traditional cultural elements—ethnic and mainstream, rural and urban—of a geographic area that, in concert with other recognizable southern regions, lend a unique interpretation to the complex social structure of the South.

South Florida Folklife explores the area for the first time from a folklorist's perspective and firmly establishes it as a microcosm of the United States, an enticing example of the human diversity that characterizes life in this country. The three collaborating authors present South Florida folklife from the 1930s to the present in four parts: the Everglades and Gulf Coast, the Miami megalopolis, the Keys, and the seasonal residents and tourists. Together, these create a mosaic of contrasts. South Florida embraces extravagant wealth and heartbreaking poverty, constant evolution and solid tradition, tropical peace and devastating storms, settled generations and the newest Americans. Without question this is the most thorough treatment of the folklife of South Florida ever written. *South Florida Folklife* will surprise and delight readers who have previously viewed this portion of the United States as only a tourist mecca and new homeland for Northern and Midwestern retirees.

William Lynwood Montell
SERIES EDITOR

This book is the result of a collaborative effort by people who have been involved in folklife fieldwork in the South Florida peninsula that began in the 1930s. Peggy Bulger came to Florida as the state's first folk arts coordinator in 1976. During her twelve-year tenure working as a folklorist for the Florida Department of State, she documented and promoted South Florida's folk artists and tradition-bearers. Her contributions to this book are based upon state-sponsored fieldwork and research. Tina Bucuvalas first came to South Florida in 1985 as a folklife specialist for the Bureau of Florida Folklife Programs' survey of the Miami area. She continued her fieldwork and folklife programming as the Curator of Folklife for the Historical Museum of Southern Florida from 1986 to 1991, and is presently completing research for a work on Cuban American folklife in Miami. Stetson Kennedy, former director of the Florida Writers' Project Folklore Unit, started collecting folk culture materials there in 1936. The Keys chapter of this volume is based largely on his pioneering work. He is currently working on a comprehensive collection of Keys lore.

Research used in this volume was supported by the Bureau of Florida Folklife Programs, Florida Department of State, as well as by the Historical Museum of Southern Florida. We wish to thank the staff members of these institutions for their invaluable assistance, especially Dawn Hugh of the Historical Museum of Southern Florida for her aid and patience in locating images and photographs.

The authorship of the chapters in this book is as follows: Introduction, Peggy A. Bulger; Chapter 1, "The Seminole and Miccosukee," Tina Bucuvalas; Chapter 2, "The Crackers," Peggy A. Bulger; Chapter 3, "The Cubans," Tina Bucuvalas; Chapter 4, "The New Miami: Nicaraguans and Islanders," Tina Bucuvalas; Chapter 5, "Land and Sea: Traditional Skills and Occupations," Tina Bucuvalas; Chapter 6, "Florida's Tropical Islands," Stetson Kennedy and Peggy A. Bulger with additional material from Brent Cantrell and Tina Bucuvalas; Chapter 7, "Tourist Traditions," Peggy A. Bulger; Conclusion, Tina Bucuvalas; Bibliographical Essay, Tina Bucuvalas and Peggy A. Bulger.

Work on this long-distance collaboration was accomplished in the midst of job changes, moves to new residences, family crises, and other "real life" situations. We are indebted for their loving support and understanding to our families—Doug, Hannah and Meagan (Peggy), Charlie, Alexandra and Chloe (Tina), and Joyce Ann (Stetson), and are grateful for the steady and sure encouragement of Dr. Lynwood Montell, our editor and friend.

Most importantly, the generous cooperation and sharing of the people of South Florida made this volume possible. We wish especially to thank Hector Barroso, Brent Cantrell, Peter Douthit, Dorothy Downs, Michele Edelson, Debbie Fant, Edward "Huevo Frito" Frieberg, Lucille Francis Fuller, Olga Garay, Remko Jansonius, David Jumper, Liliane Nerette Louis, Alberto and Maggie Manrara, Gilbert, Henry, and Alice Ogden, Randy Reed, Mario Sanchez, Ethel Santiago, Laurie Kay Sommers, David Teems, Ana Maria Vasquez, and Patsy West.

In 1967, Gloria Jahoda wrote *The Other Florida*, in which she described the northern reaches of the state as a distinct region. Panhandle Florida was depicted as a place that was separate and different from the South Florida peninsula. It was Jahoda's contention that most Americans were familiar with South Florida, but knew little of this other part of the state. While it is true that a fantasy version of South Florida exists in the minds of most Americans—a stereotyped paradise of palm trees and flamingos—the real South Florida has remained as much a mystery as its neighboring region to the north. Most travel guides, memoirs, and other Floridiana give a portrait of South Florida that all but ignores the complex social and cultural gumbo that defines this unique place on the American landscape. The true flavor of this regional stew is found in its people.

Writing of South Florida in regional terms is somewhat arbitrary. In the past, scholars have used a broad brush to paint "the South" as a region, or they have focused more narrowly and written on "the Everglades" or "Lake Okeechobee" as cohesive areas. For the purposes of this book, the region is defined as the tropical portion of the Florida peninsula—the area that extends from Lake Okeechobee south to the Florida Keys.

Natural historians and environmentalists describe South Florida as part of Florida's vast "coastal lowlands." These lowlands were formed by marine deposits that created a sandy soil of low fertility along the coastlines. In contrast, inland from the coast, organic deposits that overlay the marine terraces have made the flatlands of Lake Okeechobee, Big Cypress, the upper Everglades, and the Redland rich and uniquely fertile. These natural features, among others, have shaped social and occupational life in the region.

More than in most places, the climate has had a profound impact upon the lives of South Floridians, from the first settlement to the present day. The lower peninsula of Florida is subtropical, being further south than the southern tip of California. There are wet, humid summers and dry, cool winters—all influenced by the waters of the Atlantic Ocean and the Gulf of Mexico, which moderate extremes of temperature. Since no point of land is more than sixty miles from seawater, maritime weather and other environmental considerations strongly affect the South

Florida peninsula. In addition, the dense tropical scrublands, isolated island hammocks, and vast swamp settings of the region have presented distinct challenges to settlers for generations.

The undisputed natural attractions of the lower Florida peninsula have amazed and excited human beings for over twenty centuries and continue to lure visitors and new residents to the region. However, it is the dynamic interaction between people and this tropical environment that has created a regional identity for South Florida. Unlike geographers who define a region in terms of natural features and environmental boundaries, folklorists take a humanistic approach to regionalism. In this study South Florida is defined in terms of its folklife—the traditional motivations, aspirations and meanings behind human activity and expressive culture. This portrait of South Florida will present the region through its rich heritage and vast human resources, focusing upon the interrelatedness of the peoples and the land.

Most regional boundaries are disputed, and certainly cultural divides are particularly hard to fix. The increased mobility of American citizens has created a state of ever-changing allegiances to place and ever-expanding links to widely scattered family and friends. To add to this complexity, all regions are part of national and international systems that resound with cultural connections. A region, therefore, is a dynamic system that is driven by the interaction of people in a particular location at a particular time.

Refining this definition, folklorist Richard Dorson wrote that a "folk region" is one that "lies in the mind and spirit as much as in physical boundaries." South Florida is a folk region with no obvious physical or political boundaries but with an identity derived from its tropical environment and the mind and spirit of the many peoples who have settled there.

This identity is perhaps best expressed in folklore, folklife and folk arts—i.e., the language, customs, beliefs, foodways, tales, crafts, and music of the folk groups who populate the peninsula. Each new group to join the population will expand the boundaries of an amorphous folk region. South Florida is truly a mosaic of folks—Seminole, Cracker, Conch, Cuban, Haitian, Miccosukee, Jamaican, Nicaraguan, and Yankee tourist—all of whom retain their integrity as distinct groups, but who add their creativity and folk heritage to this new culture called "South Florida."

Florida is both the oldest and newest frontier. The state was the first area of the United States to be occupied by Europeans, dating from the 1513 expedition of Juan Ponce de León. Ponce de León was met by native peoples who numbered over twenty-five thousand on the Florida peninsula, and these tribes had been preceded by peoples who had inhabited the land for more than ten thousand years. Despite these early habitations, South Florida has a recent cultural history and is one of the youngest regional entities in the nation. The original native tribes of Florida were lost soon after Spanish intrusion, while the early Spanish, English and French missionaries and explorers settled in the northern fringe of the state. It was not until the mid-nineteenth century that settlers came to the South Florida wilderness, affecting the environment and creating a land that quickly became rich in cultural diversity.

South Florida has been aptly called the "land of escape." The Seminole came to the Everglades to escape the terrible Trail of Tears, the African American came to escape slavery, the Cracker came to escape poverty and find new opportunity on the open range, and the Cubans came to find freedom. Today this tradition continues as generations of tourists escape the winter snows to "get away from it all" in the Florida sunshine, and new waves of immigrants from Haiti, Jamaica, the Dominican Republic, and South and Central America flee political and economic tyranny in their homelands.

South Florida's role as a haven for humanity has not only provided the region with a diversity of cultures, but has also been responsible for the extraordinarily rapid growth of the population. The traditional saying that "once you get Florida sand in your shoes, you will always return" seems to hold true in recent years. Between 1970 and 1980 Florida gained 3 million new residents, while during the same decade the northeast and mid-western states lost almost 6 million people, many of them headed for the perceived tropical paradise of South Florida. South Florida's population boom is due to many factors, including the development of highly intensive agribusiness, the return of African Americans to the South, the ever-increasing numbers of retirees seeking sunshine, and hundreds of thousands of immigrants from the Caribbean and the Americas.

Despite the rapid and enormous influx of new residents, there remain clearly defined folk cultures that thrive in the multicultural lowlands of South Florida. The stereotypical images of the region as a playground for tourists, a retirement colony for New Yorkers, or a hotbed of Cuban ex-patriots all contain kernels of truth, but they are broad generalizations.

There is no "typical" South Floridian, and each individual culture that is represented has enriched the landscape with new traditions and creative ideas. *South Florida Folklife* describes the distinctive features that bind the many cultural groups of South Florida together and outlines how each of these groups has contributed to the creation of a multicultural regional identity.

South Florida is a study in contrasts. From the vast, unpopulated grasslands of the Everglades to the urban skyscrapers of Miami, South Florida is both extravagantly wealthy and heartbreakingly poor, constantly evolving and solidly traditional, a land of tropical peace and devastating storms, a home to settled generations and the newest American citizens. In cultural terms, South Florida is a microcosm of the United States, a regional example of the human diversity that characterizes life in America.

Unlike other regions that are documented in the Folklife in the South Series, South Florida cannot claim a dominant culture. Rather, its essence is the heterogeneity of its people. This book explores the story of South Florida through the folklife of several of the most distinctive cultural communities that have converged on this narrow peninsula of land—the Seminole, Conch, Miccosukee, Cracker, African American, Cuban, and other Hispanic populations of the region. Although there are over seventy identifiable folk/ethnic groups making their home in tropical Florida, only a few populations can be explored in detail here.

In this study, South Florida folklife is presented in four parts: the Everglades and Gulf Coast; the Miami megapolis; the Keys; and seasonal residents and tourists. Together, the four divisions constitute one region, with many people sharing common land and resources.

Beginning with the Native American populations of the Seminole and Miccosukee, the Everglades is seen as a challenging environment that has shaped culture and society within the tribes. Following these early settlers, the Cracker brought Anglo and Celtic traditions to both the Everglades and Gulf Coast. Cracker culture has survived, thrived and evolved in the rural prairies of this tropical region.

Contrasting with the vast, unpopulated swamplands and open range of the inland is Miami, the urban heart of South Florida, and the heartbeat of this metropolis is the Cuban community. The rich mixture of Caribbean and Hispanic cultures that has left an indelible mark upon the Gold Coast is explored.

Further down the coast is the island of Key West, with its heritage of Conch and Cuban influences. Key West folklife is depicted as a happy marriage of African, Spanish, and British traditions on an island paradise.

Finally, we conclude with the folk culture of tourists. Both the lifeblood and bane of the permanent residents of South Florida, tourists have added their unique traditions to the patchwork of South Florida folklife. In addition, each folk group on the peninsula has been touched by the tourism industry, and regional culture has been reformulated in response to the demands of serving a visiting public.

South Florida is a folk region with a polyglot heritage and a lively, fast-paced history. *South Florida Folklife* presents the abundant variety of folk cultures that thrive in the Florida tropics yet have been little understood as part of a unified regional whole. What follows is a celebration of the many life stories and folk traditions that make South Florida unique.

PART ONE

The Everglades

The Seminole and Miccosukee

The native peoples referred to as Seminole and Miccosukee are among the few that organized after Europeans colonized the Americas. As a result of conflicts with Europeans, Americans, and their allies, fragments of many Native American groups from the areas that came to be known as Georgia, the Carolinas, and Alabama fled south. After they settled in what is now Florida, they were joined by survivors from local indigenous groups. In time they developed their own distinctive culture.

One of the hallmarks of Seminole and Miccosukee worldview is that they regard different aspects of life as parts of a larger whole rather than as separate entities. This philosophy permeates their traditional culture, daily life, and even the way they perceive themselves. For example, many prefer to be called Native Americans or indigenous peoples because those terms more closely approximate the expressions in their own languages. Moreover, some believe that the labels Seminole and Miccosukee divide people who are culturally united. In this book we will balance our use of appellations between the need for clarity when referring to politically distinct groups and the need to acknowledge a people's right to self-definition.

HISTORY

Origins

Prior to European intrusion, the most numerous among the Florida peoples were the Timucua and the Calusa. The Timucua were a settled, argicultural people whose territory extended from south Georgia to north Florida. The Calusa consisted of related towns or small tribal groups that ranged down the west coast from Timucuan territory into the Keys. Other indigenous tribes included the Apalachee, near present-day Tallahassee, and the Ais, Jeaga, and Tequesta along the lower east coast.

The Spanish sighted Florida in 1513 and launched exploratory expeditions throughout the early sixteenth century. They were interested in the peninsula only for its strategic importance in blocking British and French advances into their realms. Thus, they established a string of coastal forts staffed primarily by military and religious personnel. They gradually introduced a variety of cultural changes, largely without military force. Northern native peoples had frequent contact with the Spanish, English, and a short-lived French colony, but those in the south had little contact.

In the seventeenth century, staggering numbers of indigenous peoples died from European diseases or at the hands of Europeans and their allies. By the late nineteenth century, Florida's aboriginal peoples had all but disappeared due to disease, warfare, and enslavement. Thus, as the Seminole gradually moved down the peninsula during the eighteenth and nineteenth centuries, they encountered few indigenous inhabitants.

The core of the Seminole and Miccosukee came from about two dozen Creek towns that shared a similar culture in early seventeenth century Georgia and Alabama. The majority spoke Muskogee, which was also used as a lingua franca among the towns. A large minority spoke Hitchiti, a member of the same language family as Muskogee. By the early eighteenth century, the British began to refer to the western towns as Upper Creek and the eastern towns as Lower Creek.

After the English established Charleston in 1670, their influence among the indigenous population expanded rapidly. They supplied guns to the native peoples, and encouraged them to raid other groups to provide slaves for their plantations. Sometimes led by the English, the Creek and Yamasee attacked the Spanish missions, destroying the surrounding native towns and enslaving ten thousand to twelve thousand inhabitants.

By the early eighteenth century, many Lower Creek, Yamasee, and other native groups became disillusioned with the English. They migrated south to the Apalachee region near present-day Tallahassee, where they were joined by Apalachee and Timucua refugees. These early western proto-Seminole settlements were generally allied with the Spanish. By 1764 the more easterly Alachua region, near present-day Gainesville, was settled by pro-English Creek who had accompanied the English on raids there.

By the mid-eighteenth century, settlers used "Seminole" to designate the native peoples descended from a number of different southeastern tribes and earlier Florida peoples. The term came from the Muskogee *simanó-li*, and means "wild, runaway" in reference to animals or plants. The figurative meaning was closer to "emigrants" or "frontiersmen." The Creek probably borrowed the word from the Spanish *cimarrón*, or "runaway."

The early Seminole were hunters, traders, and warriors. As time went on they established agricultural villages and cultivated corn, potatoes, beans, squash, melons, tobacco, and orange groves. They also took advantage of the natural resources for fishing, frogging, and hunting. By the end of the eighteenth century, there were at least seven Seminole towns between northern and central Florida. The language of the majority was Hitchiti, but a large minority spoke Muskogee.

In 1763, Spain gave Florida to England in ransom for Cuba. During their brief tenure, the English granted land to numerous refugees from the American Revolutionary War and also incited the Seminole against the new stream of American settlers. Under pressure from the United States, Britain returned Florida to Spain in 1783. By that time, however, Spanish control over her New World colonies was in decline.

The composition of the Seminole changed as a result of the Creek War of 1813–14. The earlier immigrants had come from Lower Creek towns that had had substantial interchange with Europeans. After the Revolution, Americans began to settle the Upper Creek area, and the conservative, nativistic Upper Creek lashed out against them and the pro-American Creek. After Andrew Jackson's force of Georgians and Tennesseans defeated them, many fled to Florida. Though they spoke Muskogee rather than Hitchiti, these new immigrants readily merged with the others. Refugees from other northern tribes also continued to trickle in. After 1814, these new native groups banded together with the remnants of Florida's indigenous native peoples, runaway slaves, and renegade whites to form a single Seminole body about six thousand strong.

The Seminole Wars and Their Aftermath

In 1817, the United States government sent Andrew Jackson to Florida with two thousand Americans and Creek—ostensibly to recover runaway slaves. Jackson's true purpose was to retaliate for Seminole support of the English during the War of 1812 and subsequent raids into Georgia, and to claim Florida for the United States. As Jackson's army laid waste to Seminole and Black Seminole forts in the west and burned towns and fields in the Apalachee region, the people fled east and south. Jackson's actions constituted the First Seminole War (1817–18). With his success, Spain's position in Florida became untenable. It sold the territory to the United States in 1821.

After the war, the people moved toward a more definitive independence from their Creek forbears. They lived on farm and pasture land in central Florida, where they built log houses, raised horses and cattle, planted citrus groves, and owned both black and Native American slaves.

By 1823, about thirty-two Seminole towns ranged from northern Florida south to the edge of the Everglades and Big Cypress. The Seminole utilized the swamp areas only for gathering, hunting, and fishing. Although the dominant linguistic group was Hitchiti, they continued to employ Muskogee as a lingua franca throughout the eighteenth and nineteenth centuries.

As Florida's first territorial governor, Jackson instituted a policy to remove all native peoples to west of the Mississippi. When the Seminole refused, the Americans drove them out with the 1823 Treaty of Moultrie Creek. The treaty was motivated in part by white settlers' desire for Seminole land and in part by the government's interest in building a new, centrally located capital on a Seminole site. The Treaty of Moultrie Creek ordered the Seminole to give up all land except for a reservation in the south-central portion of the state. The Americans bribed a few minor chiefs to sign the paper, then evicted thousands from their homes. The Seminole could not resist United States pressure so soon after their defeat, so they unwillingly migrated further south.

Little more than a decade passed before whites once again clamored for ownership of Seminole land and the Black Seminole. The Second Seminole War (1835–42) was one of the longest, most brutal, and costly Indian wars in United States history. The Seminole evaded the Americans by fleeing into the isolated Everglades and the wildernesses of Big Cypress and Lake Okeechobee in the south. Under the leadership of Osceola they conducted a guerrilla war, and American forces found it virtually impossible to defeat them. Eventually, the Americans imprisoned Osceola when he attempted to negotiate under a flag of truce. By 1842, 4,420 of the estimated 6,000 Seminole surrendered or were captured.

During Jackson's presidency, Congress passed the Removal Act which rescinded "all the rights, privileges, immunities, and franchises held, claimed or enjoyed by those persons called Indians" and made it illegal for native peoples to live east of the Mississippi. The Americans duly marched their Seminole prisoners to Oklahoma's Indian Territory. Many died during the long, painful trek, which the Seminole and other native groups that were forced to make the journey call the Trail of Tears.

The Black Seminole deserve special attention. Beginning in the early nineteenth century, many African Americans in northern Florida adopted Seminole ways. They were primarily former slaves from Florida, Georgia, and South Carolina who had run away or had been captured or purchased by the Seminole. Under the Seminole most were free, though a few lived under a very mild form of slavery. The Black Seminole inhabited separate villages and fought under their own leaders, but recognized the authority of a local chief. They not only supported the

Negro Abraham, a
nineteenth-century black
Seminole leader
(Courtesy of the Historical
Association of Southern
Florida [HASF])

Seminole militarily, but also played pivotal roles as bilingual and
bicultural mediators during negotiations with the encroaching whites.

One American goal during the Second Seminole War was to
"recover" the Black Seminole, whom they considered runaway slaves.
The Black Seminole fought bravely against United States forces, but
resistance faded when their leader, John Horse, surrendered in 1838. The
army subsequently sent them to Indian Territory, where they had been
promised freedom. However, the federal government ruled that those
enslaved before the war would remain enslaved. Thus the army turned
over nearly three hundred Black Seminole to native peoples in the
territory who claimed them. The Oklahoma Creek kidnapped and sold

many others. In order to avoid slavery, some Black Seminole fled to Mexico.

The Third Seminole War (1855–58) was minor compared to the previous two. Trouble had been brewing for years, but war finally broke out when American troops destroyed crops owned by Seminole chief Billy Bowlegs. The Seminole fought the Florida militia and federal troops in the Big Cypress Swamp. Ultimately, American troops killed twenty Seminole and sent two hundred and forty to Oklahoma.

By the late nineteenth century, fewer than five hundred Seminole remained in the isolated wilderness areas of the Everglades and Big Cypress Swamp. Their territory extended from roughly sixty-five miles north of Lake Okeechobee to just south of Miami, and from present-day Davie in the east to Immokalee in the west. The people resided in several camps composed of extended families. Since their new land base did not support earlier agricultural and ranching subsistence patterns, they created a new way of life by relying on the abundant natural resources and small gardens.

In the 1870s, the Seminole resumed trading with white settlers. They exchanged bear and alligator hides, raccoon and panther furs, egret and other bird plumes for flour, beans, bacon and coffee, cloth, rifles and ammunition, and supplies for traditional arts. Some men began to work as seasonal laborers on nearby farms, but most Seminole believed that the government would attempt to eradicate them again.

The Twentieth Century

At the turn of the twentieth century, most Seminole still lived in isolation except for trade arrangements. However, the expanding white population changed their lives permanently. The Seminole gradually started to replace traditional artifacts such as baskets and pottery with manufactured ones, and came to regard guns, coffee, tobacco, and cloth as necessities. Their lives were further disrupted when, in 1905, the state government determined to drain the Everglades in order to bring drinking water to the coasts and increase arable land. The state cut a system of canals in the eastern and northern Everglades which unbalanced the ecosystem and depleted fish and game. After World War I, Seminole trade arrangements were upset by conservation laws that forbade the sale of plumes or alligator hides.

In 1911, the Bureau of Indian Affairs created the Big Cypress Reservation south of Lake Okeechobee and the Dania (now Hollywood) Reservation near Ft. Lauderdale in an attempt to solve the growing problems. Most Seminole were slow to move onto the reservations. However, with the South Florida real estate boom of the 1920s, the

burgeoning white communities built roads that encroached on Seminole territory. This forced many bands from their camps along the Miami River back into the Glades or onto the reservations where new folklife patterns began to emerge.

The Seminole eventually found that the tourists and settlers could provide a source of income. Seminole women began to make palmetto dolls for sale. Some men worked as guides, while others participated in seasonal occupations such as frogging, crop picking, and lumbering. Many found employment in seasonal Miami attractions such as Musa Isle and Coppinger's, which offered tourists a glimpse of traditional Seminole life.

After the Tamiami Trail connecting Miami in the east with Tampa in the west was completed in 1928, numerous native families set up camps along the road to facilitate travel and operated small tourist attractions. Unfortunately, the Trail further disturbed the ecology of the Everglades

Seminole group encountered while en route to camp at Chokoloskee, Shark River Area, August 1915 (Photo courtesy of the *Miami Herald*)

by cutting off the flow of water to areas south of the road. The road also made it easy for white sportsmen to visit the area in search of fish and game.

The 1930s were a difficult period for the Seminole. However, many were able to remain largely self-sufficient with assistance from occasional jobs in seasonal agriculture, the Civilian Conservation Corps, or highway road crews. The federal government created the Brighton Reservation near Lake Okeechobee in 1935. In addition, Florida designated 108,000 acres south of Big Cypress as a state reservation for hunting, fishing, or obtaining other natural resources.

Despite incursions by outsiders and a dwindling land base, the Seminole preserved a great deal of traditional life with little change until the 1940s. At that point, Muskogee-speaking missionaries from Oklahoma converted many Seminole. After World War II, the increasing number of roads and canals brought rapid changes in folklife ranging from economic patterns to housing, education, religious beliefs, marriage practices, and folk arts. In addition, more Seminole moved onto the reservations, which offered social services, schools, and cattle-raising programs.

By the 1950s, many of the people rejected use of the word *simanoli*, which had come to mean "wild" in both Mikasuki and Muskogee. They referred to themselves as *yá-tkitiscí* in Mikasuki and *isticá-ti* in Muskogee, which are general terms for Native Americans. Muskogee continued as the lingua franca among the Florida peoples and in their relations with non-natives until about 1920s. By the 1950s, conversations between speakers of the two languages usually took place in Mikasuki. Nevertheless, most curing songs and many personal names are still in Muskogee. The Hitchiti language has been called "Mikasuki" in English since about 1920, though the people use it only as a loan word from English. Despite language differences, most cultural traits are shared by Mikasuki- and Muskogee-speaking groups.

During the 1950s, the Seminole found their traditional ways severely disrupted by white expansion onto their land. Although they had never before had an overall political organization, they decided that a formal government would provide them with the educational, financial, and legal assistance they needed to protect themselves. The Seminole Tribe was officially recognized and granted a charter for limited self-government in 1957. Members could live on or off the three reservations under tribal jurisdiction: Hollywood, Brighton, and Big Cypress. Today, there are approximately 1,845 Seminole tribal members.

In 1976 the U.S. Indian Claims Commission agreed to pay the Seminole $42 million for the 30 million acres of land seized during the

Seminole Wars. This was granted in exchange for a promise to extinguish any further land claims. The government paid three-quarters of the money to the Oklahoma Seminole and the rest to the Florida Seminole.

Each reservation reflects a different level of acculturation. Located in the midst of mainstream communities which provide substantial opportunities for employment and entertainment, Hollywood is the most progressive. Most Muskogee-speakers reside in or near the Brighton Reservation, and they are also highly acculturated. Big Cypress residents are the most conservative among the Seminole, though the Miccosukee probably maintain more aspects of traditional life.

The community of camps along the Tamiami Trail did not join in the organization of the Seminole Tribe. As a group, they represented a more conservative and traditional branch. They eventually realized they had to establish their viability as a group in order to maintain their independence from the white world. The federal government recognized the Miccosukee Tribe as a distinct entity in 1962. Their reservation consists of an area about five miles long and five hundred yards wide along the Trail, as well as a part of the State Indian Reservation east of Big Cypress.

Today the Miccosukee number about five hundred. Most remain on the reservation and marry other Miccosukee or Seminole. Mikasuki is the first language for approximately 98 percent of tribal members, and 25 percent are monolingual in Mikasuki. The Miccosukee who live on the reservation today have maintained their preferences for nature and freedom over materialism. When the government offered compensation for their seized lands, the Miccosukee and the traditionalists refused it. From their perspective, the settlement meant selling out their right to the land from which their lives had sprung and for which they had sacrificed everything.

In addition to members of the Seminole and Miccosukee tribes, there are about 250 individuals who belong to neither tribe. These traditionalists believe the others have sold out to American culture. Most live along the Tamiami Trail or on the west coast between Naples and Bradenton. A number of Seminole and Miccosukee tribal members also live off the reservation and participate in both native and mainstream cultures. Stephen Tiger, son of former Miccosukee chairperson Buffalo Tiger and a member of the Miccosukee rock band Tiger-Tiger, reflects, "We can't live totally traditionally as in the old days. There's not enough water to live in the Everglades. Not enough game. So we have to get a non-Indian education. At the same time we try to hold on to the same ways as much as possible. We walk a tightrope."

SOCIAL STRUCTURE

Clan and Family

Traditionally, the basic unit of Seminole society has been the clan. Among southeastern peoples clan membership is derived from the mother. The people believe that at the time of creation, the Creator made sixteen different clans in order to keep human society intact and the body strong. The Creator showed no favoritism among clans, but set out basic rules for them to follow. One important rule is that clan members are not allowed to marry others in the same clan.

Most clans are named for natural phenomena. Nevertheless, they are not totemic in the sense that members claim descent from an animal, nor are they forbidden to kill or eat the animal for which their clan is named. The Snake and Big Town clans originated more recently than other clans. The first members of the Snake clan were descendants of black-Seminole intermarriage, whereas the Big Town clan was created to include non-Indian women in the system. Respected Seminole medicine man Josie Billie recounted the following origin myth: "When the Seminoles fought at St. Augustine, they found two white girls wandering in the woods, lost, tired, and hungry. They might have been Spaniards. Some of the tribe wanted to kill them, but the chief said not to, since they were women, and could be kept and forced to work. Eventually they married Indian men. As these women were not Seminole, they belonged to no clan. Thus their children had no clan relations."

In the past, clans maintained great social control over their members, often functioning as judicial entities. They also took on social responsibilities, such as helping to feed and clothe the children from broken homes. Today, clans no longer have official leaders nor do they conduct separate ritual or social events. Although most Seminole carry substantially the same cultural knowledge, members of each clan possess slightly different bodies of tradition concerning such areas as childraising, household maintenance, or folktales.

Within the past century several clans have disappeared due to death, emigration, or warfare. In combination with the population depletion stemming from the Seminole Wars, this sometimes makes it difficult for young people to find marriage partners outside their clan. As a result, there have been increasing numbers of intraclan marriages, which are tolerated but not widely approved. In addition, many have married people of other races, the result often being weakened clan affiliations. For example, at the Hollywood Reservation approximately 10 percent do not have a clan affiliation because the mother is not Seminole. Nonnative parents and their children are accepted by the community and allowed to live on the reservation.

While the clan continues to be a major organizing principle of Seminole and Miccosukee society, the nuclear or sometimes the extended matrilineal family seem to have replaced the clan as the basic unit. A typical extended matrilineal family might include a couple, unmarried daughters and sons, married daughters and husbands, grandchildren, and/or aged or dependent members of the wife's clan. The family is of central importance to the people, with the strongest bonds existing between mothers and children.

Government

In the past, the Seminole and Miccosukee lived according to traditional law and social organization. Although it is difficult to discern their early social history, there is evidence that eighteenth- and nineteenth-century leaders were chosen on the basis of ability. More recently, the broadest form of government consisted of a council of clan elders that played a judicial and legislative role during the Green Corn Dance. Otherwise, the Seminole held land in common and made decisions as small residential groups.

Current tribal organization allows the Seminole and Miccosukee to govern themselves except for certain areas of federal guardianship. The Seminole governing body, a five-member tribal council, is elected by secret ballot and majority vote. Its responsibilities include negotiating with local, state, and federal governments, managing tribal lands, making and enforcing ordinances, employing legal counsel for the tribe, and otherwise acting as a governing and advisory body. The tribal council and state of Florida have agreed to state and county jurisdiction over civil and criminal conflicts on the reservations, though in actual practice most lesser offenses are dealt with internally.

The Seminole Tribe is divided into political and business branches. The latter, the Seminole Tribe of Florida, Inc., controls the economic development of the tribe and operates the Seminole Arts and Crafts Center, Okalee Indian Village, and Bingo Hall at the Hollywood Reservation. These tourist attractions employ tribal members as managers, guides, salespeople, and demonstrators. The tribe also earns income through marketing tax-free cigarettes. The Big Cypress and Brighton reservations run successful cattle-raising programs, and the Seminole Land Development Enterprise operates a program to improve pasturage. In addition, the corporation offers technical assistance and low-interest loans to tribal members.

Each reservation has a tribal center with administrative, judicial, and educational branches. Educational centers usually offer classes in traditional arts such as patchwork, basketry, beadwork, or doll making. Although many still learn traditional arts within their families, others now learn the skills through this more formal arrangement.

The Miccosukee General Council is responsible for both government and economic development. The tribe runs elementary through senior high schools, a library, restaurant, public safety department, and cultural center. The latter is a large outdoor attraction consisting of a museum and a traditional camp with demonstrations of native arts. They also have a health clinic which provides traditional or western medicine. In order to increase tribal funds, the Miccosukee operate airboat rides and build chickees (traditional thatched, open-sided houses) for outsiders.

The Miccosukee legal system employs reservation police trained in local, state, federal and traditional laws. Their court meets monthly to try misdemeanors; state or federal courts handle felonies. Each case is presided over by both a traditional and a contemporary judge, who decide together whether the case should be treated in accord with Miccosukee traditional law, American contemporary law, or a combination of the two. Since the judges know most tribal members, the atmosphere is friendly and informal. Most defendants plead guilty. Miccosukees have suggested two converging reasons for this phenomenon. First, everyone in the small community knows what the defendant has done. Second, the Miccosukee and Seminole strongly condemn lying, so they tend to be more honest than mainstream Americans.

Despite the overlay of a modern political structure, the Seminole and Miccosukee continue to act politically in traditional ways. For example, leaders consider themselves as voices of the people or mediators with outside agencies rather than as political instigators. They recognize that their authority depends on the cooperation of tribal members, which may be withheld if they cease to serve their constituents. Moreover, the Seminole and Miccosukee still prefer to act as individuals rather than as large nonfamilial groups.

Religion

Seminole and Miccosukee religion is based on that of the indigenous southeastern peoples. It is difficult to discern more than a few precontact concepts, but it is known that they believed that the world was flat and that the stars, moon, and sun were struck on the overarching sky. The southeastern peoples associated names and stories with some constellations. They also believed that spirits lived on the sun and moon and that the galaxy was the spirits' road.

Over the long period of contact, many aspects of the indigenous religion have become permeated by Christian beliefs. For example, in the 1960s anthropologist Merwyn Garbarino collected the following origin myth from an elderly non-Christian medicine man. It reveals a synthesis of Seminole and Christian mythology:

Fishakikomechi, the Creator, made the world. Before that there was just water. Then he put animals and plants on earth and made a man he called Adam. Adam was the only person and he got lonely. So the Creator made a woman and called her Eve. There was a plant that they could not eat, but a snake told them it was all right to eat it. Eve gave it to the man, and he ate it, and then they knew they were naked, so they hid. They made clothes from leaves, and eventually they had children of all different colors. That is why there are so many different people in the world.

But later there was too much drinking and too many wives, so Noah built a boat and took animals and people away with him. Water came over the land and the other people were drowned. The people on the boat went back to the land when the water went down and had lots of children.

Jesus came and preached to them, but some people hated him and killed him. He arose and went to his followers and they had a feast with wine. Jesus said that since people had killed him, he was not going to live on the earth anymore, but first he taught people how to grow corn, and that is how the people came to have corn.

Currently most Seminole and Miccosukee hold both native and Christian beliefs. Since they do not make a distinction between the two systems, they have little conflict holding beliefs from both. Educator David Jumper from the Hollywood Reservation discloses that personal accountability to the Creator is often considered more important than adherence to a denomination. He estimates that perhaps half of those who profess Christianity still attend the Green Corn ceremonies.

Green Corn Dance   The Green Corn Dance is the most sacred event in Seminole and Miccosukee religion. This ritual cycle of purification and thanksgiving is derived from an ancient eastern woodlands tradition practiced by the Creek. The event was held annually for four to eight days at the time of the ripening of the young or "green" corn. Although observances varied among groups, there were many stable elements. Everyone in the band attended the ceremony, which took place in a ritually prepared area under the auspices of civil and religious authorities.

Until the Seminole Wars, Seminole Green Corn ceremonies appear to have followed Creek practices. Afterwards, observances focused on the display of medicine bundles containing sacred items. The medicine men who cared for the bundles officiated at the annual observance and displayed objects from the bundle in order to ensure the tribe's well-being in the coming year. By the end of the Second Seminole War, it is likely that each band of Seminoles had its own medicine bundle, which became the focus of the group's spiritual life.

The Seminole and Miccosukee believe that the medicine bundles were given to them by the Creator in order to provide for their well-being. In response to new situations, the Creator may reach down during the last night of the Green Corn Dance and place a new medicine in the bundle. The bundles consist of many different objects each wrapped individually in a small piece of deerskin and tied with a leather thong, then bound together in another piece of deerskin. The medicine is alive and has the power to do great good or evil, depending on how it is handled. Thus it is conscientiously cared for by a medicine man. The people believe that if they did not hold the Green Corn Dance, the medicine would die and the world itself would end.

Until formal tribal organization, the largest political units were associated with the Green Corn Dance. Each group had a medicine bundle, and every individual belonged to a bundle. This meant that he or she attended the dance and came under the judicial and political jurisdiction of the councils. Individuals could also visit the observances of other groups.

Currently there are six bundles: one among the Muskogee-speakers and the others among the Mikasuki-speakers. There is no longer a separate Green Corn Dance for each bundle. Instead, several medicine men may organize a cooperative observance. A single medicine man also may be responsible for more than one bundle. There now appear to be three regularly held Green Corn dances—one near Lake Okeechobee and two near the Tamiami Trail.

The Green Corn Dance consists of a sequence of events that unfold over four to seven days. The date varies but always coincides with the ripening of the corn between late April and early July. A medicine man and his assistant select a date a month or two in advance. The dance is held in a wilderness area some distance from settlements. The focal point is a central circular dance ground, which itself centers around a fire built on a raised mound. A ball pole stands near the eastern edge of the circle. On the western border is the Big House, an open-sided arbor covered with palm thatch. Each clan builds a camp in the circle around the dance ground.

Participants gather over several days preceding the dance. Dancing and stickball games sometimes begin the day or two before the event.

The traditional ball game is derived from games played by the indigenous southeastern peoples. Archaeological evidence suggests that this single-pole game probably originated with the mound peoples around 900 A.D., and LeMoyne described a similar game played by the Timucua in 1565. Archaeologist Brent Weisman believes that stickball is an important cultural element for the Seminole and Miccosukee because it provides a model of appropriate behavior towards others. The people play stickball not only during the Green Corn Dance but also at secular events.

Stickball games pit boys and young men against girls and young women. The ball is thrown into the air, is caught by one player and thrown to another, and is then in play. Males use wooden rackets with nets to hit the deerskin ball, while females use their hands. The goal is to hit the ball pole within a designated range. The ball pole is a pine sapling twenty to twenty-five feet tall, trimmed of branches and decorated at the top. The people square and smooth the pole approximately four to five feet from the ground, then record scores on the flat sides.

At dawn on each day of the Green Corn Dance, the medicine man bathes ceremonially. During the first day participants prepare the dance

Leroy Osceola prepares equipment for stickball. (Photo by Dianne Levenshon/Courtesy of HASF)

ground, then play stickball in the afternoon. After the medicine man's two assistants sweep the dance circle and light the fire at nightfall, the people perform animal and crazy dances for hours before retiring.

The second day, Feast Day, prepares men for the ritual fast. After a stickball game in the afternoon, participants dance and feast from dusk until midnight. They do not consume corn, since one purpose of the Green Corn Dance is to enable men to eat the first corn of the harvest. Men begin their fast at midnight.

The third and most important day is Court or Fasting Day. In the morning, the medicine man and his assistants bring the medicine bundle to the dance grounds and examine it. Afterwards, they make sacred black, or emetic, drinks to cleanse and purify the body. Young boys or men who must leave early receive ritual scratches to purify the blood and ensure health. Then the men drink the sacred beverages, rub them on their bodies, and retire to vomit in private.

At midday the men gather in the Big House for the annual court or council, during which they discuss group problems, make plans, and mete out punishment for serious crimes committed within the last year. In the afternoon, older boys and some men may be ritually scratched and break their fast. Then the people play stickball and sometimes perform the Buffalo Dance. At nightfall, they light the fire with flint from the medicine bundle and the medicine man ceremonially lays out the bundle's contents. During the night, boys receive adult names chosen by clan elders or medicine men from among those of the dead.

Dancing continues until dawn, when the women prepare food to end the fast. Meanwhile, the medicine man again examines the medicine bundle contents, rewraps them, and hides the bundle in the wilderness. The remaining men receive scratches on their limbs or torsos. Afterwards, young men gather in a small sweatbath to take a steam treatment believed to prevent the antisocial behavior or "craziness" to which they are susceptible. They subsequently bathe and return to the Big House to await the medicine man. Upon his return, there is a feast which includes corn from the new harvest. The people then leave for home.

The Green Corn Dance fulfills a variety of important functions: it permits males to eat the new corn without becoming sick; it fulfills essential political and judicial functions during Court Day; and the annual reexamination of the medicine bundle ensures its potency. Overall, the dance provides for the general well-being and health of the people during the new year.

LIFE CYCLE

In the past, midwives delivered babies, and the infant and mother lived in a separate chickee for the first four months. Today Seminole and Miccosukee children are generally born in hospitals and few women live in separate chickees. As in the past, however, a female medicine woman sings special songs to strengthen the mother and child after birth. The baby is cradled in a white cloth hammock hung from the rafters. Mothers often croon simple lullabies consisting of "sleep, baby, sleep" until the child falls asleep.

Seminole and Miccosukee babies are given an English first name along with the father's last name for legal purposes. In addition, infants may receive a native name, which the family uses but which does not appear on the birth certificate. An elderly person traditionally suggests these names, and the mother chooses one on the fourth day following birth.

Girls' ears are pierced shortly after birth. Newborns are often dressed in solid light colors, such as white or yellow. After four moons have passed, the babies are given a haircut and their nails are trimmed. These are preserved and presented to the child when he or she is grown, though the reason for this practice has been forgotten. After the haircut, the mother and child take a ritual cold-water bath and parents can renew marital relations. Babies may also wear clothes with prints at this time.

Mothers care for their children unless they work outside the home, in which case grandparents or older children may help with the young ones. Older children attend schools on the reservation at Tamiami and Big Cypress, while those at Brighton and Hollywood go to public schools. Children also attend summer programs on the reservation that mix academics, information about both mainstream and indigenous cultures, and recreational activities. Increasing numbers attend college, but few graduates return to any reservations except Hollywood.

The Seminole and Miccosukee consider it important to communicate traditional values and information to the younger generation. As medicine woman Susie Billie notes, "What you learn as wife and mother you must pass on to your children." Children, especially girls, often learn traditional ways by helping around the house when they are young. Little boys begin to learn hunting techniques when they are old enough to shoot. Today there is less such traditional training since children attend preschool or school at an early age.

In the past, there were puberty ceremonies for both sexes. Girls were isolated in special chickees during the first menstruation. Today there is no isolation, but some still observe restrictions against cooking for or eating with men. Boys who are nearly twelve years old may be initiated at the Green Corn Dance and receive a new name.

Young people often marry early. Contemporary Seminole and Miccosukee marriages are usually celebrated with civil or religious ceremonies. Another form of marriage mirrors the traditional arrangement wherein a couple that lives together considers themselves married. This is becoming less frequent since formal marriage facilitates a wide variety of financial and legal matters. Divorce has historically been easy and frequent. In such cases, children most often stay with the mother.

Most married couples hope for children. If they cannot have any or if their children are grown, they may follow the Native American practice of fostering or adopting children. For example, grandparents often raise one or more grandchildren, or childless couples may raise a young relative from a large family.

Many customs surrounding death and burial have been subsumed by Christian traditions. In the past, mourners transported the body to the wilderness on the fourth day following death. They broke personal belongings and placed them by the body, covered the body with logs, and maintained a fire at the head of the grave for four days and nights. A member of his or her own sex washed the widow or widower in a pond. Women dressed in black, removed necklaces, wore their hair in a single braid, and sustained mourning for between two and four years. Men did not cut their hair for four months and observed a short period of mourning. The bereaved behaved solemnly while in mourning.

Today, family members and mourners wear black clothing to funerals held at reservation churches. A Native American or white preacher may officiate, and those close to the deceased may offer fond memories. Afterwards there is often a large meal in a chickee outside the church. Mourners usually bury the deceased in a nearby cemetery.

FOLK ARTS

The Seminole created beautiful clothing, basketry, beadwork, and silverwork, and adopted many new forms, motifs, and materials during the eighteenth and nineteenth centuries. In the late twentieth century, folk arts still play an important role in Seminole and Miccosukee life. However, many arts now fulfill decorative, symbolic, or economic functions rather than utilitarian ones. Others have changed greatly from early forms. The tribes actively promote continuation of many traditional arts through demonstrations at their tourist centers and villages. Artists learn their skills from relatives or through apprenticeships or classes offered in tribal schools or cultural centers.

Many Seminole and Miccosukee earn income through traditional arts made for tourists. Women are the most numerous folk artists, though some men support themselves by building chickees, carving, or, less frequently, sewing. For many women, the work is simply an extension of ordinary family duties such as making traditional clothes.

To the Seminole and Miccosukee, traditional arts incorporate a wide range of skills and beliefs. As Ethel Santiago explains, "Just about everything is blending together. You must know how to pick your materials and how to prepare it in order to do arts and crafts." Unfortunately, many traditional artists now suffer from limitations imposed by conservation laws to correct ecological abuses by the white population and from the effect of the abuses themselves. David Jumper notes that, "We are restricted by the federal government from getting cypress and things like that. So we are limiting various things. And I think people need to understand that they are endangering the Native American people, their existence, by doing that."

Foodways

The Seminole and Miccosukee perceive foodways as closely allied with traditional concepts about women and their lives. Jeannette Cypress interprets for an elderly medicine woman:

Susie Billie is saying that a woman's place is by the fire. It's up to each woman to control her own life and carry out the cooking. It is her place to see that the meat is prepared for drying, and if it's corn she should know how to prepare that. She says when a woman grows old like she is today, with great-great-grandchildren, it is her place to have a home and to have a fire going. A Seminole woman must never stop teaching what she has learned in childhood so that she will know how to continue to be a Seminole.

The Seminole and Miccosukee base their foodways on the general diet of the southeastern peoples, which they supplement with the wild foods of South Florida and with foods grown in their gardens. Traditionally, Seminole men fished and hunted for animals such as turkey, deer, alligator, or gopher turtle. The women stewed meat and fish, and completed meals with frybread, coffee, *sofkee*, and tropical fruits. Until recent decades, they cooked most foods over an open fire of long logs carefully arranged like spokes of a wheel that did not meet in the center.

When they lived in camps, the Seminole and Miccosukee usually ate a morning meal before beginning work. During the day, they left a pot of stew on the fire so that family members or visitors could partake when they became hungry. The evening meal was a relaxed social event, often followed by storytelling.

Today, most Seminole and Miccosukee purchase their food at grocery stores and eat a diet similar to that eaten by non-Indians. However, they also prepare a number of traditional foods. Corn has always been a particularly important food for the people. Fresh corn is eaten boiled or roasted. Some women still grind dried corn with mortars and pestles made from hollowed cypress logs and large wooden sticks, then shake the ground corn through a palmetto sifting basket before use in a variety of dishes. The corn beverage sofkee is one of their most basic traditional foods. Like other corn-based drinks found among Native American groups in the United States and Mexico, sofkee is made by boiling corn and water into a thin porridge. Many drink it warm or cold with meals, sometimes adding pumpkin or tomatoes for flavor. Men used to carve long-handled sofkee spoons to serve the beverage.

Swamp cabbage is the heart of the sabal palmetto bud, also called heart of palm. The bud is the top portion of the tree, and the people obtain it by slitting a stalk lengthwise, then removing one layer at a time. The Seminole and Miccosukee eat it raw, boiled, or sauteed. Raw swamp cabbage tastes like celery.

Frybread is made by many Native American groups as an accompaniment to meals, or as a sort of large tortilla in which to wrap or on which to heap other foods. The Seminole and Miccosukee make frybread by combining flour, baking powder, salt, shortening, and sometimes pumpkin, then forming the dough into a sort of thick tortilla and frying it.

Baskets

The Seminole and Miccosukee make two types of baskets, each of which fulfills different functions and requires different materials and construction techniques. Derived from southeastern traditions, the woven basket is the original type. Although the Seminole made early woven baskets from cane, palmetto stems were easier to gather, and their use eventually surpassed cane.

In the past, all married Seminole women knew how to weave the square, shallow grain sifter and collecting baskets needed for everyday use. Ethel Santiago explains that the grain sifter "was useful for gathering big peas or vegetables from the garden and some had little holes, and then when you grind your corn you shake it and get the best part. That's what it was used for." The Seminole also wove pack baskets for transportation of goods, but these were quickly supplanted by manufactured items.

Since modern plastic or metal household goods now meet everyday needs, only a few older women still know how to weave palmetto baskets; however, traditional homes may display them in a decorative manner.

Today the coiled decorative basket, a form derived from African American basketry traditions, is the most common type made by the Seminole and Miccosukee. Judy Bill Osceola says that it was adopted specifically for the tourist trade, that "it wasn't used in everyday life. It was just a matter of people making it to make a little bit of money. That's how it was started. Not for any use, the other one was for everyday use." Gradually, coiled basketry has become traditional among the Miccosukee and Seminole. Ethel Santiago remembers, "I learned it, how to make baskets from my mother and my step-grandmother."

Before starting a basket, the artist gathers her materials. Santiago explains that sweetgrass is best harvested in summer:

Start in late spring, till . . . late September. But when it goes into October they will start getting spots and brown. June and July and August and September are the best times because they grow long and green.

You go to a certain area. You just don't pull everything right there. You pick 'em. That's why it takes so long. You probably have to go all day to get a whole bunch of grass, if you want any.

Then you bring it back and you wash it clean. Then you dry it, let's say, six or seven hours a day till about four or five days, then you can tell when it's ready because the grass be kind of light.

When the materials are ready, the artist coils bundles of grass into a spiral and stitches them together onto a round palmetto fiber base. People used to make the thread from a local plant, but today they use colored embroidery or crochet thread pulled through beeswax to prevent tangling. Some baskets have lids, though Santiago recalls, "I was told if you are young and if you are not married or even if you're married and have children that you should never make a basket with a top on, because they say you are closing it, just like closing a coffin."

Folk Architecture

Until recent decades, most Seminole and Miccosukee lived in camps built on hammocks in the Everglades and surrounding areas. The camp, which refers to both the residential site and the members of the household on that site, constituted the basic economic unit in society. The camp size ranged from a single individual to extended families or clan groups. In an extended family camp, each nuclear family had its own sleeping chickees but shared other structures, such as the cooking chickee, as well as the garden. As children married, they simply built another sleeping chickee to accommodate the new family.

The chickee is a traditional structure unique to Florida. The Seminole developed the chickee when the Seminole Wars and the migration to South Florida made it impractical for them to build more permanent dwellings. Two men can build a chickee within a few days, and a well-made structure will endure ten to twenty years. Roofs must be recovered about every five years.

The basic chickee is a rectangular pole shed, though circular and square chickees also exist. Four posts set into the ground support a rafter system that is covered with palm thatch. Many chickee roofs have an overhang on three sides that increases the covered area. The Seminole and Miccosukee construct the chickee from local materials: cypress for posts and rafters, cabbage palm or palmetto fronds for thatch. Men cut large cypress logs for the frame and smaller poles for the roof, allow them to dry for several days, and strip the bark. Meanwhile, they gather fronds for the thatch. Starting at the bottom, the men nail or tie the palm fronds close together in order to make the roof strong and impermeable. They sometimes add extra cypress poles or tar paper on top to keep the roof in place.

Admirably adapted to the hot, humid climate of South Florida, the chickees' open sides allow for maximum exposure to cooling breezes. Chickee floors are usually packed dirt. During hurricane season, a chickee that blows over is easily resurrected the next day. Today, many enclose chickees with palm leaves, boards, or paneling to create a more protected space. They build permanent furnishings such as platforms and counters on small posts sunk in the ground. This allows for the seasonal rise of water and discourages snakes. Families traditionally built several chickees in a cluster, each intended for a different purpose. A cooking chickee was at the center, with sleeping, dining, and working chickees creating a circle around it. Chickee sizes and designs vary according to the intended use. For example, a recreational chickee may be twenty by eight feet, one for dining fifteen by thirty feet, and a sleeping chickee may measure ten by sixteen feet.

In the sleeping chickee, the sleeping platform occupies most of the area and provides a clean, dry space two or three feet above ground. People hang clothes, insect netting, or hammocks for babies from roofing braces and beams and also lay boards across them to form storage lofts for bedding. The cooking chickee features a central open fire. It has an extended roof and low eaves to allow smoke to escape and to afford protection from the elements. Shelves, counters, and cabinets built along the low side eaves facilitate cooking and provide storage for utensils. The dining chickee is equipped with a long table and benches, and the work chickee has shelves, cabinets, and sometimes a counter.

Great changes have taken place in Seminole and Miccosukee housing in the last half century. Today, few live in chickees and fewer still in isolated camps. Over time, camps have grown into small towns. Moreover, modern housing has made it difficult to accommodate large extended families. Although many men still build chickees, the structures are used primarily as outbuildings for work, recreation, or storage or as second homes for vacation retreats. Construction techniques have also changed as nails have replaced pegs and tying, and many modern chickees have electricity.

In the past, men knew how to build a chickee by the time they married. Today, some young men still learn the skill by helping older male relatives. With a growing demand for recreational chickees by non-Indians, a number of Seminole and Miccosukee have established successful chickee contracting businesses. Since some designs requested by outsiders are Hawaiian or Polynesian, native builders have expanded their repertoires. Due to government restrictions on obtaining cypress and palmetto fronds, many journey a great distance for materials.

Although their daily use is diminished, chickees still have important cultural significance. They are the only buildings allowed at the Green Corn Dance, where they must be built in the traditional way. Young men who study traditional medicine are required to reroof their chickees according to the old methods. No doubt this continued ritual usage, in conjunction with secular use, will ensure that the chickee will endure for a long time.

Clothing

Like many other aspects of their culture, early Seminole clothing styles resembled those of other southeastern peoples. However, the Seminole gradually transformed styles in response to new environments, historical trends, and cultures. In the early eighteenth century, English colonists distributed trade shirts to the Creek. From them the Creek developed a male clothing style consisting of long trade shirts worn with breech cloths, fur robes, moccasins, and eventually with cloth leggings and wool blankets. With these changes, trade with the white settlers to obtain wool and cotton calico, needles, thread, and glass beads for clothing gradually became very important.

In nineteenth-century northern Florida, the Seminole wore clothing made either from leather or from cotton calico fabric. Women wore printed cotton dresses that were modeled after settlers' styles. Male clothing consisted of loose knee-length shirts with appliquéwork at the neck, over which they wore calico coats adorned with rows of appliqué. Other decorative accessories included turbans, headbands, beaded straps, pouches, sashes, silver jewelry, leggings, and hide moccasins.

After emigration to steamy South Florida, the Seminole wore cool, loose cotton clothing. By the 1890s, women had adopted ruffled two-piece dresses consisting of a long-sleeved blouse and a long skirt made from several print fabrics. They also donned multiple beaded necklaces, with the lowest necklace made from silver coins. Men continued to wear long shirts and coats, accessorized with vests and watch fobs. Children wore adult styles.

Since the early twentieth century, women's traditional dress has consisted of long, full skirts, a short square underblouse, and a cape. The light, hip-length cape, which evolved from the earlier ruffle on women's blouses, was designed to protect their arms against sunburn. The long skirts are not only modest, but also provide protection. Ethel Santiago explains, "The reason they wear long dresses and capes in Florida, I was told, you go through the bushes, it protects you from the mosquitos and it protects you...Have you ever walked through the Everglades where the sawblade grass is? You know how they cut you up in little pieces—they also protect you from that."

Men's clothing has changed greatly in the twentieth century. By the 1920s, men wore a loose, collarless, long-sleeved big shirt buttoned down to a waistband, from which a skirt fell below the knees. The big shirt was practical for men who spent time in canoes. When they began working in Miami in the 1930s, Seminole men started to wear a shirt with a shorter skirt which they tucked into pants. Eventually, they developed collarless shirts and jackets without attached skirts.

There are several junctures in the annual and life cycles that call for special clothing. For instance, it is customary to make new traditional clothing for the annual Green Corn Dance. In the past, widows wore black mourning clothes until they remarried or until the husband's family allowed them to resume wearing colors. Today, most wear black for limited periods. At a recent funeral, the widow and others wore traditional skirts and jackets with patchwork designs against a black background.

Women and girls continued to wear the traditional long patchwork skirts, short cape, and beads until the 1960s. At that time, many began wearing jeans and shorts though the older people considered it immodest. By the 1960s, most men wore jeans and shirts. Today, clothing is largely a matter of individual taste. Men often don western-cut shirts, Levi's, boots, and hats. Young men and women usually wear such mainstream attire as t-shirts, jeans, shorts, and sneakers. In addition, many wear handmade contemporary clothing that utilizes patchwork as a decorative element, such as blouses with patchwork bands, patchwork shirts, vests, or jackets. Women of child-bearing age or older are most likely to wear traditional dress for daily wear, usually a patchwork skirt paired with a contemporary t-shirt or blouse.

When sewing machines appeared at trading posts near the turn of the century, Seminole clothing design was revolutionized. With the machines, women could integrate increasing numbers of horizontal stripes, panels, and eventually patchwork patterns, into garments to create a new and distinctive clothing style.

Patchwork consists of strips of different colored cloth that have been sewn together, then cut apart and recombined at different angles. The most complex designs are cut and resewn many times. This produces a long patterned band, which is incorporated into a garment made of plain or printed cloth. Patchwork garments usually incorporate manifold strips of patchwork, colored cloth, and/or rickrack.

The Seminole create patchwork patterns and select colors in accord with personal aesthetic preferences. Designs are not written down, and may be created extemporaneously. For instance, an artist may select unusual colors to create a patchwork band and later decide the type of garment in which she will use it. When an individual creates a new pattern, others are free to share it; thus patchwork constantly evolves as designs rise and fall in popularity.

Miccosukee and Seminole women traditionally learn patchwork skills

Seated inside a chickee, Gloria Cypress Osceola demonstrates the art of Miccosukee patchwork. (Photo by Michele Edelson/ Courtesy of HASF)

when female relatives teach them to make their own clothes. Ethel Santiago recalls, "When I learn how to make clothes, I didn't know no other clothes to wear. Also they told us the patchwork was a symbol of a woman's work, like a part of cooking and garden, keeping home, doing patchwork, doing a basket, and was a woman's part of education of which we should be proud. The more you make clothes, the patchwork you do, what you make is like the proud you have in you that is going out. That's what I was taught."

Dolls

Historically, the Seminole made two types of dolls for their children. The earliest was a simple doll carved from a piece of cypress. It had a round painted head, a tubular body with articulated arms, and traditional clothes. The Seminole also made palmetto dolls, which they started to sell to tourists early in the century. This latter type predominates today.

Seminole and Miccosukee artists most often create female dolls, which consist of a simple palmetto fiber trunk covered with a couple of patchwork bands for the shirt and cape. Their attire often reflects the traditional styles of the early twentieth century. With arms, legs, and feet made of cardboard covered with palmetto fiber, male dolls are more difficult to make. They are often clothed in the style of the 1930s, with big shirt, turban, and neck scarf.

Doll makers gather the mesh-like palmetto fiber from the trunks of palmetto trees in isolated reservation sites. Mary Billie's daughter Claudia describes her mother's methods:

If you are planning on making dolls, first of all you have to find the palmetto fibers. And for that you have to have a knife and a axe and a file and maybe some water. And you don't know where you're going to find the palmetto fibers. You got to look for the nice ones. So you have to go twenty or thirty miles to look for that stuff. . . . If you're lucky maybe it take her half a day to find it, or if you can't find it, sometimes it takes her all day. Sometimes she has to go out the next morning to look for it again.

She said if she can find it early enough, she sometimes gets about fifty, but it depends on the day. If she finds it late in the afternoon, probably she cuts around fifteen. She's looking for the ones that's smooth. You have to cut it and . . . take it apart and see if it's good, or if it's not she'll just go on until, you know, she'll look for it until she finds it.

One palmetto yields enough fiber for four or five dolls. The best fiber is obtained from recently burned trees. However, forestry officials have lately forbidden the practice of setting fires for that purpose. After Mary locates a good palmetto, she extracts the fiber:

First you have to cut them leaves that are standing on that thing and then, after that, you just cut that thing off. You use the smaller kind of knife to take the palmetto fibers off.

She have a cloth with her and after she cuts them and gets that thing off it, she wraps it and brings it back. If it's dry enough, she goes ahead and makes the dolls. But if it's kind of wet, she has to let 'em dry out for a day before she can make it. She'll go ahead and cut 'em to what size she needs to make the dolls. She just goes ahead and cuts, like, some for the four-inch, and some for the six-inch, and you know, the body. It's always been like that, different sizes.

For the head, Mary sews a smooth piece of palmetto fiber over a palmetto fiber ball. Next, she makes the body from a rectangular piece of fiber that she stitches into a tubular shape. Mary stuffs the body with cotton to maintain its shape, then "she puts that cardboard and wraps that palmetto around it and put it on the bottom so them stuff wouldn't come out when it stands. She'll cut that cardboard out and make a circle big enough where she stuffed it, uh, cotton in. And then she'll take that palmetto fiber and put it around that cardboard where she make that circle, cut that circle. And then she'll, uh, put it on the bottom of that doll and then sew it up so it can stand straight." Finally, Mary sews eyes onto the head with black and white thread, eyebrows with black thread, and mouth with red thread.

Doll making incorporates a variety of traditional art forms because the dolls wear patchwork clothes and beaded jewelry. Mary makes the

Palmetto dolls made for sale to tourists at the Miccosukee Indian Village (Photo by Michele Edelson/ Courtesy of HASF)

clothes in advance. She simply wraps small pieces of cloth or patchwork around the four-inch dolls, but dresses dolls eight inches or larger in tiny patchwork garments. Mary sews the clothes on so that they will not fall off.

Many doll makers recreate the high hairdo popular fifty years ago by covering a tiny frame with black cloth. They may also employ yarn to create modern ponytail or braided styles. To complete their work, doll makers sew earrings and piles of old-style beaded necklaces into place.

Folk Medicine

Among the Seminole and Miccosukee, medicine refers to a combined religious, philosophical, and medical system that promotes physical and spiritual health. The people believe that the rituals, songs, and herbal remedies are handed down from the Creator. Although the practice of some rituals is restricted to men and others to women, both sexes are free to learn the entire body of knowledge so that they may pass it on. Women may gather herbs and leaves to prepare medicines, but may not practice medicine until after menopause. Some believe this restriction arose because women are considered more susceptible to disease during menstruation.

There are different levels of specialization among healers. The medicine men, who may care for the medicine bundles, carry the most extensive knowledge. They deal not only with physical and mental ills, but also with ceremonies, magic, and the preservation of traditional knowledge. Medicine men often act as spokespeople for their group. Traditional doctors practice healing but do not have access to the full body of ritual knowledge possessed by medicine men. In addition to the medico-religious system, there is a secular type of traditional medicine that everybody practices. This involves cures for colds, earaches, and other simple problems. Songs for the sick are often taught to children as soon as they can understand them.

Among the most important beliefs underlying the native medical system are the double soul and the direct relationship between dreams and illness. For instance, it is commonly held that the soul journeys north during sleep and returns at dawn. If the spirit ventures too far east on the return, the person becomes ill. If the soul journeys west along the Milky Way to the city of the dead, the person dies. The medicine man questions the patient about his or her dreams. When he learns the location of the soul, he gathers herbs for medicine, blows through the medicine pipe into the medicine, and chants to entreat the soul to return.

The Seminole and Miccosukee identify many distinctive illnesses. In the 1940s, scholar Robert F. Greenlee found that their categories included sun sickness, which is prevalent during the summer; moon sickness, or sleeplessness; headaches caused by the morning and evening stars; fire sickness connected with a high fever; deer sickness, or loss of feeling on one side of the leg; giant sickness; and dog disease, which includes stomach ache, loss of appetite, bad dreams, and vomiting. In the following myth, medicine man Josie Billie explained the origin and behavior associated with giant sickness:

There is a large hammock up north of Lake Okeechobee where the tall men live. They are as tall as trees. Some of them stand up. Though they have bones like ordinary people, no living Indians have ever seen the giants. A long while ago there was a man, a very smart man, who went up to the cabbage woods and saw the giants. He told the rest of the people about them. These giants stand still all the time like a tree. Others lie down all the time like a log. They are dangerous and have the power to make a person sick.

People go far off into the woods as if they were crazy when they have the giant sickness. They act as though something had hit them, but they have no idea what is the matter with them. They talk about seeing giants. If a person talks about looking at a giant the medicine man knows what the trouble is.

Some healers still use ritual and herbal medicines in connection with major life events such as pregnancy, birth, puberty, love, and death. For example, to induce pregnancy, doctors give certain medicines to the woman and man. Medicine men and doctors conduct special ceremonies to strengthen newborns, especially if the mother has lost previous babies. In 1933 ethnomusicologist Frances Densmore recorded Susie Tiger singing a song for a dying patient. The text refers to various stages on the spirit's journey to the city of the dead:

Come back.
Before you get to the king tree, come back,
Before you get to the peach tree, come back,
Before you come to the line of fence, come back,
Before you get to the bushes, come back,
Before you get to the fork of the road, come back,
Before you get to the yard, come back,
Before you get to the door, come back,
Before you get to the fire, come back,
Before you get to the middle of the ladder, come back.

The Seminole and Miccosukee make traditional medicines from a variety of indigenous plants, including sweet bay leaves, willow, cedar leaf and sassafras, snakeroot, and tobacco. They pick medicinal herbs from the north and east sides of the plant. If taken from the south or west sides, the medicine could cause bad luck or death. Doctors and patients often face the east during treatment, and doctors never make a medicine in advance.

Although many reservations now have trained nurses in residence, the Seminole and Miccosukee often employ traditional cures or see a medicine man. In many instances, they engage in folk medical practices in combination with western medicine. Indeed, some reservation nurses have concluded that certain illnesses, such as alcoholism or rashes, respond better to traditional than western medicine.

Since the 1950s few have seriously studied traditional religious or secular medicine. Only rare individuals are willing to undertake the minimum of seven years of dedicated training and personal sacrifice necessary to become a medicine man. In the last decade, one or two individuals have apprenticed themselves to medicine men and a small group on the Miccosukee Reservation has recently begun more informal study with a medicine man.

Verbal Arts

When the Seminole and Miccosukee lived in isolated camps, they often looked forward to a storytelling session after the evening meal. Today, the people still tell mythological tales concerning origins and supernatural beings, folktales about trickster characters such as Rabbit, and legends about place names and historical events to educate children about their history, religion, and the rules for daily life. David Jumper emphasizes the way the Miccosukee and Seminole view these arts:

All of it together... they are all interwoven together where you can't separate. We try to teach our kids that you don't separate things and label things, and that's what I'm trying to get across to you.... Some of our tales may involve a lifestyle or then again it may involve the way you want to go hunting, maybe the way you travel, or maybe the way you treat your relatives or maybe some who are not relatives. So it covers a variety of things. It's just like a blanket covering a number of things that's under it.

Josie Billie was a respected Seminole medicine man from Big Cypress who often acted as a cultural mediator between the Seminole and outsiders during the early twentieth century. In this role, he sometimes recounted Seminole myths and legends so outsiders could better understand their worldview. Billie presented a mixture of southeastern religious beliefs and Christian influence in the following myth:

A long while back the Breathmaker blew his breath toward the sky and made the Milky Way. This white way leads to a city in the west where the Big Cypress Seminole go when they die. Bad people stay in the ground right where they are buried. Every time you go through the woods and step where a bad person is

The late Seminole
medicine man and
cultural mediator, Josie
Billie (Photo courtesy of
HASF)

buried you feel afraid even though the grave is covered over with bushes and trees.

Good people walk over the Milky Way to a "city in western sky." Animals take the same path when they die. Long ago animals of an Indian—dogs and horses—were killed so they might go with their masters.

Many Native American tales focus on a mischievous trickster figure who tries to outwit others but is a victim of his own outrageous actions. These tales both teach and entertain. Frances Densmore heard Josie Billie narrate the following story, which combines origin myths with a tale about Rabbit, the Seminole and Miccosukee trickster figure:

At first the Indians were under the ground, in a big hole, then they all came out. When they came out they bathed in a little creek. When they got through bathing they had nothing to eat and no fire.

One man told them what to do and how to make a fire. He told them to take dry, soft bark, twirl a stick between their hands, and then a spark lighted the bark. He got some dry punk. One made made the spark, another caught it on the punk, then they made a fire, but they had no pots or kettles.

The man heard a noise a half a mile or so toward the north. He thought some animals were there. He sent two men to get little trees and out of these he made bows and arrows. He got ready, then sent the boys and men to find something to eat.

They found deer, turkey, and bear and brought them back to camp. Then they had plenty of meat but nothing else. The man tried to find something else and found swamp cabbage. He cut it down and told the people to eat it raw, as they had no kettles. Then he taught them to roast it in the ashes of a fire. The two men talked it over. One man had made the bows and arrows and the other had taught them to roast the swamp cabbage and to cook meat in the same way, putting some in the fire. One man said to the other, "What shall we live in?" They had been sleeping in the grass, so they made themselves a house, like those the Seminole live in now. Then a horse and dog talked to the man, talking like people. At that time the rabbit stayed with people and he told lies all the time, but the dog and horse told the truth.

Somebody found out that the rabbit lied. Then the rabbit tried to do something all the time. He would go away, and when he came back he would say he had seen things that he had not seen. He would say he had seen snakes, alligators, and turtles.

The man said to the rabbit, "If you find a snake, kill him and bring him back to camp." The rabbit killed a snake and brought it to the camp, and he sang a song with words that meant "On his back . . ."

When the rabbit was bringing back the snake he saw an alligator. The man said, "You kill the alligator and bring him back." The alligator talked too, at that time. The rabbit said, "Somebody wants to see you up at the camp." The alligator believed this and went along with the rabbit. When they had gone about halfway the rabbit tried to kill the alligator; he beat the alligator but did not kill him and the alligator went back to his cave.

Then the rabbit came home.

Then the man said, "If you see a turkey, kill him and bring him home." So the rabbit started out to get a turkey, but he went to a wildcat and said, "You kill a turkey for me." Wildcat went and found a turkey and killed him. Rabbit brought the turkey back to the camp and told the man that he had killed it. The man believed it.

Then the rabbit wanted to get married. The man thought the rabbit had killed the turkey and given it to the girl. But when the rabbit got married he didn't bring any food at all. The people found out that the rabbit did not kill the turkey, so they drove the rabbit away from the camp. That is why the rabbit is wild today.

Music, Dance, and Musical Instruments

Seminole and Miccosukee music currently exists as accompaniment to songs or dances. Most music and songs are based on Creek traditions, though the people have preserved Calusa Corn Dance songs from the days when they camped nearby.

The people sing for a variety of reasons: dances, healing rituals, entertainment, or to assure success in hunting. Many songs, such as those for making medicine, are not melodic. Instead they resemble a spoken chant, with occasional high nasal tones that slide forward. Certain melodies are associated with specific conditions or activities.

Before undertaking a hunting trip, men sometimes sing unaccompanied songs to encourage the animals to feed nearby. The leader intones the first phrase, which the men repeat, then they all sing together. The songs characteristically end on a downward glissando followed by a sound that resembles clearing the throat. The following song, recorded by Frances Densmore, describes the movements of a bear:

> Yellow nose, small eyes
> round ears, dark body,
> big hindquarters, short tail.
> It moves about as it feeds.

There are special songs to bring success in stickball. The night before a ball game, women may sing all night while men accompany them with a rattle and drum. Lyrics of stickball songs concern defeating the opposite side, such as, "You Tallahassees are afraid to bet on yourselves." Friends of each team also dance to help bring success.

Traditional Seminole music is accompanied by rattles, drums, and flutes. Some believe that the coconut shell rattle is the oldest Seminole instrument. It consists of a coconut shell mounted on a stick, drilled with lines of holes, and filled with canna seeds. Similar but smaller rattles were made from box turtle shells filled with dried mud pellets. Women used to wear strings of rattles tied around each leg for the Corn, Stomp, and Catfish dances. Beginning sixty years ago, these were replaced by strings of small tin cans filled with mud pellets.

Different drums accompanied various native dances, such as the cypress knee drum for the Stomp Dance and the water drum for stickball songs. The people formerly made the water drum from cypress bark or a hollow cypress section covered with buckskin, but now often fashion it from a tin can. Long ago the Seminole played an unusual type of flute made from cane or deer bone, but knowledge of the instrument is now rare.

The Seminole and Miccosukee perform a variety of dances that fulfill different ritual and social functions. They dance at the Green Corn Dance or social events, but infrequently perform for outsiders. Children are encouraged to join in the dancing at an early age. Some dances, such as the Lightningbug, Little Bug, Little Fish, and Little Boys' dances, are specifically for children.

The Corn Dance accompanies the most important ritual sons at the Green Corn Dance. The dance and song leader heads a long line of alternating men and women who link hands and walk rhythmically counterclockwise around the fire. Women tie rattles around their knees to provide emphasis and accompaniment.

Dance movements sometimes imitate the actions of birds or animals, as in the Chicken, Quail, Blackbird, Buzzard, and Catfish dances. For example, dancers mimic fluttering wings in the Chicken Dance or fins in the Catfish Dance. Among the many dances associated with birds or animals, the Alligator Dance is one of the most important. Josie Billie explained: "A long time ago all animals talked like people. The alligators made up this dance at that time. There is an old story that when the people all die maybe the animals will come back again as they were before, talking like people."

Another distinctive social dance is the Stomp Dance, which is performed to several different songs. At night, a singer beats a cypress knee drum to one side of a line of alternating male and female dancers. The dance motion consists of quick and heavy rhythmic walking. The dance leader does not play an instrument, though the women wear rattles on their knees.

Despite the blending of their own culture with Americanized beliefs, the Seminole and Miccosukee respect and retain many aspects of their Native American heritage. By passing down their knowledge from generation to generation, they are able to keep alive a valuable part of South Florida's history.

CHAPTER 2

The Crackers

THE "GLADES"

The Everglades is the nation's most extensive swampland, covering most of the South Florida peninsula. The Glades area encompasses 4,472 square miles from the southern shore of Lake Okeechobee to the tip of Florida's southwest shoreline. Known as *Pay-hay-o-kee* (grass-water) to the Seminole, the Everglades is actually a slow-moving and shallow river that flows southward through extensive acres of sawgrass, sedge, and aquatic vegetation. The river is dotted with small hammocks—islands on slightly higher ground that support cypress, palm, live oak, coco plum, custard apple, and other trees. These hammocks are the only ground that remains above water during the summer rainy reason.

For centuries the Everglades has been home to a wide variety of exotic flora and fauna that have flourished in this tropical swamp environment. Orchids and other air plants proliferate, Spanish moss drapes the cypress tops, and the water is filled with duckweed, floating heart, sagittaria, bladderwort, and bonnets. Animals such as the Florida panther, the alligator, and marsh rabbit are found here in the southernmost interior. Birds are plentiful and diverse—herons, egrets, wild turkey, redwing, rail, gallinule, and ibis all have rookeries and make their nests in the Glades.

Into this tropical and forbidding wilderness only the most desperate or adventuresome people came to start a new life. Early white settlers began to arrive before the Civil War years, although no survey of the Everglades and South Florida was done until 1912. By the time of this first survey, many pioneer families had conquered the odds and carved out a living as Florida "Crackers" in the sawgrass and peat. Beginning as hunters of plumes and pelts, then establishing vast open-range ranches, year-round produce or citrus farms, and lucrative fishing businesses, South Florida Crackers tamed the tropics and brought their unique culture into what would become a truly multicultural region.

WHAT IS A CRACKER?

"They are dirt-poor and eat cracked corn."

"They live in little cracker-box houses."

"They are skilled at cracking a cow whip."

Theories abound concerning the origin of the word "Cracker," but it is generally conceded that Crackers are the white settlers who first came to the South Florida wilderness—most arriving from Alabama, the Carolinas, north Florida and south Georgia. The early white settlers of the Deep South were different from the Colonial New England pioneers, who had strong Anglo-Saxon roots. The settlers in the South were of Celtic stock, and scholars have outlined how Cracker culture closely resembles traditional Celtic culture—habits, customs, values and occupational choice all point to a Celtic heritage. Being herdsmen with strong kinship ties, the first Florida Crackers had a lifestyle that paralleled that of the Highland Scots clans and the fiefdoms of Ireland. Of course, just as there are vast differences between the English and the Irish in the British Isles, the settlers of the American North and South were culturally distinct, with the southern Cracker looked upon with contempt as rustic and lazy by the puritan Yankee.

George M. Barbour, a New England Yankee who travelled to Florida in 1882, described his first encounter with Crackers this way:

The entire trip that day was through an unsettled region, the only human beings living anywhere along the road being four or five families of Florida natives, the genuine, unadulterated "cracker"—the clay-eating, gaunt, pale, tallowy, leather-skinned sort—stupid, stolid, staring eyes, dead and lusterless; unkempt hair, generally tow-colored; and such a shiftless, slouching manner! Simply white savages—or living white mummies would, perhaps, better indicate their dead-alive looks and actions. Who, or what, these "crackers" are, from whom descended, of what nationality, or what becomes of them, is one among the many unsolved mysteries in this state. Stupid and shiftless, yet sly and vindictive, they are a block in the pathway of civilization, settlement, and enterprise wherever they exist.

This Victorian perception of the Cracker has improved over the years, but the term has remained largely a derogatory one, synonymous with hillbilly, peckerwood, honkie, doughface and redneck in the Yankee lexicon. It is impossible to paint an entire group of pioneers with the same brush, but the Florida Cracker developed a culture that was for the most part rural, clannish, leisure-loving yet combative—Celtic in nature. This culture thrived in the wilderness that was South Florida and has been handed down to the Crackers of today. As native white Floridians

Early Cracker families made their livings from the land, fishing, hunting, and farming. (Photo courtesy of the Florida State Archives [FSA])

have reclaimed their heritage, "Cracker" is a label they wear with pride, proclaiming their origins by covering their car bumpers with "Florida Native" stickers. Florida Cracker E.A. "Frog" Smith was asked a few years ago what he would be if he wasn't a Cracker. His instant reply: "Ashamed."

RANCHING

The defining features of Cracker culture are set by the three major occupations that sustained life in South Florida before the advent of tourism—ranching, farming, and fishing. Of these three, it was ranching that brought the first settlers and most likely gave the Crackers their name.

Many people have no idea that Florida is the largest beef-producing state east of the Mississippi River, with unique ranching traditions suited to the tropical climate. By the time Florida became a state, the Seminoles of the Everglades already possessed extensive cattle herds, and white settlers soon followed their example. In 1990 Florida boasted twenty-one thousand working ranches that produced almost 2 million head of cattle, with most of these ranches located on the southern peninsula of the state. This cattle boom in South Florida started in 1865, right after the Civil War, and the industry has continued to be a regional occupation that is distinct from the stereotypic western cowboy culture with which we are more familiar. Frederic Remington, one of the greatest artistic chroniclers of the western cowboy, visited Florida in 1895. He made only a few paintings depicting the Florida cow hunters, and observed that they "lack dash and are indifferent riders, but they are picturesque in their unkempt, almost unearthly wildness."

British-based Florida cattle-raising traditions contrast sharply with western cow culture, which is influenced by Spanish and Mexican practices. Unlike the western plains cowboy with his lariat and pistol, the Florida "cow catcher" uses dogs and a long whip to herd a hybrid cattle that thrives in hot, humid weather. In this way, cattle breeding and ranching traditions of South Florida were developed over the years in response to the climate and terrain of the tropical scrub country, which in many ways was more frontier and wild than the West.

Many of South Florida's ranching folkways were transplanted from coastal South Carolina traditions when settlers from the Carolinas came south to the tropics. In turn, these traditions have their roots in cattle-herding practices from England, Wales, Scotland and Ireland. In the British and Celtic homelands, cow culture thrived in small villages or farms, and animals grazed on unfenced range with sparse forage. In order to identify their herds, farmers marked or branded them. During the fall, owners sold most of their herds to drovers, who used dogs to drive the cattle to market. This system of cattle raising proved to be easy to reproduce in the American South, and Florida ranching retains many Anglo and Celtic practices. For instance, in the British Isles herders would burn the moors each winter to remove old growth and encourage new growth to feed their free-range animals. In South Florida, ranchers often burn their flatwoods range in winter to remove old growth and encourage new grass and palmettos to grow. As fourth-generation South Florida cattle rancher Seth Alderman explains, "The grass—after it gets old and tough—it's not much good. There's a lot of wiregrass; and when it's fresh burned, it's real good grazing. Then, I guess it kept down the palmetto some. . . . And when the palmetto's young and tender [after a fire], they would eat it."

A wild, frontier life continued to be the norm for Florida herders, cowmen in the region being ex-soldiers and ex-gangsters in many cases.

Yet, despite their relative isolation and small numbers, Florida Cracker cowmen ruled the state legislature until very recently; Florida, for instance, remained an open-range state up until 1949, whereas the western states passed fence laws in 1927.

The first cattle raised in the Everglades were known as "scrub cattle" and were bony, but hardy with a woods sense. Although their meat was tough, the scrub cow was known to be tolerant of the severe heat of southern Florida, able to survive on the sparse native forage, immune to the constant insect bites, and good at dodging snakes and gopher holes. Florida scrub cows were bred from Andalusian cattle introduced by the Spanish in the sixteenth century and British breeds from the upland South. Most recently, the Brahman from India has been cross-bred with Angus, Hereford, Shorthorn, Charolais, and Limousin to produce the "Brangus" and other hybrids suited to the tropics.

Florida cattlemen still rely upon "catch dogs" to herd errant cows from the scrub. Catch dogs are trained to find, herd and hold cattle. They are indispensable, especially on fall roundups, for they will jump into difficult areas (ponds, palmetto patches, or swamps) to retrieve strays. In the past, before the danger of screwworm infection, a dog was trained literally to "catch" a cow and hold its ear or nose in his teeth until the cowman arrived. Today a good cow dog continues to be a vital part of Florida ranching, able to find cows in the dense underbrush and separate them as needed. Seth Alderman remembers that catch dogs "were mostly 'cur-dogs.' . . . They were just good old dogs. [But] a good dog was worth two or three men, really."

Aside from a good dog, a Florida cow catcher needs two whips—one that is twelve to eighteen feet in length for horseback use, and an eight to ten foot length for use on foot. The pop or crack that results from the skillful use of a cow whip sounds like a rifle shot and will resound for several miles. Florida Crackers manage a cow's movements by cracking their whips near the animal's ear, nose, or leg, thus producing the necessary shock to keep a cow on course. The name "Cracker" is most often attributed to this skill, which continues to be a feature of Cracker life in the Deep South.

South Florida ranchers today combine traditional and modern technology. Most continue to ride horses, train cow dogs, and use whips. However, cow whips today include synthetic materials and have been refined over the years. George Altman of Manatee County is a whipbraider who still fashions his whips from strips of latigo (oak-tanned cowhide, or cull buckskin), but weights are now braided into the belly of the whip to give it stiffness and heft. Some whipmakers today use nylon tubing from parachute cords in place of latigo, for it is cheaper yet strong and resistant to rotting. Florida whipbraiders have also developed a

A Florida cow hunter is never without his whip. (Photo by Peggy A. Bulger/ Bureau of Florida Folklife Programs)

unique socket system for attaching the handle, giving it more flexibility.

One of the few traditional whipbraiders left in Florida is Vernon Ryan McDonald from the Okeechobee area. Now in his eighties, McDonald has been braiding whips for so long that he cannot remember who taught him or how old he was when he started. He laughs, "I've been doing it so long, I could do it with my eyes closed." Mr. McDonald needs only a few tools to make his whips—shears, a cutting knife and a clamp. He cuts strips from a hide, and braids the center with four strips. Next he covers it with eight strings, then another twelve to achieve the correct weight, with copper-coated BB shot in the long whips to add weight. Although the market for cowwhips has diminished, McDonald confesses that he continues to make whips purely because "I get pleasure out of making them and it's about all I can do now."

Florida Crackers have of necessity discovered specialized solutions to the challenges of ranching in the tropics. For instance, techniques that have upgraded the rangeland in South Florida have made it possible to raise a cow on three or four acres, whereas forty acres were required a few generations ago. As ranch foreman Coot Wilson says, "A successful rancher is nothing but a grass farmer." Another invention developed in response to South Florida environmental conditions is the buzzard trap. Since buzzards are plentiful in the South Florida peninsula and prey upon newborn calves, cowmen have responded by fashioning large four-foot-high and ten-foot-square wood and wire traps baited with carcasses. The carrion-eating birds land at a trap and walk around it until they finally crawl in through a tunnel leading to the bait. After eating, the birds keep walking around the inside edge of the trap, but they are not smart enough to leave through the tunnel. Today ranchers still make and use buzzard traps; however, they must obtain a special state permit to do so.

Until the recent advent of good roads, most cattle in South Florida were worked in "cow camps"—pens that were placed a day's ride from each other. The camps provided a place to keep the cattle at night and gave shelter for the hands on the long cattle drives to the Gulf Coast market town of Punta Gorda. Today, trucks are used to bring cattle to market, but the hands still often live in bunkhouses on large, isolated ranches. Despite many twentieth-century modifications, Florida cowmen (and women) continue to live a traditional lifestyle that includes Cracker ranching skills, foodways, and oral culture—especially tall tales and legends.

Florida ranchers tell tales of the legendary cowboy hero, Napoleon Bonaparte "Bone" Mizell, who was said to "outrope, outride, outshoot, and outdrink" any cowman in the region. Historian Charlton Tebeau collected this tale in the early 1950s:

Zibe King was a big rancher in South Florida and he hired two cowmen, Ed Fewell and Bone Mizell to run his cattle. Bone decided that he would quit and start his own ranch up by Kissimmee, but that didn't sit too well with Zibe. King promptly got the law out after Mizell for rustling his cattle. Bone admitted to the lawmen that he'd taken a few cattle from Mr. King, but that he'd rustled over 40,000 head *for* King while he worked for him, without ever having trouble with the law. King and Mizell patched up their differences and Bone again became part of King's staff.

Another version of the rustling tale is recounted by Gene Burnett:

Bone was arrested one day for allegedly stealing a few cows, and he was convicted by a court of law. But Valley settlers, aware that many of the big cattle kings were guilty now and then of a cow theft or two, raised a protest. They got up a petition to have Bone pardoned. Authorities were sympathetic, but had to point out a technicality; he could not be pardoned until he had served "time." No problem. The good folks dressed Bone up properly and sent him on the train to Raiford [where the state prison is located]. Here an official greeted him, escorted him through the prison buildings, and then gave a dinner for him, at which Bone gave a short speech affirming that he found no fault with the management. Having served his "time," he picked up his pardon and left for home.

Zibe King, the Hendry family, and Jake Summerlin were the most wealthy ranchers to pioneer in South Florida, and their fame spread as oral tales passed from cowman to cowman. King himself was known as a true "cowpuncher," who was reportedly over six feet, six inches in height, with a girth to match. It is said that once Zibe was so angered by a wild steer that had attacked him that he swung a haymaker and hit the steer near its heart, killing it instantly. Another legend that is still remembered is told about Jake Summerlin, who became a millionaire before he turned forty. Summerlin made his millions by exporting cattle to Cuba, receiving Spanish gold in payment. It is said that at one time the gold doubloon was the region's primary currency. Oldtimers insist that Jake would travel in disguise as a cowboy to ranchhands' homes throughout South Florida and would distribute gold pieces to the children as he left. Summerlin is still referred to affectionately as "The King of the Crackers," not because of his wealth and generosity, but because he could "decapitate a snake or gut a hen" with one pop of his whip.

Florida cattlemen now use a host of modern techniques to facilitate their work, such as calf tables, bull squeezes, and electric branding irons. Western skills and styles have been introduced through rodeos, and several of the traditional Cracker ranching practices are now obsolete. However, Cracker ranchers continue to view their work as unique and rewarding. As seventy-four-year-old cowboy Junior Mills sums it up, "It [ranching] wasn't a money-making deal. But one thing about it, I enjoyed living an outdoor life. I wouldn't trade it for nothing, really. The best part was you seen something different every day."

FARMING

For the Cracker settlers who were not ranchers, South Florida's fertile land and year-round growing season often provided a living. Many, like Peter Douthit's family, came south after the freeze of 1896 that destroyed citrus groves in north Florida. Douthit, now living in Big Pine Key, remembers that his father came to South Florida to plant a lime grove on the Keys, and his family became quite successful growing vegetables and tropical fruits and shipping them by boat up north. John Weeks, Ted Smallwood, Dick Turner, and G. M. Storter were a few other pioneers in the Everglades who came to farm and became successful and wealthy landholders.

Aside from growing vegetables for the winter market up north— tomatoes, new potatoes, sweet potatoes, squash, pumpkins, cucumbers, eggplants, cow peas, peppers, strawberries, cabbages, melons, onions, okra, and cauliflower—South Florida Cracker farmers could grow exotic tropical fare. Pineapples, coconuts, oranges, avocados, lemons, bananas, mangoes, limes, guava, kumquats, grapefruit, sapodillas, and sugar cane thrived in the South Florida heat and humidity. These tropical crops still provide a living for many Cracker farm families.

As in other parts of the world, South Florida farmers are dependent upon the weather and other unpredictable conditions for success. It is not surprising that the folklore of farming in South Florida includes traditional beliefs and practices handed down for generations. Eighty-three-year-old Peter Douthit recalls: "You can get a lot of farmers, won't plant a pea unless the moon's right. They call it planting by the moon. I've known lots of people that religiously wouldn't plant unless it was the right time to plant . . . the *Farmer's Almanac*, you can get all that stuff out of there. And it's interesting. Yessir, they'd watch that thing there and plant their crops accordingly."

Sugarcane is now grown by large agribusiness concerns, such as U.S. Sugar, but cane cultivation began with the first Cracker families who settled the land, and most families still grow a small crop for personal use. George Storter was famous for his sugarcane, which he reportedly grew for over twenty years "on the same land without fertilizing or cultivating." It is said that twenty-five acres of Storter's land was planted in cane, producing seven hundred gallons of syrup per acre.

For the Storters, as well as for all other South Florida families, cane grindings and syrup boilings were a major form of entertainment, in addition to being a necessary process for food production. Today grindings are not as common, but a few Cracker families continue the seasonal tradition to provide syrup for the year. Thanksgiving is the traditional time to grind the harvested cane, while extended families are gathered together and can assist in the all-day task. A mule (or tractor) is hitched to a long pole that turns in a wide circle, creating the motion that grinds the raw stalks of cane through the cane mill, which sits at the center. As the stalks are fed through the press, cane juice is collected in fifty-gallon drums and then transferred to the boiling kettle. The juice is stirred over a low fire until it thickens into syrup, providing a long, hot, but social occasion during which people swap stories, tell jokes, and feast on the "polecat" froth that rises to the edge of the boiling kettle.

Although the land is fertile in South Florida, natural hazards are common. Besides worrying about drought and excessive rain, farmers in South Florida must always be wary during hurricane season. Hurricanes not only destroy property and take lives but can ruin the land. Since South Florida is barely above sea level, the flooding caused by a hurricane can "salt" the land, leaving it barren until heavy rains can wash the salt out. A good Florida Cracker who is considering buying

A traditional sugarcane grinding, ca. 1920s (Photo courtesy of FSA)

land for cultivation will often "taste" the soil first, to detect the presence of salt.

The other ubiquitous hazard of South Florida life is the presence of "swamp angels" or mosquitoes. Peter Douthit remembers that when he was a boy, before he could enter the house, someone would have to beat the mosquitoes off him. At night, despite screens, he would sleep with a pole under the sheet that raised it over his head and body. If the sheet touched his skin, the mosquitoes would bite right through the fabric. A favorite Cracker saying is that the mosquitoes are so bad in South Florida that "a man can swing a pint cup and catch a quart" of them.

Insects or no, the agriculture business became so successful in South Florida that, after 1915, "Negro labor" was imported to supplement the settlers' workforce. There was fierce opposition to this by the native Crackers. It is said that there was a black cook at the Moore Haven Hotel on Lake Okeechobee who feared for his life because of the Cracker terrorism directed against blacks in the region. Another story has it that black workers who were brought in to lay the railroad tracks in South Florida were targets for "Crackers who hid in the underbrush along the right of way and took pot shots as they worked."

Despite their bigotry, South Florida Crackers would soon share the farmland with people from many diverse cultures. Today, agriculture is second only to tourism as Florida's largest industry. South Dade County is especially rich, having a district known as the "Redland" that is an agricultural basin of over eighty thousand acres. The folk culture of the Redland is Cracker, African American, Caribbean and Hispanic. This diversity has been created by a migrant labor pool that harvests the winter crops destined for northern markets. Migrant laborers from Mexico, Nicaragua, Jamaica, Haiti, the Dominican Republic, and across the southern United States travel to south Dade County for the six-month harvest season, coinciding exactly with the winter tourist season. Many of the farm owners, the foremen, and the pickers are Florida Crackers who have had to adjust to the new international flavor of South Florida's agribusiness.

The largest row-crop production takes place around Lake Okeechobee, with its rich Everglades mucklands. Sweet corn, celery, escarole, iceburg lettuce, radishes, and other crops are grown in the fall, winter and spring. Okeechobee, the Everglades, Palm Beach County and Dade County each have distinctive crops to harvest, yet they share a common migrant workforce that is composed of many ethnic groups. Each crop harvest requires specialized techniques and skills. Many growers maintain that different ethnic groups have crop-specific talents and are best at certain kinds of harvesting. It is true that, for instance, tomatoes, avocados and star fruit are often harvested by Mexicans, limes by Bahamians, beans by Haitians, and sugarcane by Jamaicans. However, whether this is a function of personal preference, ethnic heritage or imposed segregation is not clear. What is clear is that the Crackers of South Florida share the rich farmland and agricultural opportunities of this tropical region with an international workforce that has added new and complex cultural traditions to the South Florida landscape.

FISHING

Fishing is the third major source of livelihood for the Crackers of South Florida. Surrounded by ocean coastline and dotted with rivers, lakes and swampland, Florida ranks fifth among the states in seafood production and is rich in expressive maritime culture. Skills and occupations that revolve around the fishing industry are an important part of Cracker folklife in South Florida. Boat building, net making, and fishing-gear production provide a living for many South Floridians.

Aside from leading fishing parties for tourists, commercial fishermen have been important in the region since the 1860s. Before the invention of refrigeration and the arrival of railroads, South Florida Cracker fishermen salted fish and shipped them to the Cuban market. Eventually, ice and advanced transportation networks allowed the South Florida fisheries to become a source for markets all over the world.

Mullet has always been the staple fish in the Florida Cracker diet; however, commercial fisheries also sell mackerel, kingfish, bluefish, red snapper, weakfish, sea trout, redfish, catfish and snook. A Cracker pioneer, Robert Storter, is credited with inventing a fishing spoon to lure snook, but a Cracker narrative tells of how an unscrupulous Yankee tourist later patented it as the "Wilson spoon."

Florida leads the nation in catfish production, an industry that developed on Lake Okeechobee during 1906–10. In the early days, there would be fifty or more men fishing the lake, catching catfish that could weigh up to thirty pounds. Captain T. A. Bass and the OK Fish Company took the catch to the mid-western markets of St. Louis and Kansas City, where they were in great demand. Today catfish are raised on "farms" and sold to restaurants throughout the country where they are fried and served with hush puppies and grits.

A technique of fishing that may be unique to South Florida is known as "dry stop fishing" and is done only at the high spring tides. During the spring months, at high tide, ocean fish go into the sawgrass and mangrove swamps of the Everglades, and fishermen can stake out nets like big fences in the water. When the tide goes out, the mangrove will be dry and the fish that are lying in the mud can be picked up.

Adding to the maritime catch are shellfish that are abundant in the region. Stone crab claws are harvested in Everglades City and Chokoluskee, Gulf Coast centers for this lucrative catch. Although the crabs used to be caught by hand for personal consumption, stone crabbing is now a commercial business. Crabbers use long "lines" that will hold four hundred to eight hundred traps each. A commercial crabber will have six of these lines and pull in one line a day, breaking off one claw on each crab and returning it to the water, where it will live to grow a new appendage.

In South Florida's Everglades, maritime folklife is shaped by the distinctive nature of Cracker culture, as well as by the environment. The communities of Clewiston, Crescent City, Cortez and Big Pine Key are major centers of maritime Cracker culture. Fishermen in these communities are great sources of traditional knowledge and oral lore—anecdotes, jokes, names, weather lore, legends, oral history and folk beliefs abound in the Cracker fisherman's storehouse of folklore.

The packing houses that are part of the commercial fishing industry function like the general store and post office of other rural communities. Workers congregate and swap jokes, retell narratives, and generally pass on the local folklore and history. Listening at such a gathering, one hears expressions such as "on the hill," meaning "on land," or "he bought a new kicker," meaning "he bought a new outboard motor." In Cortez, when fishermen refer to "cream and honey," they are describing a particular place in the Sarasota Bay that is muddy (cream) and has excessive mosquitoes (honey).

Fishermen like Albert Mora of Clewiston depend upon the elaborate belief system that is part of maritime culture. Mora fishes "by the moon," believing (like most Crackers) that the full or new moon is the time to catch the most fish. Most Cracker fishermen also observe a myriad of traditional taboos to ward off bad luck. For instance, it is bad luck to leave dock on a Friday, say "alligator" or "banana" on board, have a woman on board, whistle on board, turn the hatch upside down, or bring a black suitcase on board.

Folk beliefs are abundant in maritime South Florida, but they are only one aspect of a rich oral lore. Cracker fishermen have developed a legendary stature in Florida, for it is said that at one time or another, "every serious offender against the law south of Atlanta sought asylum on or near Florida's waters." One fisherman who became a legend is William E. Collins, or "Pogey Bill." Bill was a scrapper, often getting into fistfights and once having his finger bitten off by an opponent. His exploits as a freelance "enforcer" became so well known that the justice of the peace appointed him the sheriff of Okeechobee County, a position that he held for fourteen years.

Pogey Bill acquired his nickname when he took a boatload of bony, inedible menhaden to market, to the accompaniment of hoots from his fellow Cracker fishermen. Menhaden, also knows as "pogeys," were used in industries for their oil, and Bill found that his folly was very lucrative. He returned with new stature, as well as cash. Despite his reputation as the "toughest and meanest" fisherman in Okeechobee County, Pogey Bill reportedly had a heart of gold and served as the head of the Boy Scout movement in South Florida. He was also indispensable during the 1928 hurricane, for he knew everyone in the region and he helped to identify bodies for the authorities.

Natural disasters often acquired a folk explanation in the fisherman's oral history. Clams once were harvested on the southwest coast of Florida until they were killed by the "red tide" algae. Since this disaster occurred during World War II, the natives reasoned that Germans had poisoned the water. Tales are still told of German submarines and their shellfish sabotage.

Many Crackers living near Lake Okeechobee, or in the Everglades, go frogging. (Froglegs, a special treat in the South Florida diet, really do taste like a cross between chicken and fish.) Norman Padgett of West Palm Beach has hunted frogs ever since he was a boy. As a young man, his first job was as a net fisherman on Lake Okeechobee, but he soon specialized in frog gigging. Padgett explained that to catch frogs, he would go out on the lake at night in an airboat or small motorboat. Some people would also hunt frogs from canal banks in the Everglades. Hunters carry a large flashlight or miners' hat light, a frog gig, rubber boots and pants, a big sack, and a cooler. The frog gig itself is a folk tool, consisting of a handmade cylindrical steel head with several prongs, which is mounted on a long pole. Froggers stop their boats in swampy water where frogs are plentiful. When the frogs begin to croak, the hunters shine their lights on them, causing the frogs to freeze. The hunters quickly spear them with the gig, throw them into the sack, put the catch into the cooler and finally return home to clean and sell the legs.

Closely linked with fishing and frogging is the distinctly South Florida occupation of alligator hunting. Since the 1880s, traffic in alligator hides has been a brisk business. At the turn of the century, Cracker hunters were selling over fifty thousand hides annually. Alligator hunters are a colorful breed, with a few who have achieved legendary status in Florida folklore. Tales are told of "Ferguson" who could call 'gators by barking like a dog (alligators love dog meat). He was said to kill the 'gators for their teeth, which he sold for five dollars a pound. "Alligator Platt" was said to be so cheap that he would save his gunpowder and shells by hiding on the bank of a creek until a 'gator floated to the surface, then dive under, wrestle the animal and reappear "with his thumbs hooked in the gator's eyes, and in triumph ride to shore."

Historian Charlton Tebeau collected a 'gator story from Cracker pioneer Ted Smallwood, who lived in Chokoloskee until his death in the late 1950s. The year 1898 was very dry in South Florida, and a huge number of alligators migrated to Roberts Lake. Thomas Roberts, who gave the lake its name, was hunting and found the water just "teeming with alligators." He went to get some friends to help and a load of salt for the hides, and returned to harvest ten thousand alligator hides to sell to the Fort Myers market that day. Another version of that story credits Tom Roberts's brother, Bill, and a friend with finding the 'gators. According to the tale, the two men decided that they needed a cart and lots of salt to deal with the number of reptiles. They wanted to keep their competitors out, so they built a very high and narrow cart, then cut a narrow road with high stumps so that their cart was the only one that could navigate to the lake shore.

Other tall tales describe an abundance of 'gators, with hunters who were said to have gathered over four thousand hides in a day along the Tamiami Trail in "the old days." Peter Douthit of Big Pine Key remembers hunting as a boy with his father when the alligators would be so thick in the lakes that his father would shoot a rifle and "millions of heads would all come up."

Tall tales aside, it is common knowledge in Cracker folklore that alligators love two foods especially—marshmallows and dogs—and using either for bait is a sure way to attract the beasts to their lairs. Today, alligator hunting is strictly regulated and "alligator control agents" are the only persons licensed to kill a 'gator beyond the short hunting season. One control agent, who was called to kill a "nuisance" alligator that had floated too close to civilization, attests to the food preference of the animal. When the 'gator's stomach was autopsied, six metal dog tags were found, the only remains of six tasty meals.

The alligators harvested by control agents are carefully monitored; the skins are labeled, and then sold, and the tails are tagged and sent to South Florida restaurants that serve alligator tail as a specialty. Although they are less numerous today, the alligators that exist are a strong symbol of the Florida wilderness and a source of narrative material to Cracker, Seminole and African American raconteurs.

UNDERGROUND OCCUPATIONS

Other tales told by Florida Crackers have to do with storms, supernatural happenings, personal experience and danger, buried and sunken treasure, and illegal activities. Of South Florida's "underground" (illegal) occupations, poaching, moonshining and smuggling have figured prominently in the region's folk culture.

"Low bush lightning" is the Cracker term for moonshine, and the Everglades area is said to be "alive with moonshine stills" to this day. One Cracker pioneer, C. G. McKinney, moved from Columbia County in north Florida to the Everglades "for his health" and became a renowned moonshiner and bootlegger. Tales are swapped of the time that McKinney used too much Red Devil lye in his brew and "the stuff was so strong, it would lather like soap when rubbed in your hands." This batch was said to "eat up a common man's gizzard."

South Florida has also been, and still is, known as a center of smuggling—liquor during prohibition, illegal aliens for many years, and most recently illegal drugs. The vast undeveloped coastline and maze-like waterways of South Florida make it a perfect place to import and hide illegal cargo. Bootlegging of Cuban rum to Florida markets was quite common in the 1930s, while cargoes of Chinese, Cuban, Jamaican, Haitian, and Bahamian immigrants have been smuggled into Florida for several generations.

South Floridians recount escapades of "the Ashley gang," an early Cracker family who made their living as bootleggers. John Ashley and his five sons and four daughters were notorious in the region, beginning their underground careers with the bootleg business, then advancing to bank robbery, and finally committing a few murders. Most raconteurs agree that the lawmen left the Ashleys alone up until the murders, for "like the Ashleys, the lawmen were Crackers—and Crackers stick together."

FOODWAYS

Pioneer Crackers who settled in South Florida survived on a diet of wild game and fish, garden vegetables and tropical fruit. Although they killed alligators for their hides, Crackers never ate 'gator until recently. However, turtles, turtle eggs, and frogs' legs were favorite game dishes in the Cracker diet. Today turtling is illegal, but catching the freshwater "cooter" (a soft-shell turtle) and frogging are still popular.

Another favorite dish in the Cracker diet is mullet, which is either fried, roasted over an open fire, or smoked, with an old refrigerator used as a smoker. Most Crackers agree that smoked mullet is the preferred way to serve the fish, even though it takes about eight hours to properly smoke a refrigerator full of the fish. Most Crackers maintain that mullet is the only fish you can eat every day without getting tired of it. In fact, grits and mullet is still often the preferred daily breakfast meal.

Catfish is another staple, with the channel cat reigning as the "king" of good eating fish. Lake Okeechobee is known to be the best source for the coveted channel cat, but Florida Crackers also enjoy the red cat (named for its reddish tinge), spotted cat, butter cat (with yellow skin), and the butt head (with an extremely wide head). Mullet roasts and catfish fries are the most common celebratory gatherings for Florida Cracker families. Served with hush puppies and grits, these fish are eaten throughout the region.

When times are hard, Crackers can always rely upon fish to keep the table full. David Teems recalls how "grits and grunts" kept people alive in South Florida during the Depression. Grunts are small fish that are easy to catch "from the shore and off of the bridges." Today you can often see people fishing for grunts on the bridges of South Florida. Peter Douthit maintains that Conchs (Key Westers) love grunts more than any other food. "If you let the Conchs get into your fish box, they'll take out the grunts [to eat] and leave the snapper and yellow tail there."

Most Florida Crackers are adept at using the tropical abundance that surrounds them to supplement their diet. The Teems family made all of their own jellies and jams out of fruits growing wild in the South Florida glades—guava, sea grapes, and mulberries. Teems recalls that his family "had lots of trees—grapefruit, oranges, lime, mango, bananas. . . . We would slice mangoes and make ice cream. It was quite common—most Florida families would have sliced mangoes on the plate as a side dish." Today families continue to have tropical fruit trees in their yards, and guavas can still be found growing wild. A favorite dish for the Teems family is homemade coconut milkshakes. They "get the coconuts and shred them and put it in ice cream, made with a hand-turned ice-cream maker."

Peter Douthit recalls another unique South Florida delicacy, heart of palm salad. "These old palms, we made cabbage out of them . . . throw a little bit of tomato in it, a little side belly, and they'd make a right good pot." To make heart of palm salad, one cuts the tender center out of a cabbage palmetto, slices it thin and boils it like cabbage. The dish is delicious, but it kills the palmetto.

Aside from these South Florida dishes, the Crackers of the region brought foodways from the upland south. Hoecakes, biscuits, fatback stew, possum, rabbit, and other foods that are common throughout the South survived the move to South Florida.

One place where Cracker delicacies can be sampled does a thriving business. Carl Allen of Auburndale is a native Florida Cracker, born in 1919. Today he operates Allen's Historical Cafe on U.S. 92 West, and he prides himself on serving "exclusively Cracker cuisine." Alligator tail, armadillo, rattlesnake, shark, fried pickles and watermelon soup are just a few of choice menu items.

TRANSPORTATION

Though traditional craft skills such as blacksmithing, basketry, fishnet making, saddlery, quilting, and needlework abound in Florida Cracker culture, boat building is perhaps the most important folk craft in South Florida. Boat types, which are distinctive to each region, are named

Glen Simmons in his Glades skiff (Photo by Michele Edelson/Courtesy of HASF)

according to their place of origin (Okeechobee shipjack) or for prominent builders. One type of shipjack is known, for instance, as the "Gillis boat" after its creator, Leo Gillis of Okeechobee.

Although most South Florida boats are now mass produced, some craftsmen continue to make boats by hand. Glen Simmons of Florida City is one such craftsman. Simmons is a native Floridian who recalls when the Everglades ran free, before the establishment of the Everglades National Park and the dredging of canals. Since the Glades often held only a few inches of water (depending upon the rainfall), South Florida Crackers had to develop unique forms of transportation to navigate in their marine environment. Like the shallow-draft canoes of the Seminoles, the Glades skiff is long and narrow, so that it can skim the surface of the water. A boatman stands poling in the middle of the boat.

Glen Simmons, a master builder of the Glades skiff, remembers when almost everyone in Florida City owned one for use in travel. Born near Homestead in 1916, Simmons created his first skiff at the age of twelve when the boats were still made of cypress that could be bent to a pointed bow. Although this basic design remains the same—sixteen feet long, twenty-six inches wide, eleven inches high on the sides—Glades skiffs are now made of marine plywood or fiberglass. In the highest compliment paid by modern technology to the past, local boat builders have used Simmons's skiffs to make molds for the fiberglass skiffs marketed in the area. These boats, developed for specific needs, are still useful for navigation on the "river of grass."

In addition to being a skiff maker for over sixty years, Simmons is a hunter, fisher, banana farmer, and Everglades guide to writers and naturalists. In 1986, he was part of the Florida Folk Arts Apprenticeship Program, teaching his young apprentice, Don Edwards, the skill of fashioning these region-specific boats in the traditional manner (from wood) before the art was lost.

Today, the Glades skiff is rare, with "swamp buggies" and "Glades buggies" being folk innovations that are preferred. The swamp buggy is an amphibious craft with a lightweight powerful engine, low-speed transmission and oversized tires. Hunters in the Glades have customized these vehicles, and they have become a favorite with the Seminole who live on Big Cypress Reservation. The Glades buggy is similar to the swamp buggy, but has caterpillar-like traction.

On the western side of the Everglades, where the water is slightly deeper and covers most of the land, the airboat is used to transport people through the watery environment. With a flat bottom that draws only a few inches of water, the hull of an airboat is riveted from aircraft aluminum. Near the stern, bolted to a cypress frame, is an exposed airplane motor and behind the engine is a large, two-blade propeller encased in a metal cage, looking like a giant fan.

Like all folklore, the origin of the airboat has been orally passed on and is disputed. Some claim that aviator Glenn Curtiss designed the first

Jimmy Swait cruising the Everglades in his airboat (Photo by Michele Edelson/ Courtesy of HASF)

airboat in 1920 before he went on to develop the cities of Hialeah, Miami Springs, and Opa-Locka. Others maintain that the airboat was invented in the 1920s by a stunt man named Hubert Richmond who was hired by the Florida Game and Fish Commission to design a craft that they could use in the Everglades. It is also said that two Everglades frog hunters became tired of navigating the Glades in a skiff, and independently designed an airboat with a seventy-five-horsepower engine in 1933. Frogger Johnny Lamb remembers that "we figured we'd be the only ones that would ever need one."

Whatever its provenance, the airboat soon was adopted by alligator poachers, game wardens, Seminole guides and Cracker hunters as the preferred means of Everglades transportation. Today a ride on an airboat is a thrill for tourists, with the propeller making earsplitting noises and the driver racing over the grass with "no brakes, keel or reverse. You stop by decelerating and executing a quick ninety-degree turn, like a hockey player on skates."

Despite its recent invention, this vehicle is a South Florida folk artifact, for airboats are designed and made by individuals for their own use, with designs passed from one builder to another. The boats are modified according to buyer specifications and constructed in small backyard workshops throughout the region. There is a great deal of variation and dispute among airboat makers as to the preferred types of engines, shapes, and sizes of boats. Airboaters use rebuilt Buick, Ford V-8 and Volkswagon engines to power their crafts, which they christen with names like "Hurricane" and "The Gator." Some builders rely upon making airboats for a living, fashioning vehicles that can carry up to twenty people. These larger craft are often employed for sightseeing or to lead forays into the water wilderness for night fishing, frogging and hunting.

Jimmy Swait's airboat workshop, located on the eastern edge of the Everglades, is typical of most. Swait has been repairing and making airboats for about twenty-five years. Previously, he worked for the Coast Guard as a civilian mechanic, then made and ran airboats for Holiday Park in the Everglades. Today, Swait concentrates upon the commercial market, making large boats that are sold to diverse customers, including cranberry boggers from Massachusetts. He claims to have been the first to design and make large two-engine touring airboats.

Like other traditional craftsmen, Jimmy Swait and his son, John, do not use formal plans; Jimmy explains that "they're all in my head." In addition, the Swaits modify each boat to fit the customer's needs, since "everybody wants something different." When these two traditional boat builders want a visual reference to communicate their ideas, they simply draw the design on brown paper and tack it to the wall. Large airboats from the Swait workshop run up to twelve thousand dollars, while smaller craft cost about seven thousand dollars. In addition to the domestic market, Swait supplies airboats for wetlands industries as far away as Bolivia and India.

Airboats, a traditional innovation that developed in South Florida, have now found a mass market. In South Florida alone there are more than three thousand airboats registered in the wetlands, and the Airboaters Association of Florida boasts over three hundred fifty members.

ARCHITECTURE

What is now recognized as the "Florida Cracker house" dates back to the mid-nineteenth century when early settlers brought knowledge of different house types from backgrounds as diverse as the Deep South, the urban Northeast, Europe, the Bahamas and Key West. From this eclectic mix, architectural features that were best suited for Florida were selected.

Crackers who settled in this tropical wilderness also relied upon new materials that were readily available on the Florida Peninsula, as well as traditional technologies that had developed here. For instance, before the advent of concrete, the pioneers in South Florida made structures out of "tabby," a lime-and-oyster-shell mixture that they combined with sand. This technique was common in the Caribbean, and the materials were all readily available in the South Florida wilderness. Many buildings on the Florida landscape today are made of this durable mix.

Cracker architecture evolved in response to the hot, humid climate of South Florida. Cracker houses reflect the open, rural nature of life in the region; often large in scale, they take advantage of the plentiful open land. The typical Florida Cracker house is a clapboarded one-story rectangular bungalow or hall and parlor two-story structure, with a large, wraparound porch. High ceilings and many tall windows maximize ventilation. Houses are usually elevated off the ground, with stone or brick supports that discourage termites and snakes and also protect against the strong winds and high water of tropical storms.

The front and back doors are often aligned in the center of the house and connected by a long breezeway. During warm weather, both doors can be open, allowing air to flow from front to back. The houses traditionally face east so that occupants can take advantage of the eastern breezes. Many Cracker homes also have tall peaked roofs with wide overhangs and Bermuda shutters over floor-to-ceiling windows—all features designed to maximize air ventilation and minimize sun exposure. In

The Thomas Culbertson house in Coconut Grove, ca. 1890s (Photo courtesy of HASF)

all, the Cracker house is an excellent shelter for the South Florida tropics.

David Teems explains that the wood used to make most of South Florida's original Cracker houses was virgin pine, known as "Dade County pine" in South Florida, but called "lighter" or "heart" pine in north Florida. The wood that was cut from these trees is full of resin. It could be worked easily while it was green, but when it aged the resin hardened, making it almost impossible to hammer a nail through the wood. The positive side to this is that termites won't eat the wood; the negative side is that if there is a fire, the resin-filled wood is extremely flammable—thus the name "lighter."

Today, windows, doors and porches on Cracker homes are screened, but before screens were easily available, Crackers had to deal in other ways with the ubiquitous insects. David Teems remembers that "people would burn smudge pots outside and sit outside on their porches at night. They would burn oil, rubber, turpentine, or anything with a dark, oily smoke to keep the mosquitoes away. It kept the mosquitoes down to a tolerable level, but never rid them totally."

Older Cracker homes were roofed with cypress shingles. These allowed air ventilation that many feel was lost with the advent of tarpaper and asbestos shingles. Peter Douthit insists that it was not until he replaced his cypress shingle roof with new materials that he had to install air conditioning, for "it didn't allow the heat to escape like the cypress roof."

ORAL LORE

When the Federal Writers Project of the 1930s sent fieldworkers to South Florida, they found that the Crackers spoke "a mixture of Old English provincialisms, local slang, and a variety of home-invented words." Language is a fluid and changing art form, and Florida Crackers continue to exhibit inventiveness in their speech. The saying that has been used by President Bill Clinton, "Anyone knows, that dog won't hunt," is a common Cracker way of expressing skepticism. Crackers in Florida refer to a particularly cold evening as "a three-dog night," reportedly meaning that it would take sleeping with three dogs to keep warm. "I done drunk outta fruit jars so long, I got a ridge across my nose" explains a man's economic status with folk humor.

Similarly, jokes are a way to deal with the nuisance of tourists. Crackers delight in telling visitors that the way to make a good living is to "fish in the summer, and live off the Yankees in the winter." Crackers refer to the seasonal tourists as "snowbirds" who live in "bird nests" (condominium high-rises). Cracker jokes and folklore abound concerning the idiocy of tourists, especially the Yankee tourist. One story, told in Stetson Kennedy's *Palmetto Country*, goes this way:

There is the tale about the Yankee who approached a Cracker's cart of covered wares, and sniffed suspiciously. "What have you got there?" he asked. "Guavas," replied the Cracker. The Yankee sniffed again. "Ye Gods!" he exclaimed. "How long have they been dead?"

Aside from jokes and folk idiom, many Crackers are excellent raconteurs. The most pervasive tales are told either as personal experience narratives or as oral history. Cracker narratives often deal with the isolation and wildness of South Florida life, before "civilization" overtook the peninsula. Charles Pierce recounts the story of "the barefoot mailman":

There was a mail route from Palm Beach to Miami by way of the ocean beach. It was called the barefoot route because the mail carrier went barefoot in order to walk at the water's edge, where the sand was firmer. He would have to walk 25 miles straight walking at times. The whole route was 136 miles long and took the carrier six days, sometimes rowing, sometimes walking, but 80 miles of the route was done barefoot.

This story was later expanded and used in Theodore Platt's novel, *The Barefoot Mailman*. Other stories deal with the frontier-like justice in South Florida, and colorful characters who populated Cracker settlements. The most notorious was perhaps Edward J. ("Ed") Watson. As Charlton Tebeau outlines the facts, garnered from oral accounts, Ed Watson was a bad man, who became legendary in Cracker folklore—"He was generous, kind-hearted, friendly, and ready to do a favor, but he had a fearful temper when aroused."

Watson moved to Chatham River in the Everglades during the 1890s and became a successful farmer. It was said that he moved to the remote Everglades to escape reprisals. When he was a boy, growing up in central Florida, he supposedly "shot and killed a Negro, because he feared the Negro would tell his father about his carelessness in pea-picking." It is said that he fled to Arkansas, where he met Belle Starr, the infamous outlaw. "Watson had a premonition that the Starr family was about to do him in, so he shot her and fled." He settled then in Oregon, where he married and fathered four children. Unfortunately, he shot and killed another foe there and fled again, leaving his family behind. One more murder down the road, and Watson arrived in the Glades with his violent reputation preceding him.

Watson's temper continued to be a problem in South Florida. He seriously injured another Florida pioneer, Aldolphus Santini, when he got into an argument and "cut" him outside a Key West auction house. As his notoriety grew, an unsolved double murder on Lostman's River was blamed on Watson in the gossip mill. Two men were killed in Columbia County, in north Florida where Watson also owned land, and again the killings were attributed to the now legendary "bad man."

Watson finally met his own end in a bizarre manner. When he became angry at a group of his neighbors, he reached for his gun and attempted to shoot two rounds. The bullets were wet from the October 17, 1910, hurricane and misfired. However, the group of men standing near were all armed and sped into action, firing a fusillade of shots that killed Watson and cemented his fame in Florida's list of legendary characters. When asked fifty years later why Watson's neighbors were so quick to kill him, one onlooker said simply, "They were scared of him." The life of Ed Watson is detailed in a 1990 novel by Peter Matthiessen, *Killing Mr. Watson*, which is based largely upon oral accounts and local folklore.

Peter Douthit tells the tale of Lostman's River, which he claims was named by his father. Peter remembers his father telling the story this way:

There was a couple living there [Lostman's River area] with a little boy about six years old. They lived there at the mouth of that river, and they farmed, they had some high land. He done anything he could to make a little money—make a little charcoal, fish and farm. That was good onion land, for some reason, salt didn't bother the onions. My daddy's brother-in-law was in the store business in Key West. Anything you could think of, he would have in that store. If you wanted a pair of shoes, or a horse collar, or groceries, he had it. Key West at that time was the largest, most thriving city in the state of Florida. They had all the sponging industry and all the cigar industry. Anyway, getting back to this Lostman's River story, my daddy run the mail every two weeks, and people would give him written orders for the store in Key West. They'd fill these orders, and he'd run that mail on schedule, weather permitting, and people would come in [to his father's house] to pick up their groceries and mail. And this guy didn't come in for three or four days. So they decided something was the matter with him. So my dad and about three or four others decided to go see about him. It was a pretty good trip around there in a sailboat, you know. Sometimes a man can get killed, maybe get snakebit or something, and the woman would be there by herself. So they went around there to see. Now, his boat was still tied up to the dock, it was a sailboat. They had another small boat, a skiff and they both were tied up to the dock. And they went on into the house, the house was all open. There was a half-cooked meal on the table, and not a soul around. They went out in the garden, and nobody in the garden. Someone had been hoeing and just throwed the hoe down. But nobody around there, no sign of nobody. The boats were there, so they couldn't have gone off. And what they figured happened, that tide had gone out—you had a pretty swift, deep channel in there. They figured the kid fell overboard [into the river from the bank] and screamed for help. Mama, she was cooking dinner, and she run out there to get the kid, and of course she screamed too, and the man run out there to save both of them. And instead of getting in a boat to save them, he jumped overboard and figured he'd swim back, but he couldn't. And that's what they figured happened, that all three of them drowned in that swift current. It swept 'em out to sea, and they never found no sign of them. They stayed around there for a day or two, but they didn't have facilities for looking, you know. But I've heard my daddy tell that story several times down through the years, he's a good storyteller.

Since tropical storms hit the South Florida peninsula regularly—there were severe storms in 1873, 1910, 1921, 1924, 1926, 1935, 1938, 1944, 1948, and 1992—a rich body of hurricane lore has evolved. Such lore includes descriptions of traditional warning signs of an approaching storm (e.g., the snakes begin moving to high ground), "black humor" jokes about hurricane damage, tall tales about the extent of damage ("mullet blowed in on the shore and were two feet deep, ready for the fry pan"), and a host of personal experience stories. Peter Douthit tells about the hurricane of 1928 that killed thousands in the Lake Okeechobee area:

Peter Douthit of Big Pine
Key (Photo by Jan Belland)

Well, I had gone up there [to Belle Glade, a farming community on the edge of
Lake Okeechobee] with my daddy and another boy. He had bought forty acres of
muck up there—virgin land. And that's what we were doing, we were clearing up
that muck, where we could farm it. We were about three or four miles out of
Pahokee, on the main road out there. And we had built a shack, a good, big
shack, about a twenty-foot deal. And we had it up on blocks, just four-by-four
blocks, up off the ground. During the first half of that storm, well, it blew the
house off [the blocks] and set it down in the muck. And we had carried over a

bunch of two-inch pipe, we were going to irrigate an acre, for strawberries or something, I don't know. But during that lull [as the eye of the hurricane passed over], we had one of those old Coleman lanterns hanging up in the middle of the shack, and we'd cook and eat and slept just out in the open place in there, it was just one room. And during the lull, I guess it must have been fifteen or twenty blacks come in—they seen the light of that old Coleman lantern. Of course, the tarpaper had blown off the house. But when that thing come back [back side of the hurricane], that water come out of the lake. That was in '28, before there was any dike. And within fifteen minutes, that water was just about titty-deep in that shack, and all those blacks in there, Saturday night. And they was drinking, some of them, and they was scared. They done had their shacks blowed down, most of them just had little old lean-tos and stuff. They was praying and drinking, and we was up on the table. We had a table there and the three of us got up on it, because we didn't know how deep that water was going to get. And there wasn't no way for us to get out of there if it kept getting deeper. We were afraid that those blacks would try to get up on that table with us, and that would have broke *it* down. So we decided that the best thing for us to do was to get out on the road, the road was the highest thing around there. So we got out and fortunately, we had took some supply lines, some rope, and we tied ourselves together, about six feet between us. And we got out there, and you know those storms will build up and build up and build up, and then they'd drop down. Well, we'd been through the '26 storm here in Dade County, so we got out and made it across the bridge, well, we had to swim across the bridge. And we made it up on the road. And the only way we could stay on the road was to get down on our hands and knees, one right behind the other. That water was just like an open sea, and that water was *full* of rubbish. That virgin muck would float up in chunks, there'd be chunks as big as that chair come by, you know, and it'd just about knock you for a loop. We wasn't hurt. When that storm was over that next day, I still had both shoes, but both the others had lost one shoe and all we had left for clothes was a belt, with pieces of flayed cloth. That's how much trash was in the water. But you know, we couldn't comb out our hair for about three weeks.

Cracker tales such as this impart a sense of belonging, a sense of place to families who pioneered in a wilderness area and continue to feel a link with the land that survives despite development and seasonal tourist invasions. Multicultural South Florida continues to grow and change, each new group adding its folklore to the mix of cultures on the peninsula. However, Florida Crackers maintain a strong claim upon a land that was sparsely inhabited until the twentieth century. Their culture—oral lore, architecture, foodways, religion, social events, occupational lore, and music—demonstrate a unique combination of white southern traditions and adaptations to life in a tropical land.

Miami

The Cubans

Florida and Cuba have been fated to a long, intertwined history. From the time of early European contact to the present day, their peoples have moved back and forth across the narrow passage as the tides of history have turned. In the process they have profoundly changed and influenced each other.

HISTORY

Prior to European contact, the Taíno, Ciboney, and Guanahacabibe peoples hunted, gathered, and raised crops on the island they called Cuba. Columbus landed on the island during his first voyage in 1492, and the Spanish conquered Cuba between 1511 and 1513. Harsh treatment by the invaders and diseases brought from Europe resulted in the demise of most indigenous peoples by the mid-sixteenth century. Nevertheless, their presence lingers in such musical instruments as the *maracas* and *güiro*, and in the *bohío*, or typical rural dwelling.

Cuban culture is primarily a synthesis of Spanish and African traditions. Beginning in 1522, the Spanish brought African slaves to Cuba to supplement the indigenous labor force. By 1532 blacks made up 65 percent of the population. Slaves and free blacks maintained a majority until the late nineteenth century, when European immigrants dominated the population. When Castro's revolution propelled over a million people to leave the island, among the exiles were a disproportionately large number of whites. Today, some estimate that people of African descent again constitute the majority in Cuba.

Cuba and Florida have been linked since the Spanish settled the Americas. Throughout the Spanish colonial period, Florida came under Cuba's governmental and religious jurisdiction. Cuba also provided most settlers and supplies to the Florida frontier, so there was a constant flow of people and trade between the two.

Due to its strategic importance and economic value, Cuba was one of the last Spanish colonies granted independence. The first struggle for independence began in 1868, but was not successful. A subsequent brutal backlash by Spanish military forces and vigilantes led to substantial Cuban emigration to Key West and New York.

At the same time that many Cubans sought political refuge there, some cigar manufacturers relocated to nearby Key West to avoid paying American tariffs. The cigar establishments in turn attracted more Cuban workers. By the mid-1870s, forty-five factories employed fourteen hundred workers who rolled about 15 million cigars each year. The cigar workers' custom of listening to *lectores* read from a variety of newspapers, essays, and political tracts while they worked created a highly educated and politically aware society. As the century drew to a close, they became one of the key groups supporting Cuban independence.

In the mid-1880s, many cigar manufacturers moved to Tampa or returned to Havana in order to avoid strikes by militant Key West workers. The transplanted industry flourished in Tampa/Ybor City, and by 1900 a Cuban population of over thirty-five hundred worked largely in the cigar factories or related industries. In 1892 the United States consul to Cuba, Ramón Williams, noted, "The people here look upon Florida as so much a part of their own country.... Between Key West and Havana people go as between Albany and New York."

Cuba's war for independence lasted from 1895 to 1898. Florida Cubans provided supplies, ammunition, and men to the effort. Although the Cuban people were largely responsible for winning the war against Spain, intervention by the Americans at the eleventh hour allowed them to take credit. After the U.S.S. *Maine* exploded in Havana harbor, the United States declared war in April 1898. American troops fought beside the Cuban rebels until the Spanish surrendered in August. The United States installed a military government and occupied Cuba until power was transferred to a new president on May 20, 1902. However, it forced the new government to accept permanent restrictions on self-government so as to preserve special privileges for the United States.

The period from independence to the Revolution was characterized by moderate overall prosperity, though governments ranged from corrupt to reformist. Americans flocked to Havana to enjoy the beaches and nightlife. With the additional presence of large numbers of American businesses and property owners (many from Florida), Cuba in general and Havana in particular came under strong American influence.

By the Batista era of the 1950s, there was a significant economic gap between the upper and lower classes. Moreover, Batista's government alientated the large middle class with its repression and disrespect for democratic processes. As a result, revolutionary forces toppled Batista on January 1, 1959, and Fidel Castro instituted a government that turned increasingly left.

It is estimated that a million Cubans emigrated as a result of the profound social and political changes instituted by Castro's government. They fled to Spain, Mexico, Venezuela, Puerto Rico, Peru, and other

Spanish-speaking countries, but mostly to the United States and especially to Miami. The first wave of 280,000 political refugees arrived between 1959 and 1961. They were predominately middle-aged, white, well-educated, and affluent. The second wave of 273,000 arrived in Miami between 1965 and 1973 as part of a weekly airbridge designed by the American and Cuban governments to reunite Cubans with their families. Immigrants of the second wave were less homogeneous than the first. Among them were many non-whites, blue-collar workers, intellectuals, and academics.

The third wave of more than 125,000 Cubans came by way of the Mariel boatlift in 1980. This massive exodus was the result of worsening relations between the United States and Cuba, combined with a movement by disaffected Cubans to leave the country. The Mariel Cubans represented a more diverse cross-section of the national populace than previous waves. Their arrival precipitated a revitalization of many Cuban folk traditions.

In recent years there has been another, largely hidden wave of immigration by Cubans who enter the United States on temporary visas. For instance, in August 1991, the State Department noted that a third of the thirty-six thousand Cubans admitted as tourists in the previous ten months had overstayed their visas and might not return. In addition, thousands of Cubans have attempted to sail to Florida on small boats or rubber rafts. Between January and August 1991, over fourteen hundred made the perilous trip and many more perished at sea.

The number of Cubans and Cuban Americans in the United States today is estimated to be over 1 million, with about eight hundred thousand residing in southeast Florida. Cubans have worked hard to establish new homes and businesses, and in doing so they have created powerful commercial institutions with links to Latin American and Caribbean countries. Through their efforts, they have created a prosperous and dynamic world financial center in Miami. Although integrated into the American economic mainstream, they have not abandoned the traditions that make their folklife unique.

SOCIAL STRUCTURE

Life Cycle

Childhood   The *canastilla* (literally, a small basket or layette) refers to the Cuban tradition of giving a new mother the necessary clothes and linens for her newborn infant. Women use the needlework skills taught them by their mothers and grandmothers to fashion elaborate baby clothes for female relatives. Tiny smocked or embroidered dresses and jumpers, lace-decorated christening gowns, knitted and crocheted sweaters, hats, and booties are among the items still made by these folk artists.

Today in Miami, stores called canastillas carry manufactured baby items patterned after the traditional ones. Some also offer their clients the opportunity to purchase handmade items. La Canastilla Cubana is the largest, and perhaps the quintessential, Cuban children's store in southeast Florida. The business started when seamstress Esther Martín emigrated from Cuba in 1967, and started sewing baby clothes and bassinet skirts in order to earn a living. In addition to standard baby gear, the store offers traditional Cuban items such as the *moíses*, frilly bassinets with lace or eyelet tiers that come replete with *mosquiteros*, or mosquito netting. The moíses and other items are made to order by a back room full of seamstresses.

Baptisms are important occasions not only for their religious significance, but also because they are the occasion on which the *padrinos*, or godparents, are designated. Parents dress the infant in a long white baptismal gown, and family and friends wear formal attire for the church service and ensuing party. The party is often a grand affair with tents, catered food, and a band. Traditional pink or blue sugar-covered almonds wrapped in festive fabric packets usually await guests at the tables.

Cubans choose godparents carefully, usually selecting siblings, cousins, or extremely close friends. They perceive padrinos as an extra set of parents who will look after the child, listen to his or her troubles, and make a fuss on birthdays, holidays, performances, and other meaningful occasions. Padrinos have additional significance since the church regards them as sources of spiritual guidance. Moreover, the relationship between parents and godparents as *compadres*, or coparents, is very close. Godchildren pay their respects to godparents with visits on Easter Sunday (also called *el día de ahijados*, or godchildren's day), Mother's Day, and Father's Day.

Children's birthdays are important events in the Cuban community, reflecting the culture's high regard for children. The birthday party is more than just a social event for children—it marks the presentation of the child to the community. This is particularly true of the first birthday. Children's birthdays are usually observed with elaborate festivities to which dozens, sometimes hundreds, of children and parents are invited. It is not unusual for these occasions to start in the afternoon with games and clowns, and last until early morning, as the adults share conversation and refreshments while the children sleep.

Cubans commemorate a child's first five or six birthdays with a huge *merengue* cake and a large decorative *piñata*. Cuban piñatas are different from those made in other countries. Instead of making decorated clay or papier mache receptacles, Cubans construct large cake-shaped piñatas of cardboard and hang them by wooden handles. Decorations of crepe paper and toys reflect themes often based on popular fantasy characters, such as Big Bird, super heroes, Little Mermaid, or clowns. Dozens of multi-colored ribbons dangle from the bottom of the piñata. The entire group of children pulls the ribbons so that the bottom falls out, spilling the candy and prizes. Cubans maintain that this type of piñata is safer and easier for small children, and promotes cooperation rather than competition.

For many Cubans, the smell of violet eau de cologne is almost synonymous with childhood. Parents often sprinkle children and babies with the fragrance after baths. Isabelle Blanco has fond memories of a childhood ritual. In order to cool the children down after playing, their mother would bathe them, then rub them with the violet fragrance, dust them with powder, and dress them up. They passed the late afternoon sitting outside the house and greeting passing friends.

When children lose a baby tooth, they write a letter to *el ratón Miguel*, then place both letter and tooth under the pillow when they go to bed. Cuban parents tell them that while they sleep el ratón Miguel (sometimes also called Mr. Rat or Mr. Perez Mouse) will give them money in exchange for the tooth. With the teeth, el ratón Miguel will build himself a nice little house. Today, Cuban American children often write their letters in English and may expect as much as a dollar per tooth.

Adolescence: **La Quinceañera**   One of the most important events in a woman's life is her fifteenth birthday celebration, or *quinceañera*. In traditional Cuban society, the fifteenth birthday marks the point at which she is first presented to society as a potential wife and companion. Young women are generally perceived as very beautiful at the time of their *quinces*. In fact, a common saying is that an unattractive woman *"nunca tuvo quinces"*—that is, she never had a quince.

In pre-revolutionary Cuba, the upper classes especially observed this milestone. They often celebrated the quinces of several girls simultaneously with a joint party or a chaperoned trip to Europe. During the quince party, the young woman would dance the traditional *danzón* with her father.

In South Florida, Cubans from many socioeconomic backgrounds have achieved a high level of affluence. In such cases, quinces may be celebrated more lavishly than in Cuba. However, young Cuban American women approaching their fifteenth birthday are given choices, and not all elect to have elaborate parties. Some families offer the girl an opportunity to travel, perhaps accompanied by friends. The ultimate choice depends upon the outlook and finances of the family or the nature of the girl.

Miami quinces are often extravagant, choreographed, and catered affairs that take place at large resort hotels, such as the Fontainbleau. The honored young woman is specially schooled in social arts for the occasion. She often wears an elaborate dress with hoop skirts, which may be rented, bought ready-made, or made to order. Special shops employ rooms of seamstresses to make new quince dresses or to alter existing ones for rental. They also offer the services of a photographer and videographer to record the event, then present the celebrant with a photo album.

The young woman celebrating her quinceañera is attended by fourteen girlfriends in matching gowns, and they are escorted by tuxedoed young men. The celebrant wears white or a light color, while her female companions wear matching dresses in another color. They may arrive in a rented limousine, though some young women have arrived in helicopters at the most lavish quinces. As the band plays, hundreds of guests dance and dine until dawn.

Marriage   Most Cuban parents expect their children to live at home until marriage. Although some young Cuban Americans assert the American ideal of independence, traditional family values remain remarkably strong. Most young people remain at home until a much later age than mainstream American youth, though many marry early in order to create their own homes.

When a couple decides to marry, a bridal shower often precedes the wedding. For many, this simply consists of a party for the couple. However, for some younger couples the shower is a major production organized by a professional and held at a club. It may include games, a deejay, and an emcee who narrates the history of the couple's courtship.

Invitations to Cuban weddings are unique. There are often two sets of invitations: one set sent to Americans and one to Cubans. The Spanish-language version announces the wedding time as a half hour earlier then the English-language version. When people plan to conduct the wedding promptly, they give the hour and add "American time." These invitations politely accommodate the differences between the time conventions in the two cultures.

In the Cuban community marriages are often celebrated with formal Catholic weddings that incorporate several old traditions. The couple typically chooses the best man and maid of honor from among close relations, and the father or another male relative accompanies the bride to the altar. During the ceremony, the man gives the woman *las arras*, twelve gold coins that symbolize the merging of the wealth or fortunes of the couple. The couple often hires a professional soprano to sing Schubert's "Ave Maria" during the communion. At that point, they bring out a *mantilla*, or veil, which has often been in the bride's family for generations. A special friend or relative drapes it from the woman's head to the man's shoulders to unite them symbolically. When the wedding mass ends, they unpin the mantilla and return it to safekeeping for future weddings.

After the wedding there is often an extravagant reception. Tables frequently offer napkins or other little souvenirs with the couple's names and wedding date. Guests are also given the traditional lacy packets of white sugar-covered almonds. Some weddings have special themes for the decorations or activities. For example, a recent wedding featured images of doves on many decorative items, and the couple released a pair of white doves at the reception. Most weddings are videotaped.

Death Death is always a matter of great emotional travail, and many customs have arisen to cope with the loss. When there is a terminal illness, Cuban families draw tightly together. Relatives crowd the room of the afflicted in order to provide support and care. When the person dies, friends and family members come from all over to pay their last respects. Often the deceased is buried within three days.

To many families, it is important to announce a death. Spanish-language papers such as *Diario de las Americas* carry the *esquelas*. These short obituaries written by the family incorporate personal messages to the deceased, a list of family members, and information about the funeral home and burial.

In Cuba, people often held the *velorio*, or wake, in the home, though in Havana and the larger cities some held it in funeral parlors. Cubans in Miami usually place their deceased loved ones in funeral parlors that accommodate their customs. Many Cuban American funeral parlors stay open all night so that mourners can maintain the velorio. Some also have small cafeterias to provide sustenance for the families and friends who stay all night.

The funeral homes usually lay the deceased in an open casket, providing a place nearby for mourners to kneel and say a prayer. The closest family members maintain a vigil in recliners that line the walls of the room. A priest frequently arrives to say a rosary at eight o'clock. Visitors often pay their respects later in the evening, and sign a special book to indicate their attendance. The velorios serve as reunions for old friends and acquaintances, so many eventually gather in the cafeteria to exchange greetings and news. In the early morning hours, those closest to the deceased or the family doze in the recliners as they maintain the velorio.

On the day of interment, the mourners attend a funeral mass. Everyone waits to enter the church until the casket is carried inside. Afterwards, they travel in a motor procession to the cemetery. Some feel that a long procession honors the dead. The grave site is frequently marked with a plaque inscribed with the name of the deceased, dates of birth and death, and a commemorative statement such as "You always will be with us." Some bear the image of the Cuban flag or the *Virgen de la Caridad*.

After the interment, family and friends gather at the home of a relative. They may talk about the deceased, or spend time catching up with friends and relatives who have come from out of town. Food is not part of the process, since there is a belief that grief robs one of appetite.

Long after the death of a loved one, families show their devotion by visiting and caring for the gravesite. Many visit their departed family members on weekends, but especially on their birthday, Mother's Day, Father's Day, and All Saints' Day.

Folk Religion

All formal religions include rituals, material culture, celebrations, and beliefs that are maintained and communicated outside official church doctrine. Moreover, some religions are based wholly upon shared beliefs and customs learned outside of formal institutions. Both levels of traditional religious belief and practice are folk religion.

Among Cubans of European heritage, Catholicism is the dominant religion and many traditions closely associated with the island derive from it. There are also a substantial number of Cuban Protestants. Some converted in the nineteenth century after settling in Key West or Tampa, and others were baptized at Methodist, Episcopalian, and Baptist missions in Cuba. Many Cuban jews (known affectionately as "Jewbans") emigrated to Miami, where they have established a large temple. In addition to the Judeo-Christian religions, Afro-Cuban *Santería* has many adherents in Cuba and southeast Florida.

Catholicism Although Catholicism is a very formalized religion, many ethnic groups contribute elements of their culture to the observance of Catholic rituals. Cubans have developed many unique ways of celebrating holy days in the annual calendar.

Among Cubans, the week before Easter—*Semana Santa* or Holy Week—is more important than Easter itself. In Cuba, most institutions closed on Good Friday and children would often go to their grandmother's house to say the rosary at the holy hour of three o'clock. Maggie

Manrara remembers the beliefs and customs from her childhood in Oriente Province:

Generally what we do is on Good Friday, we will go to one or more of the services...at three o'clock...I remember, when you were small you went to your grandmother's house at three o'clock. And everybody started saying the rosary. And that day you're supposed to have codfish, *bacalao*. And I mean it's a tradition, and that day bacalao runs out in any store because you're supposed to have it....

During Lent in Cuba, it was like—music was all sacrosanct music, and you're not supposed to do this and you're not supposed to do that. As a child you were not supposed to play, because what would happen if you fall? You would bleed to death. And the tradition on Good Friday, I remember this, it never happened to me anyway. But at noon you were supposed to go outside and have an egg, and open it up and that egg would turn red. And I don't know how many eggs I went through every Good Friday—it never turned red....And there was a special tree that you were supposed to cut it and it was supposed to bleed. There were a lot of things that happened, mysterious things that happened, on Good Friday. And God forbid that you did any work in the house. You couldn't sweep the floors, you couldn't do anything other than cook and eat. And pray. And what would happen? The wrath of God would come upon you, and you would get sick, and that type of thing.

Then in Miami, I think some families still keep very much the tradition of the Good Friday, to revere that day, not to do something like go to the beach or do any party type of thing. You do go to church. One of the problems I think is that you can go at different hours, so the three o'clock is not necessarily such an important time. Then you still have some families that get together and do that.

On Easter, Cuban children often dressed in new white shoes, hats, and clothing for church. Although baby chicks and ducks were associated with the holiday in Cuba, there were no bunnies, eggs, or special foods. In southeast Florida the Cuban community has adopted mainstream traditions to celebrate Easter, but many American institutions and business establishments now close on Good Friday in acknowledgement of Cuban customs.

Most Catholic countries venerate a particular saint who is tied to the history of the people. In Cuba, Catholics feel a special attachment to *Nuestra Señora de la Caridad del Cobre*, or Our Lady of Charity, whom they nicknamed Cachita. In the seventeenth century, three sailors huddled in a small storm-tossed boat in the bay of Nipe. As they prayed that they would not drown, a small statue of the Virgin floated toward them on a piece of wood. When they picked her up, the seas suddenly calmed. The sailors believed that the Virgin had saved them through her intervention. They took the statue ashore, where it is kept in a shrine atop Mount Cobre in eastern Cuba. La Caridad del Cobre gradually became the patron saint of Cuba and the Church recognized the manifestation of the Virgin.

In 1961, a refugee smuggled a replica of the Caridad del Cobre statue out of Cuba. The exile community feels a special attachment to this statue and has built a shrine, *La Ermita de la Caridad del Cobre,* overlooking Biscayne Bay. The shrine contains a fine fresco illustrating the history of the Cubans. Rows of traditional *taburetes,* or rustic wooden chairs with leather seats and backs, provide seating. The shrine is popular with the devout or those reaffirming their links with the past.

Each year at 6:00 P.M. on September 8, members of the exile community take the statue from the shrine to reenact the legend of the Caridad del Cobre. Thousands crowd the shrine, cry, sing the national anthem, and throw flowers into the sea as four men carry the statue onto the small boat of the man who started the tradition. A flotilla of private boats accompanies her around the bay and then to Miami Marine Stadium on nearby Rickenbacker Causeway. More than eight thousand faithful—many of whom have traveled from the church to the stadium—greet the Virgin by singing, praying, and waving handkerchiefs. Finally, they attend a special nighttime mass to demonstrate their devotion. This occasion allows those who have children and grandchildren born in Miami to convey a whole world of belief and a strong sense of national identification.

In the Cuban community, the winter holiday season extends from Thanksgiving through *El Día de Los Reyes Magos* on January 6. During this time there is a constant round of parties and dinners hosted by family, friends, and co-workers.

There are a number of decorative traditions associated with the Christmas season. In many parts of Cuba, people decorated their homes with Christmas trees, and that tradition is universally followed in South Florida. As in Cuba, most Cuban Americans also feel it is important to have a *nacimiento,* or nativity scene. Children are often allowed to set up the little lambs, angels, and other figures that compose the scene.

For Cubans, *Nochebuena,* or Christmas Eve, has historically been more important than Christmas Day. In Cuba, Nochebuena was celebrated with large family gatherings. In the rural areas, men often roasted an entire pig while women made other traditional dishes. During the day, family members would go from house to house, visiting neighbors, viewing their pigs, and accepting small holiday treats. At night they ate the roasted pig and, as a special treat, the youngest child received the tail.

Cuban Americans who have sufficient money and space continue the old traditions. They travel to the rural areas of Homestead or Davie to buy a pig and have it slaughtered. At home they dig a backyard pit, cover it with palm leaves, and roast the pig. However, many have modified the traditions because of circumstances in urban Miami. They may buy a pre-cooked pig, or simply roast a leg of pork in the oven. Cuban Americans have also created a new baking method using a *caja china*, or Chinese box, so that those with small yards can cook an entire pig. With the pig in an aluminum bottom covered by coals on a top of heavy metal, the hot air created by the coals cooks the animal.

Cuban Americans celebrate Nochebuena with a large, traditional family dinner. The menu usually includes roast pork, white rice, black beans, boiled yuca, Cuban bread, dates, and fresh figs. Certain sweets are very traditional during the Christmas season. For instance, the Spanish nougat candy called *turrón* is always available in a number of different flavors.

In Cuba, Christmas gifts were only for the children. Cuban American children generally believe in Santa Claus, so many families do not open gifts until the morning of December 25. Otherwise, Christmas is like a second Nochebuena on which the family enjoys leftovers and visits family and friends.

Hispanic tradition focuses more heavily on the arrival of the Three Kings than on Christmas. In Cuba, January 6, or *El Día de los Reyes Magos*, was celebrated with gifts for the children. Boys and girls would write letters to the Three Kings asking for certain toys, then leave the letters out for the Kings to see. Many would also leave grass or hay for the camels. When they awoke in the morning, there would be presents near the bed.

Few Miami Cubans keep the tradition of El Día de los Reyes Magos. Those that observe it reserve the larger presents for Christmas and give only a few small toys on January 6. Families commonly keep their Christmas trees until after this date.

In 1971, Castro banned Christmas and Three Kings Day celebrations in Cuba. Although there was no parade in Cuba, Radio WQBA-La Cubanísima organized the first *Parada de los Tres Reyes Magos* in response to Castro's actions. Over the years it has become a Miami tradition. In 1992, 250,000 people watched floats, Hispanic celebrities, politicians, high school bands, and dancers march down Calle Ocho. The high point for the children is always the appearance of the Three Kings accompanied by their camels.

Santería   *Santería* is the growing Afro-Cuban folk religion practiced by an estimated fifty thousand to seventy-five thousand Cubans, both black and white, other Hispanics, and Americans in southeast

Florida. It is based primarily on Yoruba religious practices brought to Cuba by West Africans. A variety of factors, including the late termination of the slave trade in Cuba and the popularity of *cabildos*, or African-based fraternal organizations, encouraged the preservation of many African religious traditions. Thus, features such as divination, the use of stones, herbs, sacrifices, and the Yoruba language (Lucumí) have remained much the same as the religion still practiced in Nigeria.

Contact with Catholicism had a strong influence on Santería. During the era of slavery, people of African descent had to profess Catholicism in order to qualify for freedom. As a result, many religious practices were hidden behind a Christian veneer. For instance, Santería deities are called by the Spanish term *santos* (saints) as well as by the Yoruba word *orishas*. Each orisha is identified with a Catholic saint on the basis of similar characteristics: African Chango with Catholic Santa Barbara, Babalu-Aye with San Lazarus, or Oshun with La Caridad del Cobre. Candles, flowers, prayers, religious cards, amulets, and other Catholic religious elements were also adopted.

For those familiar only with European religions, Santería can perhaps best be understood through its similarities with the classical religions of ancient Greece and Rome. Many Santería practitioners, or *santeros*, believe that the world exists on two planes—an earthly realm and a spiritual one where the orishas live. The orishas are roughly equivalent to the pantheon of gods in the classical religions. Santería practitioners conduct a moral life by living in harmony with the orishas, other people, and the environment. A complex hierarchy of priests guides the actions of the devout by teaching them the tenets of the religion and revealing the wisdom of the orishas through several forms of divination. The most important divination system is *Ifá*, in which the priest throws a chain of eight seed pods, called an *opele*. Each pod may land up or down, resulting in 256 possible combinations—each associated with verses, stories, and prescriptions for behavior.

Music and dance are essential features of Santería. Religious parties called *bembés* are held to honor a particular orisha, celebrate the initiation of a practitioner, or mark the birthday of a santero into the faith. At the bembé, one of three types of musical ensembles may perform music and songs in praise of the orishas: the *guiro* ensemble, the bembé drum ensemble, or the *batá* drum ensemble. The guiro ensemble consists of three *chekeres*, or dried gourds covered with a net of beads; a *guataca* (hoe blade), which a musician plays by hitting it with a metal instrument; a conga drum; and a singer specializing in ritual songs in the Yoruba language. The bembé ensemble has three congas, a guataca, and a singer. The batá ensemble, composed of three double-headed, hourglass-shaped drums and a singer, plays the most sacred type of music. The drums are

Ritual objects offered in
a Little Havana botanica
(Photo by Michele Edelson/
Courtesy of HASF)

ritually consecrated so that, in the hands of skilled initiates, they
"speak" with the gods through a repertoire of different rhythms. Moreover, the variety of drum tones and the rhythmic repertoire of the batá
ensemble is more extensive than those of other groups, thus allowing
greater possibilities for musical dialogue with or praise of the orishas.

An intrinsic part of Santería religious life, dance cleanses participants
of negative influences and builds the intensity of sacred events. Ritual

dancing plays various roles ranging from personal expression and enjoyment to a form of salutation or a way to induce trance. Participants in a bembé gather near the musical group in parallel lines, circles, or semicircles and repeat a brief line dance for extended periods. From time to time, a santero enters the center to dance more expressively.

A wide variety of material folk culture accompanies the practice of Santería. Many objects are important to devotional activities, and santeros learn to make, use, and understand them during their initiation period. Some specialize in certain aspects of the religion, such as making the *collares*, or necklaces bestowed upon initiates. Each collar contains the protective power of the orisha it represents and is beaded in the pattern and colors symbolic of that deity. Other santeros make *ropa de santo*, the special clothing worn during certain ritual events. Many ropa de santo styles are derived from traditional Afro-Cuban dress, such as women's tiered gingham skirts, though others are based on African apparel.

Santeros employ both manufactured and handmade artifacts in ritual events or on home altars that honor the orishas. These items may be purchased at a *botánica*, or religious goods store. Botánicas stock a variety of herbs, roots, candles, oils, beads, ropa de santo, statuary, flowers, books, and other items. The staff also instructs clients in the use of religious objects and refers them to priests for further help or education.

Because of Santería's unfamiliar African underpinnings, there has not been widespread acceptance among the American public. In recent years, several groups have attempted to educate the public and formally establish Santería as a religion.

Formal Organizations: *Los Municipios de Cuba en el Exilio*, Cuban Municipalities in Exile

Like many other immigrant groups, Cubans in Miami have reconstructed parts of their social and political structure. The organization of Cuban *municipios* (counties), is the largest network of voluntary sociopolitical associations in the Cuban American community. Mutual aid organizations have a long history both in Cuba and Florida. In Cuba, people of Spanish and African background established separate fraternal orders or clubs that maintained their cultural heritage and provided them with economic assistance. Clubs in Key West and Tampa organized social events and provided education, financial assistance, and sometimes health care to those who needed it.

Los Municipios de Cuba en el Exilio was created in 1962 by former members of several different municipios who believed it would be a good vehicle for get-togethers with others from the same town. Today, Los Municipios boasts about sixty thousand active families. Although participation varies considerably among municipios, most meet at least two or three times a year to recognize national holidays or patron saints' days. More than twenty possess permanent meeting places.

While it is not unusual for immigrant groups to form voluntary mutual support societies, the Cubans have maintained a remarkable degree of organization. Of the 126 municipios in prerevolutionary Cuba, 117 have organized in Miami. Each elects a president, secretary, and treasurer. In addition, they elect representatives to provincial and national assemblies—a structure that follows the pattern of pre-Castro government. Although each municipio functions independently, there is also an umbrella organization with elected officials.

Most activities undertaken by the municipios are in the social sphere. As independent entities, they arrange social events that promote group cohesion and act as mutual aid societies to assist recent immigrants from the municipio. Many also publish newsletters to communicate information about members or document the history of their municipio. Since 1982, the umbrella organization has sponsored an annual festival with rides, concerts, and other entertainment. However, the festival centers around the seventy-odd stands built by individual municipios, which offer a range of their traditional specialties. The *municipalistas* usually provide picnic tables where festival-goers can eat, enjoy a beer or coffee, and chat with old friends.

A few municipios have revived their annual *fiestas patronales* celebrating their town's patron saint. For instance, the former residents of San Antonio de las Vueltas observe the feast day of their patron saint, La Virgen de la Candelaria. For Vuelteños the event not only serves as a reunion, but also as a celebration of their traditional festival arts. Preparations often go on for a good portion of the year, for Vuelteños must raise funds, train dancers, and create special festival arts.

Vuelteños have adapted their festival to fit the new conditions in Miami. They cannot close the streets for their traditional parade, so they hold the event in a large church hall. Since floats will not fit through the doorways, they have been replaced with *comparsas*—a sort of choreographed conga group. Although not originally part of the Vueltas celebration, comparsa was known from nearby towns. Another addition is the *trabajos de plaza*, large stationary works depicting typical Cuban sites or themes. In 1992, over seven hundred Vuelteños and their friends attended the fiesta patronal. After enjoying a dinner of regional dishes, they listened to speeches and watched comparsa groups dance through the hall. Many joined to conga to the infectious music. Finally, Vuelteños danced to a salsa orchestra until the early hours of the morning.

Isaac Dueñas is a master at making the *farolas* and *muñecones* that are important elements of the Vueltas fiesta. From the age of nineteen, Dueñas participated in the Vueltas festival and assisted master artists. Dueñas began to work on the Miami festival six or seven years ago. For each celebration he creates a new set of farolas, decorative lanterns that rest atop tall poles carried by the comparsa group, and a muñecon, a giant fantasy figure with a papier mache head.

FOLKLIFE

In South Florida and especially in Miami, Cubans and Cuban Americans sustain a vast array of folklife drawn from their heritage. Moreover, with the increasing length of their stay in South Florida, they are gradually combining many Cuban traditions with American customs to form new expressive folkways.

Foodways

Like most national cuisines, Cuban foodways were the result of the intersection of environmental, historical, and cultural factors. Cuba's tropical climate was moderate and the land fertile, so a wide variety of crops and livestock were raised. In addition, the waters around the island produced an abundant marine harvest. Perhaps the most powerful influence, however, was Spanish foodways. Like the Spanish, Cubans usually eat a light breakfast, large midday meal, and light, late supper. Moreover, most Cuban food is well-spiced and cooked in oil or wine. There is also a lingering influence from the indigenous inhabitants in the form of foodstuffs such as yuca, corn, beans, and squash. The Africans influenced Cuban foodways through their use of yams, plantains (a banana-like fruit), and grains, often eaten stewed or dipped in sauces.

Cubans and other Hispanics have transported many foodways to Miami, thereby establishing a Latin ambience in many sections of the city. Little Havana and other Hispanic neighborhoods are dotted with open-air fruit and vegetable stands similar to those in Latin America and the Caribbean. They offer tropical fruits and vegetables such as mamey, plantains, and carambola.

Most Cubans shop at American-style supermarkets, but a majority also frequent small local grocery stores called *bodegas*. Bodegas, which are often within walking distance of customers' homes, stock staples such as black beans, rice, and Cuban coffee. In addition, they purvey traditional items and brands not available in mainstream markets. For instance, many include a *carnicerta*, where clients may order special Latin

An open air market in Little Havana with a wide range of tropical fruits and vegetables (Photo by Michele Edelson/Courtesy of HASF)

cuts of meats. Bodegas often have a sidewalk counter selling pastries, coffee, cigars, and Spanish-language newspapers. Besides distributing essential goods, bodegas serve as local gathering spots and sources of community information.

During hot afternoons, street vendors ply their wares from brightly painted hand- or bicycle-driven carts or small stationary stands. Their products are those common throughout Latin America and the Caribbean: peeled oranges, pineapples, or melons; *granizados*, snowcones with exotic flavors such as tamarind, coconut, and mamey; *churros*, long, crisp fried dough strips dipped in sugar; pumpkin or coconut candies; and roasted peanuts in paper sacks. Some of these vendors announce their presence with traditional cries.

Cuban coffee is a staple of daily life. *Café cubano*, strong, sweet, and concentrated, is drunk in tiny, thimble-sized servings. On any Cuban commercial street in Miami, numerous coffee shops serve Cuban coffee for clients seated indoors or standing at the small window counters that face onto the street. Cubans share café cubano in many contexts, such as daily work breaks, while playing dominoes, or on social occasions.

Many other beverages are integral to Cuban foodways. People enjoy a variety of fruit juices: *guarapo* made from sugarcane juice, *coco frío* or coconut milk, and orange, mamey or papaya juices. *Batidos* are shakes made from ice cream and a variety of tropical fruits. Coca-Cola is a common vice.

In homes and restaurants, Cubans cook traditional dishes. Pork, chicken, beef, seafood, rice, and beans form the basis of their diet. These foods are prepared in diverse and delectable ways, often with fried plantains, malanga, or yuca as side dishes. Typical recipes, such as stews, vegetables, meats, or rice, are often based on a *sofrito*. The sofrito is a sauce made from olive oil, garlic, onion, green pepper, tomatoes, oregano, and vinegar. Meat may be marinated in oil and lime or sour orange juice before it is cooked. Meals are often accompanied by fresh Cuban bread, which is slightly softer than French bread.

Pork is the preferred meat in Cuban cooking. Roast pork is the holiday food of choice, and other favorite dishes include *masas de puerco*, or fried pork chunks, and *lechón asado*, roast pork. The renowned sandwiches, such as the *media noche*, Cuban sandwich, and *pan con lechón*, all have pork as the base.

Beef is second in popularity. It appears in a wide variety of dishes, including the thin *palomilla* steaks, *tasajo*, or dried shredded beef, *boliche*, or pot roast, and *picadillo*, a beef hash. One of the most popular traditional dishes, *ropa vieja* (literally "old clothes"), is made from flank steak boiled with carrots, onions, garlic and green pepper until tender. The meat is cooled, pounded until reduced to thread-like strips, then cooked with sofrito, broth, the cooked carrot, cooked peas, white wine, and pimento juice.

Two dishes that reflect the influence of African traditions are *fou fou* and *bollitos*. Fou fou is a main dish in which the cook adds fish, shrimp, or ham as well as okra to a sofrito. The cook then boils the plantains in their skins until tender, removes the skin, mashes them, and forms them into balls. Finally, the balls are added to the sauce, and the mixture is seasoned to taste. Although the Cuban version is somewhat different, fou fou comes from the ubiquitous West African dish of the same name. Bollitos are appetizers made of black-eyed peas. The cook soaks the peas overnight, peels them, then mashes or blends them with garlic and salt until a paste is formed. Spoonfuls of the paste are then fried in hot oil until crispy. Bollitos are almost identical to a West African dish called *kosai* (from Hausa, a lingua franca in West Africa) which consists of fried bean cakes made from mashed beans or bean flour seasoned with garlic or hot pepper.

Cuban cuisine tends toward heavy vegetables, the most popular being beans and rice. *Moros y cristianos* is a combination of black beans and rice, while *congrí* uses kidney beans and rice. Cooks boil various tropical tubers, especially yuca, malanga, and boniato. *Papas fritas*, thin fried potatoes, are very popular. In addition, fried plantains—whether ripe and sweet or green and salted, are a common part of the meal.

Some claim that desserts are the best part of Cuban cuisine. The ornate *merengue* cake is created for weddings, quinceañeras, and other festive occasions. The stiff merengue, or egg-white frosting, holds the most fanciful shapes and often becomes a work of art. Pastries, puddings, and custards, especially *flan*, are among the most common desserts. Puddings include *arroz con leche* (rice pudding), *pudín de coco* (coconut pudding), *boniatillo* (sweet potato pudding), and *pudín diplomático* (a pudding flavored with liqueur). Guava shells with cream cheese and guava-filled pastries are especially popular.

Restaurants are central institutions in the Cuban community. Some preserve unusual foodways, but their most important function is providing an opportunity for people to share, enjoy, and reaffirm their heritage. Restaurants run the gamut from tiny sandwich shops to the most elegant and exclusive clubs. In addition to restaurants, small businesses called *cantinas* specialize in delivering hot Cuban dinners to working couples or those unable to prepare meals. The collision of Cuban and American cultures has also resulted in Cuban fast food outlets at food courts in malls or downtown. They typically offer Cuban sandwiches, croquetas, *caldo gallego* or other bean soups, Cuban tamales, Cuban coffee, *pastelitos*, and desserts such as flan.

There have been many changes in Cuban foodways within the Miami context. The popular line of Cuban Classics frozen dinners, which are sold in most area supermarkets, offers some of the most popular Cuban dishes, such as roast pork with yuca, black beans, and rice or ropa vieja with rice and beans. Enterprising Cubans have founded diet clinics that specialize in Latin clients. Iraida Cazadilla runs Shape Lovers workshops in Spanish and offers *cubano light* dinners from her catering service.

Folk Medicine

Traditional remedies flourish in all cultures, and many Miamians continue to use cures they learned in Cuba. It is not uncommon for medicinal bushes and trees to be planted in yards so that supplies will be on hand.

A *cocimiento* is essentially a tea made from herbs, sometimes served with a little sugar. Some mothers administer a cocimiento of *tilo* (linden) or onion skin to their children at bedtime to induce sleep. Others calm children by boiling verbena, then add it to a warm bath. A cocimiento of five-petalled jasmine, or *jasmín*, also quiets the nerves. For stomach-aches, many prescribe a tea of camomile, apple core, or tilo. Local grocery stores carry small packets of the most common medicinal herbs.

Home remedies effectively treat many minor complaints. Eucalyptus leaves are considered good for a sore throat. Hot lemonade, sometimes with whiskey, cures coughs or sore throats. For headaches, people may simply lie down with a damp towel on the head. For bee stings, they may rub garlic or mud on the afflicted area to stop the stinging. *Ponche* is a remedy for the flu. People prepare it by boiling milk with a cinnamon stick. They then separate an egg, add sugar to the yolk, whip it well, pour the boiling milk on top and sometimes add rum.

Empacho is an illness that is recognized by many Cubans and other Latin Americans. When a person is *empachada*, a hard lump or obstruction in the stomach or intestines causes pain and constipation. The condition may be caused by improper digestion. Curers called *sovadores* massage the stomach, abdomen, back and legs to encourage the lump to pass.

Most peoples whose culture stems from the circum-Mediterranean region recognize the illness termed the evil eye, or *mal de ojo* in Spanish. The sickness most commonly afflicts infants. People may inadvertently cause an infant to become ill by complimenting it. Thus, beautiful, healthy babies are particularly at risk. A baby upon whom the eye has been cast suddenly becomes listless and feverish. When this happens, the mother may remove the eye with a special prayer. Many guard their babies against the evil eye with an *azabache*—a small faceted ball made of jet. Babies wear the azabache on a chain or pinned onto their clothes. Some mothers also thwart the eye by saying to themselves *"cuerno para tus ojos"* ("a horn for your eyes") or *"maldita son tus ojos"* ("curse your eyes") after someone compliments their baby.

Folk Architecture

Cubans brought with them a wealth of practical skills and customs acquired in their homeland, where architectural style is dominated by the Spanish heritage. Today many elements of Cuban architectural construction, materials, and style are common in Miami, perhaps due to the environmental similarities.

The earliest Cuban architectural influences came to Florida during the colonial period. Although that heritage was lost, the 1920s Mediterranean Revival style favored by South Florida developers utilized such Cuban architectural elements as tiles and landscape plants. The Cubanization of the Miami environment did not truly get underway until the mid-1960s, when Cuban immigrants gradually transformed the Riverside area near Flagler and S.W. Eighth streets into a markedly Latino residential area.

The transformation started with applied ornamentation such as murals, signs, and decoration. Numerous signs displayed references to famous Cubans, places in Havana, landscape traits such as royal poinciana trees or rural scenes with *bohíos*, and religious trappings. As they became more economically stable, Cubans started to purchase ornamentation that was typical of or made reference to Cuba. For example, they planted tropical fruit trees such as the guava, *anón*, or *caimito* in yards. Some expanded their porches to create space for two rocking chairs, thus increasing social interaction. Miamians also developed yardshrines to house statues of saints and orishas.

Commercial areas were particularly transformed. In addition to incorporating architectural details such as fake tiled roofs and eaves, businesses employed Cuban advertising techniques. For example, many establishments featured large, bright signs painted directly on the wall. The sidewalk became an integral extension of many commercial enterprises. Open-air markets stocked tropical produce in bins facing the sidewalk, furniture stores displayed their goods on the sidewalk, and cafes placed tables and chairs outside. As previously mentioned, markets opened sidewalk counters to offer café cubano, pastelitos, cigars, and other sundries to passersby. Small-scale street vendors also utilized sidewalks and parking spaces to sell from brightly painted trucks and carts piled with tropical fruits or sweets.

Finally, the immigrants established a wide variety of larger establishments named or modeled after places and things in Cuba: La Floridita Restaurant, Veradero Supermarket, Mi Bohío Restaurant, and others. The transformation was remarkable—Riverside had become Little Havana. As Cubans have gradually become more affluent and moved to newer areas in western Dade County, they have created areas that combine Latin American and American traits.

Although techniques and styles may differ in Miami, an assortment of traditional Cuban architectural crafts still flourishes. For example, iron grillwork has become a common feature on houses and commercial establishments. Grillwork has both decorative and utilitarian functions: it provides an aesthetic dimension at the same time that it prevents burglaries. Due to the high cost of handmade wrought iron, most grillwork is assembled from preformed pieces to match the needs of the homeowner and the proportions of the house. However, a few traditional Cuban ironworkers create finely crafted gates, doors, fences, and window guards.

In Cuba, most houses possessed clay tile roofs and floors. Cubans have brought tile-making skills to Miami and adapted them to the local

A Cuban company manufacturing roof tiles in Miami (Photo by Tina Bucuvalas/Courtesy of HASF)

environment. Since South Florida has no native clays, roof and floor tiles are made from cement. This development is highly functional because cement tiles last longer in the hot, moist climate. Roof tiles are hand-molded from cement that is a natural gray or tinted red with iron oxide.

Cuban floor tiles provide coolness and freshness to a house during the hot days. Craftsmen create floor tiles in a variety of sizes, shapes, and textures. Surfaces can be made irregular, smooth, natural, or precise. Tiles may be gray, colored with pigments, or sometime stenciled with designs after they dry. Colors vary from vivid to subtle and delicate. Shapes range from the simple square to hexagons, octagons, elongated hexagons, fleur de lis, and other shapes up to twenty-four square inches.

The hundreds of religious shrines that adorn yards in Cuban American neighborhoods are distinctive features of the Miami landscape. All but unknown in Cuba, yardshrines seem to have arisen after exile. The shrines may be erected in fulfillment of a vow or as an expression of the owner's devotion to a particular saint or deity. They range in size from two to ten feet high and may sit atop a pedestal or on the ground. Craftspeople make shrines from many different materials in rectangular, circular, or octagonal shapes, but a saint's statue is always visible through a glass door or walls. Although the statues are always those of Catholic saints, the yardshrines may be dedicated to either a Catholic saint or a Santería deity.

Music

Cuban musical forms have had a tremendous influence on the music of other Latin American countries, the United States, and the rest of the world. Cuban music falls roughly into three categories: music that is primarily Spanish, music that is primarily African, and music that is a fusion of both. The latter category is by far the largest and most influential.

In sixteenth-century Spain, the ten-line, octosyllabic *décima* was a particularly popular lyrical form. In Cuba, the peasants, or *guajiros*, adopted this form to compose songs about love or daily life that came to be called *punto guajiro*. They sometimes competed in improvising songs within the form. Musicians usually accompany punto guajiro with instruments derived from both the Spanish and African legacies. These include the Cuban *tres*, a small guitar with three sets of double or triple strings, the *laud*, or Spanish lute, *claves*, wooden sticks which are struck together as a time keeper, and the güiro.

Social discrimination against the Africans in Cuba sometimes had the effect of keeping them together and thereby reinforcing their traditional culture. In particular, many music and dance forms associated with Santería flourished.

From the combination of Spanish and African musical traditions have emerged manifold types of Cuban music: the *son, danzón, habanera, guaguancó, mambo, bolero, guaracha, conga, rumba,* cha-cha-cha, salsa, and *songo*. Many Cubans consider the *son* their national musical style. The son originated during the nineteenth century in the mountainous

Cuban Americans performing *punto guajiro*, a traditional musical style from the Cuban countryside (Photo by Tina Bucuvalas/Courtesy of HASF)

region of Oriente, where the culture had been strongly influenced by immigrants from Haiti, Jamaica, Puerto Rico, and other Caribbean islands. In the 1920s, the genre gained international popularity through recordings by Cuban dance bands.

Today salsa is the dominant musical form among Cubans and other Spanish-speaking peoples of the Caribbean. It is also gaining popularity among other Latin Americans. The term "salsa" was first used in the title of a 1960s recording, and came into popular usage in the 1970s. It refers not so much to one musical style as to a variety of styles that resulted from a long process of syncretization. As anthropologist Jorge Duany explains, "Essentially it is an amalgamation of Afro-Caribbean musical traditions centered around the Cuban son. Its main characteristics are a call-and-response song structure; polyrhythmic organization with abundant use of syncopation; instrumental variety with extensive use of brass and percussion, and strident orchestral arrangements; jazz influence; and . . . a reliance on the sounds and themes of lower-class life in the Latin American *barrios* of U.S. and Caribbean cities."

Salsa is built on the *son montuno*, which features an alternation between the chorus and the main singer, who improvises within a set theme. Lyrics often follow the verse patterns of the Spanish *copla* or *romance*. Instrumentally, salsa relies heavily on the trombone or trumpet, and reinforces the percussive vitality of the bongó and conga with timbales, cowbells, and claves. The three main types of salsa, *charanga*, *conjunto*, and big band, have different orchestral forms. The traditional Cuban form, *charanga*, includes violins and flute.

Miami boasts many popular salsa bands, most of whom employ musicians from throughout the Caribbean and Latin America. Some, such as Hansel y su Orquesta Calle Ocho, feature Cuban American singers/bandleaders and perform charanga or other Cuban versions of the genre. In 1991, talented Cuban American salsa star Willy Chirino garnered tremendous praise for a song that has become an anthem of the Cuban community. Entitled *"Nuestro dia ya viene llegando"* ("Our Day is Coming"), the lyrics provide an excellent description of the immigrant experience intermixed with rich layers of references to exile life in Miami.

Holidays and Celebrations: The Annual Cycle

Holidays and celebrations commemorate sacred and secular events. In ethnic communities, they may also provide a shield from a strange environment, a reason to socialize, and a symbol of cultural identity. Among Cuban Americans, the annual cycle of secular holidays begins with *La Fiesta de Año Nuevo*, or New Year's Eve parties celebrated in homes or night clubs. By early December, people frequently ask each other, *"Dónde vas a esperar el año?"* ("Where will you await the New Year?") It becomes a matter of importance to line up a party, find a date, and purchase an appropriate dress. New Year's celebrations typically include *cidra*, an alcoholic Spanish cider. The principal custom associated with New Year's Eve is the eating of twelve grapes—one for each month—as the clock strikes midnight. The host provides guests with little bags of grapes in anticipation of the hour. Often the celebrants conclude by declaring, "Next year in Cuba!"

Some households celebrate New Year's Day with a full holiday dinner: turkey, black beans and rice, *masitas de puerco, turrones, cascos de guayaba,* and cream cheese. In many parts of Cuba and occasionally in Miami, people sweep out of their houses with water on New Year's Day. When they empty the bucket of dirty water outside, they believe they have cleansed their house of all the bad luck and troubles from the old year.

January 28 marks the birth of Jose Martí, Cuba's national hero of independence. Back in Cuba, people celebrated the date by closing businesses, holding parades, giving speeches, and participating in a variety of other patriotic activities. In the heavily Hispanic community of Hialeah, approximately three thousand people attended the twenty-fifth annual parade in 1993. The parade included local congressional representatives, a man resembling Martí riding a white horse, and floats and bands from eighteen schools and eleven civic organizations.

In Cuba, *Carnaval* is celebrated during the days preceding the period of Lenten sacrifice beginning on Ash Wednesday. Carnaval festivities vary from region to region. For example, the eastern province of Oriente was especially known for its wild and elaborate celebrations. Havana's Carnaval, which featured parades, floats, costumes, and comparsa, was organized along the lines of celebrations in Rio de Janeiro or New Orleans. In Miami Carnaval has become more secular than religious, since the traditional festivities have been subsumed by events sponsored by the Little Havana Kiwanis Club.

The Kiwanis Club of Little Havana first organized a week-long Carnaval Miami festival in the 1970s. Although they based it on Cuban Carnaval celebrations, many elements were changed. For example, they combined the separate comparsa and *paseo*, or parade, and invited performers and vendors who reflected the growing diversification of the Hispanic population, and they fixed the date.

On the first Saturday in March, Hispanic artists launch the festivities with a Carnaval Night concert. At midday on Sunday is the paseo. The 1993 parade featured scores of floats, trucks, convertibles, and comparsa groups, including Brazilian and Dominican representatives. Some floats represented Nicaraguans, or Cuban regions. Many people with convertibles or trucks simply pay a ten dollar fee, adorn their vehicles, and pile their families inside to take part in the parade. Spectators on the sidewalks throw *serpentina*, or streamers, at the paraders, and sometimes dance along behind the registered participants.

The culmination of the week-long event is the Calle Ocho Festival of Latin Music on the second Saturday in March. Now the largest Hispanic festival in the country, it draws over a million visitors to a twenty-block area in Little Havana. Businesses sponsor stages on which a wide variety of musical groups perform. The bands are predominantly Latino, but Jamaican, Haitian, and sometimes rock and roll or country groups are also invited. While most of the Latino musical groups play salsa, some perform Dominican *merengue*, Colombian *vallanato*, Mexican *mariachi*, and Nicaraguan *musica costeña*. Although the festival has become multicultural in many respects, the overall mood has preserved the wild exuberance of Cuban Carnaval.

In many Hispanic cultures, the bonds between mothers and children are particularly strong. Thus it is not surprising that Mother's Day is an important holiday. Father's Day is also observed by the Cuban community, but is not as significant. Maggie Manrara discusses customs associated with the day:

Mother's day is a very important day...it is a very high holiday. [In Cuba] typically, mother and daughter will dress the same. And you will have the seamstress make a dress. And of course if you had more than one daughter, everybody will dress the same. I remember the time, I had three sisters and I remember the dresses we wore.

Another tradition that we still keep in Miami...if your mother was alive you were supposed to wear a red carnation. If your mother was dead, you were supposed to wear white....So everybody will have a flower indicating whether your mother is alive or dead.

And that day of course, you will do a lot of worshipping to the mother. You will do a Mother's Day card. She will be taken out. And I remember as a child, we did something special for her—we will sing a song or write a poem, that type of thing. We all got together, and it was a formal thing. She would sit in a chair, and we would all come in and give her a little gift we had made. It was a day that you really ponder the importance of the mother. And then you will go to your grandmother's and do the same thing on a bigger scale because everybody would get together....

I think its still done in Miami to some degree. Definitely you would get a Mother's Day card, very fancy and frilly with sugary type comments. Presents also. And at that point you will also give a gift to your godmother. You keep it up and take care of all the mothers in the family. . . . It's not the rush that we see here with the bouquets. It's more like one flower.

Veinte de mayo celebrates Cuba's independence from Spain on May 20, 1902. In Miami, concerts featuring notable Cuban performers are held in local parks and stadiums. Such events are attended not only by Cubans and Cuban Americans, but also by other Latinos who love the music and celebration. Smaller groups may also observe the event with a patriotic program that includes speakers, the national anthem, and salutation of the flag.

December 28, the Day of the Innocents, commemorates the day on which King Herod ordered the male babies killed. In Cuban tradition, the day has taken on secular overtones corresponding to April Fools' Day. When friends and family succeed in playing tricks, they taunt their victims with *"Te cogí por inocente! Te cogí por inocente!"* Roughly translated, the phrase means "I caught you, fool!"

Verbal Arts

Cubans and Cuban Americans engage in many different forms of verbal arts. Especially popular are *dichos* (sayings) and *refranes* (proverbs), as well as children's rhymes, lullabies, prayers, and games.

Cuban American mothers continue to recite many traditional rhymes to their children. Among the most common is the following rhyme, during which the mother counts out the child's toes in a manner similar to the English rhyme, "This Little Piggy."

Este fue al mercado	This one went to the market
comprar un huevito,	to buy a little egg,
este le rompió,	this one broke it,
este le echó,	this one threw it,
Y este pícaro gordo	and this fat little
se le comió!	mischiefmaker ate it!

The following rhyme is one which inevitably elicits delighted squeals from small children. As the mother recites the rhyme, she points out various places along the arm, until she comes to the armpit and tickles the child.

Este que va a la canicería.	This one that goes to the meat market,
No me traigas carne de aquí,	Doesn't bring me meat from here,
Ni de aquí,	nor from here,
ni de aquí,	nor from here,
ni de aquí,	nor from here,
pero de aquí!	but from here!

Cuban and Cuban American children play a number of games. *A la Rueda, Rueda* (Around the Wheel) is similar to Ring Around the Rosie. The children hold hands and recite a rhyme as they move in a circle. At the end of the rhyme they all fall down and pretend to be asleep. In another well-known game, one child is Señor Matadiledile, and three or four children on the other side identify themselves with different professions. The group of children skips towards Señor Matadiledile singing, then they ask, *"Que quiere usted?"* ("What do you want?") Señor Matadiledile may say, "I want a seamstress," and the child who identified herself as a seamstress goes with Señor Matadiledile. The last child left becomes the new señor.

There are a number of songs and prayers which Cubans and Cuban Americans incorporate into children's bedtime rituals. One of the most common lullabies is *"Duermase Mi Niño"*:

Duermase mi niño.	Sleep my child.
Duermase mi amor.	Sleep my love.
Duermase pedazo	Sleep little piece
de mi corazón.	of my heart.
Este niño lindo	This pretty child,
que nació de día,	who was born during the day,
quiere que le llevan	wants to be taken
a la dulcería.	to the candy store.
Este niño lindo	This pretty child
que nació de noche,	who was born at night
quiere que le llevan	wants to be taken
a pasear en coche.	for a ride in the car.

The following prayer about guardian angels relieves the fears young children may have at night:

El angel de la guarda,	Guardian angel,
dulce compañia,	sweet companion,
no me desampares,	don't abandon me
ni de noche ni de día.	during night or day.
Ser me protector,	Be my protector,
ser me buenadía.	Be my well-being.
No me deje solo	Don't leave me alone
que me perdía.	to be lost.

Cubans are particularly fond of the succinct bits of folk wisdom they call dichos, or sayings. In many cases, these are the same as refranes, or proverbs. There are literally hundreds of dichos. Here are some of the more popular:

Se te va formar un Veinte de Mayo.
You're about to get into a twentieth of May, i.e., a big thing.
(This is said when someone is about to make trouble.)

Boca cerrada no entran moscas.
Flies don't enter a closed mouth.

Aunque la mona se vista de seda, mona se queda.
Although the monkey dresses in silk, she remains a monkey.

Ojos que no ven, corazon que no siente.
If you don't know about it, it won't bother you.

Los niños y los borrachos dicen la verdad.
Children and drunks speak the truth.

En la cara le cae, quien al cielo escupe.
If you spit in the sky, it will fall in your face.

No por mucho madrugar se amanece más temprano.
The sun will not rise earlier if you get up earlier.

Candil de la calle, oscurida de la casa.
Lamp in the street, darkness in the house; i.e., if you spend all your time helping others, you will be abandoning your family.

Más vale sabe el diablo por viejo que por diablo.
The devil knows more because he's old rather than because he's the devil.

Matrimonio y mortaja, del cielo baja.
Death and matrimony come from heaven; i.e., you have no control over them.

Más vale tarde que nunca.
Better late than never.

Más vale un pájaro en mano que ciento volando.
A bird in the hand is worth more than a hundred flying.

A quien madruga, Dios lo ayuda.
God helps those that rise early; i.e., God helps those that help themselves.

Amaneció con el moño virado.
She woke up with her bun askew; i.e., she woke up in a bad mood.

Mucho cacareo, poco huevo.
A lot of cackling and no egg.

Games and Sports

Many traditional sports and games enrich the lives of the Cuban community. Some are uniquely Cuban, whereas others simply inspire unusual passion among their Cuban adherents.

Cuban men playing
dominoes in Little Havana
(Photo by Michele Edelson/
Courtesy of HASF)

Dominoes   Among older Cubans—especially the men—the game of
dominoes is so pervasive that on Calle Ocho a place called Domino Park
has been dedicated to this pursuit. On any day, you may see dozens of
men passionately playing dominoes in the park as they share cups of
Cuban coffee and comment on politics, passersby, and the world in
general. The clicking of the ivory *fichas*, or tiles, is a comforting,
rhythmic sound for those who grew up with the game.

Most players learned the game as children in Cuba. The rules are
simple, but good players use strategy and try to remember what tiles
have not been played by others. Domino games are usually played by two
teams of two players. The tiles are scrambled face down; then each
participant selects ten dominoes. Players take turns matching their tiles
against those in play that have the same number of dots. The first to play
all his or her tiles wins for the team. If all dominoes cannot be played,
the competitor with the fewest dots on the remaining dominoes wins.
The winners' score consists of the number of dots on the dominoes of the
opposite team.

The Cuban domino league, La Liga de Domino Cuba Libre, is
almost thirty years old. At club headquarters, about fifteen dedicated
players attend on weeknights, and more than forty appear at weekend
games. Although most players are men, wives often bring potluck Cuban
dinners or watch the Spanish soaps in the clubhouse. The Spanish-
language media cover the annual tournament, which includes clubs from

Tampa and New York. Today, few young Cuban Americans are taking up the game.

Jojo *Fishing*   Along Miami's waterfront and bridges, hundreds of local residents use *jojo* (pronounced yoyo), or rodless, fishing tackle. It is likely that jojo fishing originated among the indigenous inhabitants of the Caribbean, but the tradition's history has not been fully documented. Until the last few decades, Cubans wound fishing line around large wooden reels or metal cans. Today, inexpensive plastic jojo reels six to eight inches in diameter are available in most area fishing stores and are popular with both hobby and commercial fishermen.

Jojo tackle consists of the jojo reel, nylon line, a hook and weights. The fisherman casts by twirling about two feet of line and hook overhead in a circle, then flinging it out to sea. When a fish bites, the jojo reel automatically blocks the release of more cord, and the fisherman pulls in the line by hand. Many fishermen feel that jojo tackle is superior to a rod and reel because the direct contact of hand on the line increases their sensitivity. Most anglers equip jojo tackle with a heavy grade of line so it will not cut into their fingers as they let it out or haul it in.

Occupational Folklife

Cigarmaking   Cuba's unique geography and natural resources fostered the growth of many traditional occupations. The rich soil produced fine tobaccos, which the Cubans handrolled into cigars that were world-renowned for their excellence. With the United States embargo on Cuban products, about a dozen small cigarrolling businesses have opened in Miami. The people involved usually learned the trade in Cuba, and many come from families that have made cigars for generations. Most techniques and methods remain the same, but Miami cigarmakers no longer use exclusively Cuban tobacco. Moreover, they tend to make cigars larger in order to satisfy the tastes of the American clientele.

In the cool and fragrant atmosphere of a cigarrolling establishment, each cigar maker sits at a table equipped with an array of tools necessary to the craft: blade, press, cutter, fixative, and rolling board. From piles containing different varieties of tobacco leaves from the United States, Central America, the Caribbean, and Africa, the cigarmaker selects a blend of heavy and light leaves appropriate to the type of cigar. Specially trained workers pull the hard stem from the leaves, then others select or cut pieces of appropriate size and roll them firmly into shape. Next the cigarmaker carefully rolls a "wrapper," or outer leaf of superior tobacco, around the cigar, using a small curved blade to trim the ends. Then the

Ernesto Perez Carrillo proudly offers a cigar made at his El Credito Cigar company in Little Havana. (Photo by Michele Edelson/Courtesy of HASF)

cigars are put into wooden molds and pressed for forty minutes so they will have a consistent size and shape. Finally, the cigars age in a cool, humidified storage room so the flavor will be enhanced and freshness ensured until they are sold.

Guayaberas   The traditional *guayabera* is a short-sleeved dress shirt with decorative tucks and embroidery work by men throughout the Caribbean as well as in Mexico, Central America, and parts of South America. Highly suited to tropical climates, it replaces the coat and tie. Guayaberas are widely worn by Latinos and many others in southeast Florida.

Guayaberas are difficult and time-consuming to make because the small tucks require great precision. Ramón and Juana Puig own the only South Florida shop that makes guayaberas. The Puigs make beautifully crafted guayaberas for special orders. Ramón learned the skills through an apprenticeship with a tailor in Las Villas, Cuba, then taught his wife. They create a pattern for each client and cut out the guayabera, but their staff of Cuban and Colombian seamstresses sew the shirts. In addition to making guayaberas, they stock a wide selection of ready-made ones from Latin America; they also tailor suits and slacks. Their clientele includes aficionados from throughout the Americas.

Sugar   There is a large sugar-growing region on the southern shore of Lake Okeechobee. With 408,000 acres of rich muckland devoted to it, sugar constitutes the state's second-largest crop as well as 22 percent of national production. Anglos own most of the land and cane cutters are generally West Indian, but Cubans dominate management, the mills, and the labs.

Although Florida has grown sugar since 1930, production expanded considerably with the breakdown of relations between the United States and Cuba in the 1960s. At that time, the most qualified assistance came from the thousands of former sugar chemists, engineers, managers, and laborers in the Cuban community. The Florida sugar industry was a blessing for the exiles because they knew the work and could speak Spanish at their jobs.

Indeed, it sometimes seems as though a section of Cuba has been transplanted to Florida. Okeelanta Mill engineering supervisor Francisco Prieto confesses, "Sometimes I feel like I haven't left Cuba. It's the same language, the same atmosphere, the same customs. It's a way of life that hasn't changed." In the offices of the Okeelanta, Osceola, and Talisman Mills, Radio WQBA-La Cubanísima blares, secretaries offer Cuban or American coffee, and daily work logs are kept in Spanish.

The sugar industry, and the Cuban way of life surrounding it, has its own distinctive work culture. Workers identify themselves by referring to the mills, or *centrales*, in which they are employed. Hundreds commute from Miami; the two closest mills provide free bus service. Despite the eighty-minute ride, many remain in the city so their children can attend better schools and their wives can find jobs. Especially for commuters, the hours are long. During harvest, or *zafra*, they work twelve hours a day for seven days a week. During the rest of the year, or *tiempo muerto* (dead time), they work the usual five days.

La caña (sugarcane) is planted in forty-acre fields. The zafra occurs from October through February or March. Before harvesting, workers practice the old custom of burning the fields to rid them of weeds, trash, snakes, rats, and spiders. The cane is so fibrous and coarse that it is fireproof. Reports about the status of field burnings are transmitted over radios to managers.

In the mill, a set of revolving knives cuts cane stalks into small pieces. The cane is then crushed by rollers called milling tandems, which extract the juice. Liquid lime is added, and the juice is heated, clarified, and filtered until it is a cloudy brown-black syrup. Next, the syrup is boiled in vacuum pans. When sugar crystals form, it is stirred and cooled. Finally, molasses and raw sugar are separated by centrifuges.

The millworkers who run the machinery that produces the sugar measure their careers by the number of zafras worked. They also divide themselves between those who worked with sugar in Cuba and those who work because of exile. Many in the latter category stay because of the steady employment and relatively high wages, rather than love of the business. Today, most Cuban mill workers are in their fifties and sixties. Young Cubans tend to enter professional jobs in urban areas such as Miami, so mill openings are gradually being filled by Nicaraguans, Dominicans, other Latin Americans, and Anglos.

Though Cubans are adopting many aspects of American life, Cuban culture remains a vital part of south Florida life. Cuban religious traditions, music, foodways, verbal arts, games, clothing, and occupations have been fostered in the state connected by history and a narrow stretch of water.

The New Miami: Nicaraguans and Islanders

In the last thirty years, Miami's demographic balance has shifted radically due to an unprecedented influx of immigrants from the Caribbean and Latin America. Between 1959 and 1980, over 625,000 Cubans fled into exile. In the eighties, hundreds of thousands of Haitians, Nicaraguans, and others from Caribbean and Latin American nations streamed into the area. By the end of the decade, additional thousands from the Middle East, Asia, and Africa quietly settled in Miami. Today Miamians are 21 percent black, 30 percent non-Hispanic white, and 49 percent Hispanic.

These figures add up to a remarkable number. Thirty years ago Miami was a small, relaxed resort city with a blend of residents primarily from the northeast, south, and midwest. Today it has been transformed into one of the fastest-moving, most cosmopolitan and multilingual cities in the hemisphere. With more than eight hundred thousand residents from the Caribbean, Miami must be considered its capital. And with a Spanish-speaking majority, Miami is one of the most influential Latin American cities. This chapter will paint quick profiles of some of Miami's largest ethnic communities.

NICARAGUANS

Although Miami is the largest Nicaraguan city outside of Managua, it is difficult to determine the exact number of Nicaraguans because many do not have legal status. Population estimates range from seventy-five thousand to four hundred thousand, but the community probably consists of one hundred fifty thousand to two hundred thousand—making Nicaraguans the second-largest Hispanic group in South Florida.

The Sandinista Revolution of 1979 compelled many Nicaraguans associated with the old regime to flee. The majority settled in Miami, with its well-established Latin America infrastructure and ideologically compatible Cuban population. Later, from 1981 to 1987, a wave of predominantly middle-class professionals and draft-age men emigrated to the city. Then, in the late 1980s large numbers of rural agriculturalists, urban laborers, and former Sandinistas left because of severe social and economic conditions.

Despite their large numbers, the Nicaraguan community has not made the same impact upon Miami as the Cubans. This is due to a variety of factors. A minority of the Nicaraguans are legal aliens and few yet are citizens. The United States government provided special assistance to the Cubans, but no such policies were formulated for the Nicaraguans. Moreover, in many instances Nicaraguans fit themselves into existing niches in the Latin American infrastructure rather than creating their own. For instance, the Nicaraguan community does not control any radio or TV stations.

Ethnically, there are three primary Nicaraguan (or Nica) groups. The vast majority is mestizo, which is culturally Hispanic. The Creoles from the Atlantic Coast, known as *Costeños*, are descendants of Jamaican settlers and often speak English as their first language. Finally, the Miskitos predominate among immigrants from several native groups. They speak primarily Miskito, though some are bilingual in Spanish or English and a few are trilingual in Miskito, Spanish, and English. Some estimate Miami's combined Creole and Miskito population at six thousand to ten thousand.

Mestizos

Mestizo Nicaraguans are of mixed European and Native American blood. Although they live throughout Dade County, many middle-class Nicas reside in west Dade's Sweetwater neighborhood, which is nicknamed Little Managua. Recent immigrants from Nicaragua and other Central American countries often live in East Little Havana.

Foodways   In Miami, Nicaraguans not only preserve their traditional foodways in their homes, but also operate many restaurants and sidewalk grills. Most necessary foodstuffs are easily available through Nicaraguan or other Hispanic stores. Indeed, some of the basic ingredients or canned goods are now made in Miami.

Many Nica women have started small cottage industries that supply traditional foods to individuals and businesses. In East Little Havana, small hand-painted signs announce the sale of *nacatamales* or other foods inside private homes. There are also informal bakeries in converted garages, where women make the large, thick Nica tortillas. Some women also distribute homemade traditional sweets through commercial establishments.

The small, informal sidewalk food stands called *fritangas* are omni-present in Latin Miami, and some have become small restaurants. They sell such Nicaraguan specialties as *carne asada* (grilled strips of marinated beef served with a tortilla, beans and rice), nacatamal (cornmeal dough stuffed with rice, prunes, green olives, pork, capers, and potatoes and wrapped in a banana leaf), *vigorón* (boiled cassava topped with pork rinds and cabbage slaw), or *baho* (beef, ripe plantains, green plantains, yuca, tomatoes, onions, and green peppers steamed in a large pot lined with banana leaves), as well as tortillas, cheeses, sausages, beverages, and baked goods. In addition, many Nicaraguan grocery stores market prepared food. They may also sell beverages such as *chicha* (fermented corn drink), *cacao, jicaro* seed drink, and *linaza con limon* (flax seed drink).

Soups are a staple of Nica cuisine. Restaurants and fritangas offer traditional soups made from a water, sour orange, onion, tomato, mint and green pepper base. Some of the more popular are *sopa de res* (vegetable soup with beef marrow and bones), *mondongo* (tripe and vegetable soup), and *sopa de albondigas* (soup with spiced cornmeal dumplings and meat). Of course, the indispensable corn tortilla is used to hold such fillings as beans, cheese, and onions. Eating establishments also sell Nica desserts like the famous *tres leches*, a delicious rich cake soaked in three types of milk (evaporated, sweetened condensed, and sweet cream) and crested with whipped cream or meringue. Other delights include *sopa borracha*, a rum-soaked sponge cake, and *pio quinto*, a custard cake also soaked in rum syrup.

A few Nicaraguan dishes have gained widespread acceptance in Miami through the influence of popular restaurants. One is the afore-mentioned tres leches, which is frequently sold in Cuban bakeries and restaurants. More widely known is *churrasco*—special cuts of marinated, grilled beef served with a variety of spicy sauces including *chimichurri*, a paste of parsley, garlic, and oil, and a *jalapeño* cream sauce with tomatoes and onions.

Nicas have brought many traditional beverages to Miami. They crush and add sugar to such tropical fruits as mangos, papayas, tamarinds, and guavas to create chunky juices called *frescos*. *Tiste* is a ground corn and cocoa drink which is often sipped from a gourd. Cereales y Cafe El Vencedor makes and distributes a variety of nutritious traditional bever-ages: *pinolillo* (toasted corn with cocoa), *fresco de cacao* (chocolate drink), jicaro seed drink, and *cebada rosada* (pink barley). Ramiro and Helen Alvarez, who owned a similar company in Managua, head this family business.

Music   The Nica community maintains a rich variety of musical traditions. Numerous popular dance bands perform repertoires consisting of recent Latin American hits and older Nicaraguan songs. Most Nica groups consist of four to six members playing such instruments as drums, conga, keyboard, guitar, and sometimes horn or sax. Among the most active are Romance Internacional, Grupo Imagen, Los Bitters de Corinto, Grupo Marfil, Los Galos de Doña Gala, and Poder Costeño. Romance Internacional, the first Nica band in Miami, is also one of the finest. The thirteen-member, family-based dance orchestra, Los Galos de Doña Gala, was one of the most popular dance bands in Nicaragua before the revolution. Though their size renders them too expensive for many club dates, they often play for parties, festivals, and other important community events.

Nicas consider *sones* accompanied by guitar and *marimba* as among their most traditional musical forms, but few Miamians specialize in this style. Rafael Jimenez performs sones, corridos, and international Latin music at Guayacan Restaurant. He learned music from his uncles and brothers, who were all musicians. In Nicaragua Jimenez played with several groups and recorded two of his own compositions. Since immigrating to Florida, he has written songs exploring Nica life, including "Tierra Prestada" ("Borrowed Land") and "Calle de Miami" ("Street of Miami").

The African-derived marimba is found throughout Latin America, but the *marimba del arco* is purely Nicaraguan. Closely associated with the Indian town of Monimbó outside Masaya, the marimba del arco is a national symbol of folk music traditions. Smaller than the Guatemalan marimba, its twenty-two wooden keys lie on top of cedar tube resonators. The *marimbero* (marimba player) uses two or three mallets to play the instrument, often as part of a trio that includes a guitar and the smaller *guitarilla*. Marimba del arco musicians usually play the types of sones classified as *jarabes* or *danzas*. The marimba accompanies such folk dances as the *baile de la marimba* or dances for Masaya's festival of San Jerónimo. Marimberos often pass on the tradition to their sons, and many make the instrument themselves.

In Miami, the marimba appears within a wide variety of events, including Purísima celebrations, festivals, and private parties. Recorded marimba music accompanies the opening of the radio program "Nicaragua Hoy," and one popular Nica dance band features a marimba button on their synthesizer. Nica restaurants often feature marimba music, though most use the larger marimba. Alonso Montalván, a mestizo from Masaya, is the only marimba del arco player in Miami. Although it is unusual to find a non-Indian marimba del arco player, his father was a famous folkloric dancer in Nicaragua. Montalván performs at the festival of San Jerónimo, private parties, community functions, and Purísimas.

Music is an important element of Nicaraguan patronal festivals. *Bandas de chicheros* perform a musical style which is traditional for religious processions, bullfights, and other such festive events. The name derives from *chicha*, the Nicaraguan national drink of fermented corn. Bandas consist of trumpets, trombones, clarinets, tubas, bass drum, and snare drum playing in a loud and boisterous manner. The chichero repertoire usually contains *sones de pascua* (Easter songs), *sones de navidad o del Niño Dios* (Christmas songs), and *cachos de toros* (music for patron saints' festivals). Los Chicheros, a Miami band headed by Abilio Sanchez, Sr., is the only such group in the United States. Sanchez' group consists of five members playing two trumpets, drum, trombone, and bass drum. They perform for the Fiesta de San Sebastian, as well as many other local fiestas, parades, and religious celebrations.

Since there are few Nica clubs, many musicians perform in Nicaraguan restaurants. They frequently perform solo, accompanying themselves with guitar and rhythm box, since their small salary would be inadequate if divided among a group. Nica groups also perform for Colombians or other Central Americans, though they play infrequently for the Cuban community due to the tremendous difference in musical forms.

Festivals In the last five years, Miami's Nicas have mounted many patronal festivals from their native cities and villages: the Purísima and *Gritería* (December 7), San Sebastian (January 20), San Marcos (April), Santiago (July), Santo Domingo (August 1), and San Jerónimo (September 30). In Nicaragua, most festivals transpired over a period of several days surrounding a fixed date. Due to American custom and work schedules, Miamians generally celebrate on the Sunday nearest the Saint's Day. Because the bureaucracy surrounding parade licenses and fireworks has discouraged Nicas from duplicating the original festivals, the activities have been generally simplified to include a mass, procession, dancing, and feast.

The most widely and fully celebrated Nica event is La Purísima. This is the feast day of the national patron saint, the Virgen de la Asunción (the Immaculate Conception of Mary). While outwardly a religious event, it has strong nationalistic overtones. The event encompasses both special masses and Purísimas, or folk celebrations in homes and public places.

La Purísima commences with the nine-day *novenario* of the Virgin, starting November 26. Nicas invite guests for private Purísima parties throughout December and into January. The celebrants light candles at a special altar before the observances. The evening begins with a rosary and traditional songs called *villancicos*. Celebrants sing a cappella or are accompanied by chicheros, organs, or marimbas. The host brings out special holiday foods and *la gorra* for the guests at various times during the evening. La gorra consists of small baskets of traditional sweets such as *gofio*, anise cookies, sweet lemons or bananas, sugarcane, and toys. The parties end with the traditional *gritería* or shout: "*Quién causa tanta alegría? La concepción de María!*" ("What causes such happiness? The conception of Mary!")

Purísima altars are an intrinsic part of the festival. Some Nicas paint or embroider an ornamental backdrop called a *telón*. The Virgin is usually represented by a statue, and candles or Christmas lights may frame her image. In Nicaragua, the seasonal flower *madroño* usually decorates the altars, but in Miami Nicas substitute a variety of natural or artificial flowers.

The small toys and other artifacts included in la gorra are an essential component of La Purísima. In Miami, many are imported from the renowned artisan town of Masaya. For example, hosts can purchase the small palm containers, the noisemakers called *matracas*, and little Nicaraguan flags at various Nica shops. In addition, some Nica artists specialize in creating elaborate Purísima altars and the other decorative items. Among them, Chony Gutierrez is an outstanding folk artist who makes exquisite artifacts and altars for La Purísima and other festive events.

La Purísima celebrations involve many special foods. In addition to the chicha, golfio and sugarcane, some women make festive sweets such as *cajeta* (a fudgelike candy made from sugar, cocoa, and rice water), *ayote en miel* (honeyed orange squash), and *espumillas* (meringues), which they distribute through Nica stores. Since many of these traditional sweets are not as widely available in Miami, Nicas may substitute American candies.

The Sunday nearest to December 7 is La Gritería. Churches with predominantly Nica congregations observe the occasion with a special altar to the Virgin, mass, and a program featuring villancicos. At night, people set up altars to the Virgin outside their homes and businesses. Celebrants stroll along the streets, visiting altars, singing villancicos, and giving the gritería. In return, the hosts give them la gorra. Sweetwater in particular creates a Nicaraguan ambience by blocking off portions of the street. In 1989, residents set up over one hundred altars in the area.

In Miami, former residents of Diriamba first celebrated San Sebastian's feast day in 1990. Although the original ten-day observance has been compressed into a single day, it is still quite elaborate. In Nicaragua, the day begins with the procession of San Sebastian to the neighboring city of Dolores, where he meets the saints from the towns of Santiago and

San Marcos. They all return to Diriamba, where the other saints and townspeople remain as guests through San Sebastian's festival. On January 20, they dance through the streets to the accompaniment of traditional music. Recently Nicas from San Marcos and Santiago held their patronal festivals, to which they invited Nicas from the other towns.

At Miami's annual San Sebastian festival, celebrants carry the saint in a procession that includes dancers and the chichero band. They wind back to a special altar decorated with the Nicaraguan flag, candles, and flowers. Afterwards, the festival highlights the fiesta queen, princess of the horse, horse show, and a social dance. Festival-goers feast on *picadillo, carne asada, tacos de carbon, nacatamales, vigorón, reprochetas, baho, buñuelos, fresco de cacao,* beer, and *flor de caña* (Nica rum).

Nicas perform the *Toro Huaco, El Viejo y Vieja,* and *Diablito* dances for the San Sebastian festival. Based on historical events or aspects of colonial life, these dances exhibit a synthesis of Spanish and indigenous cultural elements. Some dancers are *promesantes,* who dance to fulfill a vow made to the saint. The Toro Huaco dance, in particular, is famous throughout Nicaragua as a native parody of the Spanish conquistadors. Dancers wear wooden masks with European features, capes, decorative leggings, colored handkerchiefs on their arms, and beautiful, ornate sombreros covered with flowers, peacock feathers, and colored foil. One dancer playing the part of the *toro,* or bull, dons a diamond-shaped frame covered with a blanket and fixed with a bull's head in front. Except for the imported mask and rattle, the costumes are made by the dance troupe. Two lines of twelve dancers face each other, move out and back with stomping dance steps, and make crying noises that simulate communication. Meanwhile, the bull and some of the dancers chase each other.

The Nica community observes the feast day of Santo Domingo de Guzman, the patron saint of Managua, with masses and a procession from St. Michael's to San Juan Bosco Catholic Church in early August. During the procession, female promesantes perform the *Baile de las Vacas* (Dance of the Cows) in colorful costumes. The dancers wear a hoop draped with white or flowered cloth to which is attached a cow's head made of brown fabric. Holding the hoop at waist level, they take simple steps, turn, and occasionally dip the heads. Men mimic the movements of matadors by using towels or handkerchiefs to simulate a cape. Each year, folk artist Chony Gutierrez dresses the saint and makes the dance costumes.

As in other Nica festivals, Masayans celebrate the feast day of patron saint San Jerónimo with a mass, procession, selection of a festival queen, food and drink, and a social dance. This celebration is distinguished

The Toro Huaco dance, an important part of the patronal festival of San Sebastian for Miami's Nicaraguan community (Photo by Tina Bucuvalas)

from others by a traditional marimba dance, the appearance of a *gigantona* (a giant wood-and-paper figure meant to ridicule the height of the Spanish women compared to the indigenous people), and the distinctive *Las Inditas* and *Las Negras* dances. During Las Inditas, four or five couples vie with each other in grace, synchrony with their partners, and overall skill as they perform to sones de marimba during stops in the saint's procession. In Las Negras, one member in each of the four or five male pairs imitates a woman. Dancers dress in elegant pink or white costumes, masks, and wigs. Festival organizers are gradually reintroducing other aspects of the festival, such as the *torovenados* (carnivals or masquerades) after the Saint's Day.

Creoles

In the Bluefields area on Nicaragua's Atlantic Coast, American missionaries who taught in the schools provided the Creoles with an early introduction to American life. As a result, many Creoles came to the United States to study before the Revolution. In many cases, their education and ability to speak English have made adaptation to Miami easier for the

Creoles than for their mestizo compatriots. Most Creoles live in the northwest section or are sprinkled throughout Nica or Jamaican neighborhoods in the southwest and west.

For many Creoles, the Moravian Church is an important force. The church has been active in Nicaragua since the mid-nineteenth century, and the Atlantic region was especially influenced by its efforts. The Prince of Peace Moravian Church ministers to those in the northwest, and the New Hope Moravian Congregation meets at the Tropical Park Community Center in south central Miami.

Foodways   Most Creole foodways are based on Jamaican and British traditions, though mestizo dishes are also included in the regional cuisine. Typical foods include fruit buns (a yeast bread), stick to my ribs (cassava pudding), rundown (a Creole type of baho made with coconut, ripe plantains, green bananas, green peppers, and either corned beef, dried fish, or corned pork), and meat patties. Coconut milk is an important ingredient in such staples as rice and peas, white and brown breads, coco pudding, rhubarb-filled pastries, *patin* (spiced pork and beef patties), and johnnycake.

A favorite Creole beverage is ginger beer, which is made by boiling mashed fresh ginger in water, straining the mixture, then adding sugar, coloring, and cream of tartar. The result is a delicious, tangy drink perfect for a hot day. Sorrel is a choice ingredient for teas or wine. Homemade sorrel wine is particularly favored at Christmas and Easter.

Few Creoles have opened restaurants or grocery stores in Miami. In Nicaragua the Chinese or mestizos usually ran the shops, and in Miami Jamaican shopkeepers fulfill most needs. Moreover, the Prince of Peace Moravian Church sponsors many events at which Creole foods can be bought or sampled. For example, one of the church's best cooks, Gertrude Guthrie, makes and sells *guisada* (a coconut-filled tart), sweet buns, and patties after services to raise funds for the church.

Music and Dance   *Palo de mayo* is the music and dance style most closely associated with the Nicaraguan coastal region. It stems from Jamaican-derived maypole celebrations held in the beginning of May. The Creoles cut down a tree that blooms during May, then braid it with ribbons while performing traditional songs and dances. Maggie Harrison from Bluefields has this to say about its origin: "This I hear from someone who I'm sure got it from her father. She said that . . . the slaves were trying to make fun of the English people, their formal maypole. They couldn't do what they were doing, so they just cut down a tree, which was a pretty tree at the time, and then they would dance around it and sing. And they usually made up the songs that they sing. Like what they do in calypso and reggae and that sort of thing. They just make up the words." The traditional palo de mayo songs commented on significant local events. Maggie Harrison remembers songs about a Miskito woman who lost her house key and a man who capsized his boat.

Modern palo de mayo music features songs with fixed texts in English. The music blends rhythms found in the English-speaking Caribbean, such as reggae, soca, and calypso, and is played throughout the year. The traditional musical ensemble featured accordion, guitar, gut-bucket bass, mule jaw rasp, drum, and maracas, but in the 1970s the music was electrified and popularized through a government-sponsored recording. The dance has also changed through time. Older Creoles conceive of the maypole dance as a sort of sensual limbo without the pole. However, in recent years it has become increasingly suggestive.

The band Poder Costeño exemplifies contemporary Atlantic Coast musical traditions. With Caribbean influences ranging from soca to calypso, Atlantic Coast music differs considerably from mestizo music. Poder Costeño's repertoire consists of widely popular Hispanic hits, Nicaraguan favorites, and Atlantic Coast genres such as palo de mayo. Several Poder Costeño members formerly played in the band of the same name in Managua, as well as in another famous Atlantic Coast group called Dimensión Costeño.

Festivals and Celebrations   Parishioners of the Moravian churches in Miami celebrate several festivals. The Harvest Festival, held at Thanksgiving, is observed throughout the Caribbean rim. Participants offer items such as vegetables they have canned, homegrown or bought produce, baked goods, flowers, plants, and needlework in order to raise money for the church. The church is decorated with palm fronds and sugarcane decorations, and parishioners place their offerings around the altar. The congregation sings special harvest hymns during the service. Afterwards, they gather outside to purchase the offerings of hot Creole, Nica, Jamaican, and American foods.

In Nicaragua, the Creoles held palo de mayo celebrations during which participants performed the traditional songs and dances. At the party's end, celebrants sang the final song, "Tululu," then picked up the maypole and danced down the street as they escorted each guest home. In addition, school children performed a maypole dance similar to the British original, in which girls held ribbons while dancing around a pole.

Miami palo de mayo celebrations have been greatly simplified. Often people simply dance to palo de mayo and reggae recordings. In recent years, the palo de mayo dance has become so suggestive that many older Creoles scorn it as obscene. However, younger Nicas perform variations of palo de mayo at clubs, and some Nica folkloric dance troupes stage exaggeratedly erotic versions.

Material Arts　Creole women practice a variety of different needlework skills. *Hardanger* embroidery originated in Norway and came to the Atlantic Coast via the Moravian Church. Many women still practice hardanger, as the altar cloths in Miami's Moravian churches indicate. There are two types of hardanger: cut-work and solid-work. Women first embroider the design border, then cut and remove some of the threads in the pattern. They weave together the remaining threads to create new patterns. Most hardanger designs are embroidered with white thread on white cloth or beige on beige. The work is very time-consuming.

Creole women also create tatting, crochet, cross-stitch, and machine embroidery. Tatting involves the tying of tiny knots either in circles or along a foundation thread with a tatting shuttle, which produces dainty lace fabric or trimming. In Miami, tatted snowflakes are used as Christmas tree ornaments. Atlantic Coast women also crochet fine, lacy tablecloths or tablecloth insets and sew cotton gingham aprons embroidered with cross-stitch.

Miskito

The Miskito are the smallest and least-known segment of the Nica community. Most Miskito are racially mixed, culturally westernized, and Moravian by religion. They usually speak Miskito as their first language and Spanish as their second. There are some Miskito professionals in Miami, but most immigrants are young working-class men. They live throughout the area, with concentrations in Miami Beach, East Little Havana, Carol City, and Fort Lauderdale. The Prince of Peace Moravian Church sponsors a Miskito service each Sunday, conducted by a Miskito pastor.

Miskito foodways incorporate a number of Creole and mestizo recipes, but also include many distinctive dishes. *Wabul* is a porridge-like drink made from mashed ripe bananas. The Miskito also enjoy *auhbi pyakan*, a fish rundown without the coconut. Unfortunately, some foodstuffs basic to traditional Miskito cuisine, such as turtle and breadfruit, are presently unavailable.

The Miskito share many Moravian musical traditions. For instance a Miskito choir and band perform Moravian hymns in their own language during Sunday services and Saturday night youth fellowship meetings at the Prince of Peace. The band utilizes such Miskito instruments as shake shakes and a homemade bass created from a washpan, broom handle, and single string. Secular music traditions include songs that comment on local events and experiences. Although many know these songs, few actively perform them.

THE ISLANDERS

Extending from Florida south to Venezuela, the West Indies were the first land masses that Columbus discovered. Europeans quickly established colonies based largely on sugarcane cultivation. Upon the death from disease and overwork of most indigenous peoples, colonists brought large numbers of slaves from West and Central Africa. By the early nineteenth century, they had transported at least 6 million Africans to the Caribbean. To compensate for the abolition of the slave trade, landowners brought thousands of indentured workers from Europe, Africa, China and India between 1836 and 1917. This diverse cultural mix is the basis of the Caribbean's remarkable ethnic complexion.

Since the nineteenth century, limited natural resources and centuries of careless agricultural practices have made it difficult for the islands to support large populations. Thus, for generations, a significant proportion of West Indians have undertaken migrant labor to sustain themselves and their societies.

South Floridians usually refer to non-Hispanic West Indians as "the Islanders." They can be divided into two basic categories. Most English-speakers come from the Bahamas, Jamaica, and Trinidad/Tobago. They share many cultural elements and often live in contiguous neighborhoods. It has been estimated that there are about forty thousand Bahamians and forty thousand Jamaicans living in the area. The other major group consists of approximately one hundred fifty thousand Haitians, who speak Haitian Creole and/or French.

British West Indians: Bahamians, Jamaicans, Trinidadians

With only fifty miles separating Florida and the Bahamas, there were many early connections between them. Many blacks arrived in the Bahamas as slaves of British Loyalists who emigrated from Florida after the American Revolution. In the early nineteenth century, Black Seminoles settled on Andros Island, and the British made efforts to attract more black immigrants from the South. At the same time, Bahamians frequently fished and wrecked along Florida's lower east coast and the Keys, which were sometimes regarded as "another island of the Bahamas."

By the mid-nineteenth century, many Bahamians began to migrate

permanently to the Keys for better-paying jobs fishing, turtling, or sponging. When Miami expanded in the late 1890s, many men came to work in agriculture, construction, railroads, docks, gravel pits, and lumberyards. Bahamian women emigrated in greater numbers when tourist resorts and restaurants opened. By 1920, 4,815 Bahamians lived in Miami—more than 16 percent of the permanent population. From the 1920s to the 1950s, Bahamians flocked to South Florida to harvest crops from Fort Pierce to Florida City, then returned to their islands during the summer.

Bahamians have had a significant impact on Miami. They created their own communities replete with distinctive buildings, churches, fraternal organizations, and artistic societies. Today, about 70 percent of the families in the old Bahamian section of Coconut Grove are descendants of Bahamian immigrants. They have maintained their heritage in

The black Bahamian community in Coconut Grove, ca. late 1890s (Photo courtesy of HASF)

part because of the continued flow between the countries. Today a half-hour flight enables more Bahamians than any other foreign nationals to visit relatives and shop in Miami.

In the last century, significant numbers of Jamaicans have also emigrated to take advantage of better economic opportunities. Between the mid-nineteenth and early twentieth centuries, almost two hundred thousand toiled on canals in Central America. During the early twentieth century, thousands more left for sugar, banana, and coffee plantations in Nicaragua, Costa Rica, Honduras, Trinidad, Colombia, and Guatemala. When Jamaica's economy faltered again in the 1960s, many emigrated to England and later to the United States.

Today there are several Jamaican neighborhoods in Miami. In the northwest, a plethora of restaurants, record stores and other shops, and churches supply the needs of the community. There are also large Jamaican sections in Lauderhill in southern Broward County, and in west Palm Beach County near the sugarcane fields.

At the southern end of the island arc, Trinidad and Tobago were colonized by the Spanish, French, and British. Later, Africans, Chinese and East Indians contributed to the creation of a unique cultural mix. Although not as numerous as Bahamians or Jamaicans in Miami, immigrants from Trinidad and Tobago have had an important influence through a carnival tradition which brings together many different island groups.

Foodways   Commercial establishments that supply traditional West Indian cuisine and foodstuffs abound in Miami. Many fine restaurants can be found in the northwest section, such as The Pepper Pot, Pantry Restaurant, Pauline's and Callaloo. They serve such popular Caribbean dishes as rice and peas, curried goat, oxtail stew, jerk chicken or pork, fried plantains, conch fritters or salads, callaloo, Escovich fish, and ackee with salt cod. West Indian bakeries offer breads and sweets such as meat patties, sourdough and coconut breads, coconut and plantain pastries, currant rolls, and fruit cakes. Tai's Bakery, owned by a Chinese Jamaican family, also serves hot lunches. Small West Indian groceries have sprung up everywhere to purvey a wide range of merchandise: medicinal herbs, spices, imported canned goods, pharmaceuticals, and produce.

Bahamian cuisine is based on the fresh fish and tropical fruits available in the islands. Conch fritters, fish stew, pigeon peas and rice, conch salad, crab salad, fried snapper and grouper, coconut candy, and queen of all puddings are favored dishes. Conch fritters in particular have achieved widespread popularity.

Jamaicans have brought a wide variety of foodways with them.

Typical main dishes include curry goat, jerk chicken or pork, ackee and saltfish (cod), Escovich fish, and callaloo stew. Rice and peas made with coconut milk is eaten with fish, chicken or roast beef dishes, while plain white rice accompanies the curry goat. Holidays mean special festive foods, such as the dark, sweet, and heavy fruitcake made from a variety of dried fruits at Christmas time. On Easter, Jamaicans purchase special rectangular sweet buns at local bakeries and complement them with a type of canned cheese.

Until recent years, Jamaicans drank freshly made tropical fruit drinks rather than manufactured sodas. In Miami, they still make fruit drinks such as soursop juice, pineapple and guava punch, and ginger beer. With carrots, sweetened condensed milk, nutmeg, cinnamon, vanilla, and rum, Jamaican carrot juice is a delicious beverage served after dinner or on festive occasions. The non-alcoholic version is a vitamin-rich drink suitable for children.

Trinidadian/Tobagon cooking is similar to Jamaican, but there are important differences in ingredients and popular dishes. Like many others living in tropical climates, the people of Trinidad and Tobago enjoy their main meal at midday and a lighter snack of sweet breads, cheese, tea or hot chocolate in the evening. Typical dishes include rice and peas, curry chicken, stew chicken, fried fish, akra (saltfish cakes), fishhead broth, and cowfoot stew.

Many Trinidadians pre-season, or marinate, fish or meats overnight with lime, oil, and a dash of bitters. This technique tenderizes the flesh and adds flavor. Cooks often brown meats in oil and brown sugar before cooking to add coloring.

Fish are important to the national cuisine. Typically, a fish such as snapper, bluefish, pinfish, or grouper is sliced and pre-seasoned, then dried, coated with flour, and fried. Next the cook creates a gravy by browning chopped onion in oil, then adding flour and curry powder. The fish is placed in the prepared gravy and simmered an additional five minutes.

Trinidadians and Tobagons prepare a variety of special holiday foods. Like the Jamaicans, black cake is one of their specialties for weddings, christenings, Christmas, and other festive events. A cook may begin six months in advance by soaking ground raisins, currants, and prunes in a mixture of rum and wine. As they say, "The longer the soak, the better the cake." When it comes time to bake the cake, the fruits are added to a simple batter. To obtain the black color, the cook burns sugar in a little oil, then adds a glass of water and mixes it into the cake.

Although noted traditional singer and dance instructor Shirley Sutherland has been in this country almost twenty-five years, she continues to prepare traditional foods from her native Tobago for family and friends.

An exemplary cook, Sutherland's mother was a renowned vendor of sweet potato pone and corn pone. Among the dishes Sutherland prepares is coocoo, which is made from cornmeal, okra, coconut milk extracted from grated or blended coconut meat, onions, salt, and pepper. Her callaloo stew differs from Jamaican versions. She makes it with okra, green peppers, pig tails, crabs, and unopened leaves from the tuberous dasheen plant, and serves it over rice or coocoo. Until her children grew up, Sutherland baked breads, sweet breads, small cakes, and little coconut cakes twice weekly. She frequently utilizes tropical fruits such as mangos, papayas, and guavas in her cooking. For example, she often uses green papayas to add flavor and tenderize the meat. She turns guavas into jam, jelly, stewed guava, and tarts, and makes wine from oranges, guava, Tobago cherries, mandarin oranges, or tangerines.

Folk Medicine   When Bahamian settlers came to Miami and Key West in the late nineteenth century, there were few doctors to minister to their needs. Instead, they relied on knowledge of traditional herbal remedies and the many similar plants in Florida. Some brought Bahamian fruit, plants and seeds with them so they could continue their folkways. These traditional remedies, called bush medicine, are sometimes used by Bahamian Americans today. Among the more common remedies are aloe for cuts, bruises, burns, facials, or hair treatments; grapefruit juice to cure sore eyes or colds; lime to counteract the effect of mosquito or other insect bites; allspice tea as a general tonic; and gumbolimbo bark applied to toothaches.

Some Jamaicans continue to use traditional remedies to alleviate a variety of ailments. Like the Bahamians, they call specialists in herbal medicine bush doctors because they use the native plants to cure. Jamaicans use bark, roots, and leaves to create soothing teas, baths, or poultices. They obtain these directly from plants or purchase imported packets in Jamaican shops. Common remedies include a mixture of lime juice, salt and water as a gargle for sore throats; tea from cerasee leaves, mint, and jack-in-the-bush for colds; cooled tea of cerasee leaves, jack-in-the-bush, and fresh grated ginger for stomach aches; and a few drops of cooled rosemary tea for eye irritations.

Architecture   When Africans came to the New World, they continued many architectural traditions and also created new ones by combining African, European, and Native American elements. These designs have had a great impact on Miami's architectural environment.

The Bahamian immigrants to Miami added a special character to the area through their noted building skills. Early Bahamian settlers modeled their homes on those of the Bahamas and Key West. Constructed from oolitic limestone, which was also common in the Bahamas, the buildings were elevated off the ground on stone piers or wooden posts to allow air circulation and prevent wood rot. Wooden balloon frames, low gabled roofs, exterior staircases, and louvered door and window shutters enabled the structures to withstand the area's violent tropical storms. The houses were also designed with two-story porches equipped with balustrades across the front or sides. The porches shielded the house from the direct rays of the burning sun. Scholars believe porches are an African or Afro-Caribbean architectural element.

Similar in design to West African houses, the shotgun house is common throughout the Caribbean and American South. Some scholars believe it originated in Haiti from a combination of three different architectural traditions: the gable door and porch of an Arawak Indian house, the building techniques of a French country cottage, and the dimensions of a Yoruba house. Haitian immigrants brought the design to New Orleans during the early 1800s, and from there it spread widely throughout the country. The fundamental shotgun consists of a wooden frame building one room wide and three rooms deep, with doors at the gable ends and often a front porch. Some believe the name arose because a shotgun could be fired through the front door and the bullet would go out the back door without touching the walls.

The Charles Street area in old Bahamian Coconut Grove still features many old Bahamian-style structures as well as shotgun houses. At the western end of Charles Street is one of the city's oldest cemeteries, where Bahamian-style above-ground limestone graves predominate.

Verbal Arts   The Jamaican narrative impulse is very strong. Some Miamians fondly remember their childhood in rural Jamaica, when parents and grandparents would gather children around them in the evenings and entertain them with traditional stories, riddles, and songs. Many narratives, such as the Anansi (spider) tales, originated with African moral tales about animals who act like human beings. Within the context of slavery, the Jamaican tales about small animals outwitting larger ones also allowed people to enjoy a measure of revenge. Another popular type of narrative is the ghost, or duppy, tale. Jamaicans refer to spirits as duppies, a word still found in West African languages. Jamaican ghosts take frightful forms such as the rolling calf, the spirit of an evil person who spits fire and makes a terrible noise with clanking chains. Duppies also appear as the pale white ghosts of the dead.

Although the tales are familiar to most Jamaicans, Lucille Fuller is one of the few outstanding storytellers in Miami. A former teacher and principal in Jamaica, Fuller learned stories from her grandmother and parents. She is a remarkable performer, capable of enrapturing an

Jamaican storyteller
Lucille Francis Fuller
with granddaughter and
apprentice Sophia
Campbell (Photo by Tina
Bucuvalas/Courtesy of
HASF)

audience with dramatic characterizations in a wide variety of tales. Fuller
has recounted Jamaican stories in school, church, and community programs to the delight of generations of children. She related the following
duppy tale:

A rolling calf is the spirit of a person that died—that was a wicked, evil
person that died. They say that that person's spirit has no resting place, so it
becomes a rolling calf. And when you walk on the street at night, and you look
behind you, you will hear like a chain coming: "Brrrrum, burrrrrum!" And you
will look far out back there, you might see a ball of fire. And the thing just keep
rolling and coming nearer. And the nearer it gets to you, the head start getting
bigger and grow bigger and grow big. And you start sweating like you have a
fever. And start trembling. And then when you look, you feel like a heat—
something hot pass you! And you look opposite from the other end, and you see
the ball of fire going up there, and the chain rolling, "Rrumump, churrumuump,
brrrrmrrr!!"

Why? They say back in slavery they used to chain the slaves, and when—yes,
the sound of the chain, and those were the evil slaves that hated the masters, and
they were vicious and they die. So their spirit has no resting place, so they turn
rolling calves and frighten people. And some of those, coming nearer on, you
have people that died that were *obeah* men, a type of voodoo, and those spirits
have no resting place. They turn rolling calves. So our parents, going to tell us
jumbie, duppy stories, we have to be sure that everything outside finished,
because we cannot go outside for the night! No! You are scared!

You have duppies that used to walk upright, coming to you. They generally dress in white because they used to bury people in white. So you pass a graveyard . . . at night, you're sure to see a ghost. And my grandmother told me about a story of this woman, she look—a man sent her to the shop at night to buy something, and she had to pass this place, this graveyard. And when she was away down the street she saw this woman walking, coming to her in white. And the women just going up and down like this, and walking, coming down. So she said, oh, she going to get company. And nearer, when she get nearer, her head started growing big, and her head started growing big! Until when she look, she look up the woman head, you could look through the nostrils and see her brain. Just a big hole up there. And she run and pass the woman like that!!! And she look down the other end, she saw the woman going. But when she was near, she didn't see the woman, she just saw the head with the holes, the nostrils just go up in the head. So you see, that's all duppies are. They say duppies don't have any brain, you can always look through the nostrils into the head and see the duppy. Well lots of those people could tell you from time to time they have seen them. Particularly when they pass graveyards.

Fuller includes the following Brother Rabbit story in her repertoire. These stores are African survivals related to the American Brer Rabbit tales, but are now rare among Jamaican tales.

Brother Rabbit left his children home. And the bear went there and because the bear wanted to eat the rabbits, the bear tried to give them tasks to do that were impossible for them. So that when they could not perform the tasks the bear would eat them. So the bear gave the baby—the children rabbits, Brother Rabbit's children a basket to go down to the pond to fill of water.

And the baby, children rabbits took it down there. And they were there crying, and trying and trying and they couldn't get it to fill up. So a little bird came by in the tree and started singing, "If you daub it with clay and paste it with mud, just daub it with clay and paste it with mud, it will hold water. So daub it with clay and paste it with mud."

And the rabbits, they did that. The little children rabbits did that. They took the mud and they daubed it outside, and they pasted it inside with the clay. And they were able to take water to the wolf, and the wolf didn't get to eat them up.

Jamaicans love verbal contests, so it is no wonder that riddles are popular. Many of the following puzzlers involve aspects of life that are distinctively Jamaican. Some also open with the traditional "my father" formula:

Riddle: My father's children came with three eyes, but only one it sees out of.
Answer: A coconut with three holes, but you can only get to the center through one of the holes.

Riddle: My father has a shipload of people and all of them come with black head.
Answer: Ackee, whose seeds are black.

Riddle: My father has six children and all of them come with one eye.
Answer: A needle.

In Jamaica, people often use proverbs to illustrate a concept. The following proverbs exemplify some parental admonitions:

Proverb: There are many ways to harm a dog without putting a rope around its neck.
Interpretation: There are ways to discipline without corporal punishment. The saying might be used by parents who plan to take away a child's privilege in order to discipline him or her.

Proverb: Is not the same day a leaf drops in the water it rots.
Interpretation: The consequence of an action is not always immediate. For instance, a child may do something bad and the parent may find out at a later time.

Proverb: He's giving you a basket to carry water.
Interpretation: Someone has given you an impossible task. This refers to the Brother Rabbit story in which the bear asks the baby rabbits to bring him water in a basket.

Music and Dance   English-speaking West Indians have created a wide variety of musical styles, such as calypso, reggae, and soca, by combining African and British musical elements. Although each style is distinctive, there are some common characteristics. In each case, the music utilizes European harmonic systems and instrumentation. Nevertheless, African elements such as syncopation, call-and-response, heavy percussion, improvisation, and lyrics based on contemporary social issues predominate.

With its large Jamaican population, Miami's music scene is the home to many bands playing Jamaican music, especially reggae. Reggae evolved from earlier Jamaican musical forms that fused African and British elements. From the late nineteenth century through the 1950s the most favored song-and-dance form was mento, which was much like a polka with a heavy bass line. In the 1960s musicians fused mento with rock and roll to create ska and rock steady. Rastafarianism, a social and religious movement that espouses black nationalism and Afro-Christian beliefs, emerged in the 1930s and eventually grew to include many disaffected young Jamaicans. Among adherents were also members of the burru cults, which maintained a complex African type of drumming. The combination of burru drumming with rhythm and blues, mento, studio technology, and Rastafarian philosophy eventually became the basis of today's reggae. The term "reggay" ("ragged" or "everyday" in Jamaican slang) was first used in 1969 in the title of a recording by Toots and the Maytals.

Musically, reggae possesses a slow tempo, with bass drum, rhythm guitar, and keyboards emphasizing the offbeats. Lyrically, its hallmark is the attempt to stir listeners with a universal message about the evils of oppression. The result is one of the most universally popular musical forms ever created. The reggae dance style, which incorporates a dipping motion some believe originated in Africa, has also achieved great favor.

Miami is a major reggae center. To emphasize its national identity, the Jamaican community combines its annual independence day celebration with one of the largest reggae festivals in the United States. Miami boasts many excellent local bands, including Zero Crew, Ti-Shan, Spice Roots, Bigga, Benaiah, Massive Crew, and others, and concerts regularly headline major reggae bands. Several clubs are devoted entirely to reggae, others feature it weekly, and many parties and other private social events highlight reggae bands. Moreover, the city's recording industry supports studios that specialize in reggae. Miami is also home to a variety of fine reggae record shops, Caribbean radio stations such as WAVS-AM, and *Reggae Report*, a glossy magazine with international distribution.

With its indigenous steelband, calypso, and soca musical forms, Trinidad and Tobago have had a strong influence on the music of other Caribbean islands. Legend has it that Trinidadians first created steeldrums when empty oil drums abandoned by the United States forces washed up on the beaches during World War II. It is more likely that the drums have African prototypes. Pans, or steel drums, are traditionally made from special fifty-five-gallon oil drums, though Florida pan makers sometimes use fifty-five-gallon orange juice drums. Craftspeople heat the top, then hammer, chisel, and form it into a circle of distinct rhomboid-shaped areas that produce brilliant, bell-like notes. Drums differ in type and tuning; there are, for example, thirty-two notes on a tenor drum and six on a cello drum. Players strike the pans with wooden dowels wrapped at one end with rubber bands, rubber balls, or cloth.

Steelbands are composed of several pans tuned in different keys, arranged from soprano to bass. They may also employ other instruments, such as congas or snare drums. Steelbands play in a polyrhythmic, syncopated manner derived from the African musical heritage. Traditionally, the bands accompany popular calypso melodies with western harmonies to create a complex art form. Many bands today have abandoned calypso in favor of jazz or symphonic forms. Conversely, some bands performing music in other traditions have begun to include a pan for its beautiful, ethereal sound. For example, some Miami groups combine the instrumentation and arrangements of jazz, steelband, and other Caribbean musical forms.

In southeast Florida, a wide variety of clubs and restaurants ranging from dockside bars to neighborhood dance halls feature Caribbean music. Many salsa and rock clubs now offer reggae each Sunday night, perhaps because the music provides a more tranquil entrance into the working week. Festivals provide an important venue for many Caribbean bands.

Festivals and Celebrations   Miami's largest West Indian celebrations are the Jamaican Independence Day Reggae Festival, Bahamian Goombay Festival, and the West Indian American Carnival initiated by the Trinidadians. These festivals reflect European, African, and sometimes Asian folklife. Europeans brought masquerade and mumming traditions to the Caribbean, where they eventually blended with African religious masquerades. African elements and aesthetics play a major role in Caribbean festivals. They are especially evident in the vibrant costumes composed of assemblages of myriad objects and materials such as brightly colored feathers, mirrors, glitter, and fringed paper, which combine to achieve a fantastic effect.

Half a million Miamians turn out annually during the first weekend of June to celebrate Goombay—the largest black heritage street festival in the United States. Organized and directed by Coconut Grove's Bahamian American community, Goombay's central theme is the long-standing link between Miami and the Bahamas. The festival is an amalgamation of elements from the Bahamian Goombay and Junkanoo festivals, as well as from mainstream American street festivals.

Goombay opens Friday night with precision drills by the Royal Bahamas Police Band, presentations by American and Bahamian dignitaries, and a VIP reception. On Saturday many descendants of early Bahamian settlers attend a Pioneers Luncheon, which focusses on the area's history as well as on some aspect of Bahamian culture.

On Saturday and Sunday, the Goombay street festival attracts the bulk of the visitors. More than four hundred temporary kiosks offer Bahamian, Jamaican, Trinidadian, and African American foods along the central street. Other stands offer traditional and contemporary arts, including woven items from Nassau's famous straw market. At intervals, West Indian and American musical groups perform on portable stages. The most popular Goombay performers are indisputably the Junkanoo groups. The festival occasionally sponsors one of the large Bahamian groups, but it always features Miami's own Sunshine Junkanoos. A golf tournament on Saturday and a Miami/Bahamas Goombay Regatta on Sunday round out the event.

In the Bahamas, Junkanoo celebrations commence in the early hours of Boxing Day (December 26) and New Year's Day. Revelers wear costumes created from shredded strips of colored paper, glue, wire, and cardboard. Neighborhood bands perform choreographed dances accompanied by cowbells, goatskin drums, and whistles. Each year the bands create new costumes to represent a theme. Some also concoct gigantic costumes and large floats.

Sunshine Junkanoo Band founder Bruce Beneby emigrated to Miami in 1956, but returned to Nassau annually to participate in Junkanoo celebrations. There are many theories about Junkanoo's origin, but Beneby believed that "it all began in Africa with a gentleman named 'Johnny Enew,' leader of a band that traveled from house to house, from street to street during certain holidays like Christmas and New Year's, which is when Junkanoo is celebrated in the Bahamas." Like Bahamian bands, the Sunshine Junkanoos create dramatic new costumes each year from cardboard, crepe paper, and decorated clothing. Some designs display a fascinating blend of Bahamian and American symbols, such as headdresses bearing the image of Martin Luther King. The Sunshine Junkanoos play annually at Goombay, as well as at many other festive events in Miami. During performances, band members parade through the festival grounds playing horns, drums, whistles, and cowbells. Although the music is simple, it is highly infectious, and festival-goers often dance in the wake of the band. Beneby was killed in a tragic hit-and-run accident in 1990, but his son now leads the band.

Like most Caribbean celebrations, Trinidadian Carnival derives its vitality from a mixture of European and African components. Its precursors were African religious observances and pre-Lenten fancy balls and masquerades held by Spanish, French and English planters. Seventeenth-century French settlers had a particularly strong influence, but Trinidadian Carnival owes much of its current form to African freedmen who appropriated the festival after emancipation in 1834. In addition, Chinese and East Indians contributed significant elements from their cultural traditions, such as the large wheeled figures of kings and queens.

Trinidadian Carnival is a tremendous event. Carnival bands, or *mas* (for masquerade) camps, present their themes, kings, and queens in late fall. By January, activity is already frenzied as steel bands perform frequently and calypsonians release new recordings. The king, queen, calypso, and steelband competitions occur a week before Mardi Gras. On opening day, celebrants covered with mud or clothed in rags converge on Port-of-Spain's central square. Some carry palm branches signifying the renewal of life in both African and European symbolic systems. Afterwards, they eat such traditional Carnival foods as chicken pelau, black pudding, or salt fish. During Tuesday's grand finale, bands masquerade

Bruce Beneby and the
Sunshine Junkanoo Band,
1990 (Photo by Tina
Bucuvalas/Courtesy of
HASF)

through the streets in fantastic costumes as the floats blare dance music.

Miami's West Indian American Day Carnival Association has sponsored an elaborate Carnival celebration since 1984. Beginning months in advance, dozens of mas camps design and create stunning costumes and floats. Carnival commences in early March, with the Old Mas Competition Show and Dance on Saturday, the Kings and Queens of the Band parade and Individuals Show and Dance on the next Friday, and the Soca Carnival Jump Up/Show and Dance on the second Saturday. The culmination is the public Carnival parade on Sunday. Groups of dancers dressed in fabulous costumes alternate with ornate floats carrying powerful sound systems. Carnival bands display a wide range of traditional themes and imagery, such as sailors, Native Americans (especially Aztec), and Asians. Festival-goers and participants come from all over the United States, the Caribbean, and even London. When they are not watching or dancing, they indulge in Caribbean delicacies such as curry goat, jerk chicken, and meat patties sold by curbside vendors.

Llewellyn Roberts is a master costume and mask maker. Like many other West Indians, he makes an annual pilgrimage to his homeland to participate in Trinidad's Carnival. In addition, each year he creates new costumes for his mas band and the annual Miami celebration. Roberts generally makes the elaborate masks by covering a wire frame base with a variety of materials to create beautiful, exotic effects based on the annual theme. His brother, Granville, sometimes makes Carnival masks entirely of sheet metal.

Miami's Carnival mirrors Trinidadian Carnival, but includes participation by other Caribbean islanders. In 1991 groups composed of former residents of Trinidad, Barbados, Jamaica, the Bahamas, St. Lucia and St. Vincent, and Belize took part. Thus, the festival provides a welcome opportunity for English-speaking Caribbean communities to draw closer together. As Steve Fairweather from Belize states, "It is a great time, but it also helps us organize as a community. . . . It is good for us from the Caribbean Islands to come together like this. We really have no voice, though we're very large in number."

Sports and Games   In Miami, many men from the British West Indies compete on cricket teams. Players don the traditional white uniforms and shin pads each Sunday to play regularly scheduled matches viewed by crowds of fans. According to Vernal Gordon, former secretary of the South Florida Cricket Association, there are about six hundred players and twenty-five teams. He says, "We have cricketers from all over the Caribbean taking part in some very intense competitions just like back home in the islands." In fact, British teams sometimes fly to Miami to compete in events. Cricket matches are played in parks or school yards located around the city, and the results are posted each Friday in the *Miami Herald*.

Haitians

Haiti is the western third of the island of Hispaniola. Colonized by the Spanish and then the French, the island supported a rich plantation economy based on sugarcane, indigo, coffee, cotton, and the labor of large numbers of African slaves. Those of African descent came from present-day Kongo and Angola, and to a lesser extent from Dahomey and the Yoruba, Bamana, and Mande areas of West Africa. By the dawn

Reveler wearing a record
costume during the West
Indian Carnival, 1990
(Photo by Brent Cantrell/
Courtesy of HASF)

of the nineteenth century there were eleven blacks for every white.
Throughout their history, African folkways have formed the core of daily
life for most Haitians.

The Haitians mounted a successful revolution against the Europeans
and became the first independent black republic in the Americas in 1801.
Since independence, Haiti has suffered a long succession of oppressive
dictatorships that have impelled many of its people to seek better
conditions elsewhere. Beginning in the late 1970s, tens of thousands of
Haitians fled to Miami to escape the harsh political and economic

circumstances. Today, there is continued immigration, though much is illegal and difficult to quantify. Miami's Haitians frequently visit Haiti, as well as Haitian communities in New York and Canada. Through these visits, they maintain a connection with their homeland by sharing their new lives with their compatriots and returning with news and goods.

Most Haitian immigrants settled in a declining two hundred-square-block area bordered by NE 41st Street on the south, the Little River at NE 83rd Street on the north, I-95 on the west, and Biscayne Boulevard on the east. Officially known as Edison/Little River, the area is now widely known as Little Haiti, since Haitians now compose the majority of residents. As a result of their presence, the community is currently experiencing a modest revival in its residential and commercial sectors. Today Little Haiti boasts more than 135 Haitian-owned businesses, many painted with attractive, brightly colored signs in French and Creole. Haitians in the professional class have started to purchase larger homes, particularly in the northern sections of Dade County.

Many cultural and service organizations play roles in promoting traditional Haitian culture. One of the most important is Notre Dame d'Haiti, the Catholic church located in the midst of Little Haiti. The church organizes a wide variety of programs to assist community members. For instance, it helps recent arrivals find food, housing, and work. There are classes in English for recent immigrants and Haitian Creole for young Haitian Americans. Other organizations include artistic societies that stage dance, music, storytelling, and dramatic productions. Small businesses support traditional arts by selling paintings, musical recordings, food, clothing, and religious items. Some, such as Les Cousins Record Shop, serve as clearinghouses for community information.

Foodways   Haitian food provides some interesting variations upon Caribbean cuisine. The basis is African, but the French influence combined with moderate spicing renders it similar in some respects to the Creole cuisine of Louisiana. In Little Haiti, a variety of markets and specialty stores serve the needs of domestic cooks. In small groceries such as the Miami-Haiti Market, women select dried conch and fish, or scoop bags of rice from large wooden barrels. In botanicas, residents purchase herbs for medicinal or spiritual purposes, as well as newspapers, religious candles, tinwork, baskets, leatherwork, and traditional housewares. Some large supermarkets in the area also carry special produce, such as malanga, that Haitians use to prepare their national cuisine.

Among the most common of traditional Haitian dishes are *griyo*, or fried pork; *lambi*, a stew of conch and vegetables; and *mayimoulen ak pwa*, kidney bean puree mixed with corn meal. Many entrees are served

Haitian cook and
storyteller Liliane Nerette
Louis prepares a
traditional dish. (Photo by
George Chillag/Courtesy
of HASF)

with rice, beans, and sometimes *piment*, a hot relish made from peppers,
carrots, and other vegetables. Haitians prepare a yellow squash soup for
special occasions such as Sunday dinners, New Year's Day, or first
communion. *Akasan*, a porridge made from corn farina, is eaten for
breakfast with syrup or evaporated milk, or mixed with milk and vanilla
to make a beverage.

Haitian desserts and beverages are superb. Among the most common
are *pen patat*, a delicious sweet potato pudding with banana and rum; *pen
mayi*, a cake made with corn flour; *douce jus coque*, a sweet created from
coconut milk, and *beignets*. The many Haitian bakeries offer *pate*, savory
puff pastries, Haitian bread, or sweet cakes. Like other Caribbean
peoples, Haitians enjoy beverages created from tropical fruits. One
example is the delicious *jus Haitien*, a refreshing drink made from
crushed ice, condensed milk, grapefruit juice, sugar, and almond flavoring.

Architecture   Within the realm of folk art, the type of painting
that occurs on signs is an important expressive medium for the creative
vision of folk artists. This folk art form flourishes in Haiti, and seems to

derive its strength from the same vivid sense of form and color that infuses the Haitian school of naive painting. In Miami's Little Haiti, sign painting continues to be important because there are few manufactured signs available in French or Creole. As a result, the area is enlivened with hand-painted signs announcing businesses and products. They are the work of many sign painters, both known and unknown.

Religion   Haitians are a very religious people. An old saying points out that "Haitians are 80 percent Catholic, 20 percent Protestant, and 100 percent *Vodoun*." In Miami, most Christians attend Catholic churches, though a wide variety of small Protestant churches ministers to growing Haitian congregations. The churches provide a focal point for both spiritual and social involvement.

Vodoun is a powerful force in the lives of many Miamians. Father Wenski, director of Notre Dame d'Haiti, says, "Besides being a religion, voodoo is a world view that permeates Haitian culture just as secularism is a world view that permeates American culture. All Haitians are influenced by that world view." Father Wenski believes that Vodoun may be widespread in Miami because of the stresses Haitians must live with: "When uprooted and in need of making sense of a strange experience, people turn to the faith they are comfortable with."

Rodrigue Gilbert creates many of the vivid signs that announce businesses in Little Haiti. (Photo by Michele Edelson/Courtesy of HASF)

For centuries, Vodoun has been misunderstood as a form of black magic. In fact, Vodoun is a synthesis of the traditional religions of Dahomey, the Yoruba, and Kongo, with some Catholic influences. There are two basic divisions of Vodoun. *Rada* centers around a pantheon of deities under a supreme being, and is associated with peace and reconciliation. It derives primarily from Dahomean and Yoruba religions, though Catholicism's miracle-working saints reinforced the belief system. Based on Kongolese and Angolan religions, *Petro* focuses on the powerful spirits of the dead and on charms that promote healing or manipulate hostile forces.

Drums are the core of Vodoun music. During ceremonies they are played constantly in order to induce trance and invite the deities. Vodoun music is based on a fast beat overlaying a slow pulse, and devotees dance during the ceremonies with fluid, contrasting motions. Since an extended period is required for the ritual music to be effective, Vodoun masses last all night. The *houngan*, or priest, presides as participants summon the *loa* to possess them. Loa are spiritual beings who may intercede in the lives of their devotees. Some are such important African deities as Shango, Erzulie, or Legba, while others are the deceased relatives or ancestors of the participants. When a deity appears, the body of the possessed provides a vehicle by which the deity can greet devotees, ask and answer questions, or give advice.

Like Santería, Vodoun is not widely visible because historically it has been relegated to the private realm. Thus practitioners create altars and conduct ceremonies in their homes. In Miami, the most overt evidence of Vodoun is the botanicas. The stores carry a variety of religious goods, such as herbs, candles, chromolithographs depicting the loas in the form of Christian saints, Vodoun banners, sequined Vodoun bottles, and many other objects used in rites. Some shops also make elaborate ritual garments. As is the case with Santería, there is a new movement to develop public awareness and respect for traditional Haitian religion. Mission Halloumanjia, a service organization formed for this purpose, makes educational presentations and has produced a festival.

Verbal Arts   Like all peoples, Haitians communicate a great deal of cultural information through different verbal genres. Proverbs—those succinct phrases through which people express gems of cultural wisdom—are among the most common of traditional verbal forms. Haitians use a wide assortment of Creole proverbs, many of which provide insights into traditional Haitian life:

Proverb: *You sèl dwèt pa manje kalalou.*
    One finger cannot eat kalalou.

Interpretation: In Haiti, many people eat with their fingers. The stew kalalou does not stick to the fingers, so people need more than one finger to eat. The meaning of this proverb is that people must work together.

Proverb: *Roch nan dlo pa konn doulè ròch nan solèy.*
The stone in the river does not know what the stone in the sun suffers.
Interpretation: Those who are doing well cannot appreciate the plight of the less fortunate.

Proverb: *Se kouto ki konn sa ki nan kè yanm.*
Only the knife knows what is in the heart of the yam.
Interpretation: You can never know what is in another's heart.

Proverb: *Joumou pa donnen kalbas.*
A pumpkin cannot give birth to a calabash.
Interpretation: You can't make a silk purse from a sow's ear.

Most Haitians are familiar with a large body of old traditional *kont*, or tales, which were often told in the evenings to entertain children, other family members, or friends. Some of the most common are the Bouki and Malice stories, which are derived from African narratives. In the tales, the trickster Bouki usually undertakes a shameful scheme that ultimately backfires on him.

Liliane Nerette Louis is one of the few in Miami who actively maintain Haitian storytelling traditions. As a child, she looked forward to the evenings, when her mother gathered the children around her and told them tales. Louis begins all her stories with a traditional formula: "*Krik, krak.* We used to start all the old Haitian kont with krik, and the people listening to the kont will say krak." The following, one of her favorite stories, reveals many details of an earlier Haitian way of life:

The Little Boy and the Ayayay

Krik! [Krak!]

One time a little boy was living with the aunt because he had no mommy, no daddy. But the aunt was terrible to him. She used to beat him all the time. For yes or for no, the little boy was beaten. The little boy was responsible for most of the household. He used to clean, cook, clean the front and back yard, take water from the river to the house, wash the clothes, go to the market. Everything was the little boy's responsibility—even kill the chicken. But every day, the aunt would find a reason to beat the little boy, no matter how well he would do his duties.

One day he worked so hard and so well the aunt didn't find anything against the little boy—*anything* to beat up the little boy. So that day she said to the boy, "I see that you did your work pretty well, but I'm sure I didn't see something. Now come over here, I'm going to send you to the market. I'm sending you to the market to buy some ayayay." Ayayay in English means "ouch!" The little boy said, "Auntie what ouch is? I don't know ouch." "You mean you don't know ouch?! Ouch!! That's the first time I hear that. Somebody who don't know what ayayay means. Ayayay—all the time people say ayayay and you don't know what it means? Well, I don't care. I want you to go to the market and get me some ayayay. And if you don't get my ayayay, I will give you a good beating! You'll be afraid. Let me tell you something, it will be better you weren't born, because I'm really going to give it to you! You better find me that ayayay."

The little boy left the house crying, crying. He didn't know what to do. Where can he find ayayay? He didn't even know what ayayay was. He was on the street crying. A man was passing by. He said to him, "My little boy, why so much?" "Oh sir, it's my aunt who told me to go buy some ayayay! I don't know what is ayayay, and if I don't take the ayayay to her, she's going to beat me up very bad." "Oh, my little boy, I wish I could help you, but I really don't know what ayayay is. Well, ask someone else."

The little boy kept on going. He really didn't know what ayayay was. He was crying. Everybody saw him crying. Everybody would tell him—just pass by and tell him they don't know what ayayay is. Then came an old lady, a very old lady who had a lot of experience. She saw the little boy crying. She call him, "Come over here, my little boy. Why are you crying so much?" "Oh, it's my auntie. She beats me every day. And today she's going to really beat me very hard. She might kill me, because she wants me to buy her some ayayay and I don't know what ayayay is." "Oh, my little boy, come on. I'll find you some ayayay. Don't you worry. Come over there, let's go over there. Let's go to the forest." "Ohh! Is that so? Is it at the forest you can find ayayay?" "Come on my little boy, you will find ayayay in the river first. Let's go to the river."

Then they went by the river and the old lady pick up two big crabs. Fat big crabs! And she put them in the little boy's bag. Then she went to the forest and pick up big needles. The old lady pick up some pine needles—big long pine needles. And she put them in the little boy's bag. Then she told the little boy, "Do you have anything to buy?" "Yes, my aunt wants me to buy all the market for today." "Okay, my little boy, go to market now and place everything on top. When you get home, tell your auntie that the ayayay is in the bottom of the bag and she should put her hand all the way down to get it. Don't worry, she should be very happy, because that's really what ayayay is."

So, the little boy did exactly what the old lady told him. He went to the market, bought rice, peas, vegetables, lettuce, everything that the aunt told him to buy. Then he went back home. He was happy that day. So the aunt said, "Why are you so happy?! Don't you know that I'm going to beat you up for the ayayay that you haven't find?" "Oh no, Auntie, I find your ayayay." "Oh, yes, you find my ayayay? Let's come over here, let me see what the ayayay is. And if it's not ayayay, you better be prepared, because I'm going to beat you up!" "Okay

Auntie, I'm sure I find you your ayayay this time. Put your hands all the way in the bag, and you will pick up the ayayay."

So, the auntie did just like the little boy told her to do. She was so in a hurry to find that ayayay, and she put her hands all the way down to the ayayay. And—OOF!! "AYAYAY!!" she cried. "AYAYAY!! AYAYAY!!" That was the two big crabs who were beating her up and the pine needles were profoundly in her hands and blood was coming out. She yelled so loud that everybody came. Everybody. Even the sheriff came. And when they heard the story that she was the one who asked for the ayayay, she was blamed for good. And ever since she could never beat the little boy anymore, because the sheriff had the big eye on her.

When I heard all that yelling, I came to see what was happening, and they pushed me down, and I came to tell you the story.

Music and Dance Traditional Haitian music arose from a combination of European and African musical forms and instruments. Since the vast majority of Haitians descended from West and Central African peoples, their musical styles have blended to form distinct genres such as Vodoun music. French social dances such as the *contradanse, mascaron,* and *quadrille* were also popular in the past, though they gradually fused with African rhythms to create new forms.

In Miami, Haitian mothers continue to croon time-honored lullabies to soothe their children to sleep. Many, such as Claudine Sada and her cousins Kareen Sassine and Scarlett Camacho, sing the following popular lullaby to a beautiful, haunting melody:

Fe dodo ti,	Sleep little baby,
titit maman li.	mommy's little one.
Dododo ti,	Sleep little baby,
titit maman li.	mommy's little one.
Si li pa dodo,	If you don't sleep,
krab la va manjé li.	the crab will eat you.
Si li pas dodo,	If you don't sleep,
krab li va manjé li.	the crab will eat you.
Maman li alé,	Your mommy went
la riviè.	to the river.
Papa li alé	Your daddy went
peché krab.	to fish for crabs.
Si li pa dodo,	If you don't sleep,
krab la va manjé li.	the crab will eat you.
Si li pa dodo,	If you don't sleep
krab la va manjé li.	the crab will eat you.

Dodo titit,	Sleep little baby,
krab lan kalalou.	the crab is in the callalou.
Dodo titit,	Sleep little baby,
krab lan bouyon.	the crab is in the stew.
Lan bouyon,	In the stew,
Lan bouyon.	in the stew.

The folk liturgy performed at Notre Dame d'Haiti Catholic Church incorporates Haitian traditional music. Ethnomusicologist Laurie Sommers determined that the choir and drum, keyboard, and guitar ensemble play music that melds the rhythms of Afro-Cuban *yenvalu* and *congo*, French contradanse, Trinidadian calypso, and Cuban cha-cha. Parishioners show their support by attending in such numbers that the church can barely accommodate them.

In Miami, some bands perform music derived from the post-Carnival Rara celebrations. The musicians play percussion and wind instruments, especially drums and *vaccines.* the latter consist of large bamboo flutes often used in sets of three. Since bamboo of appropriate dimensions is not easy to find in Miami, Haitians sometimes make sheet metal vaccines. Rara drums come from the Vodoun tradition, and appear similar to conga drums. Rara bands also highlight the *grage*, a piece of perforated sheet metal played when a musician rasps a piece of metal across it; lengths of bamboo mounted and played like drums; gourd and metal rattles; and the *po lambi*, a conch shell played like a trumpet. Miami Rara groups Koleksyon Kazak and Konbo Guinen International now play for a wide audience.

Contemporary Haitian popular music derives from such diverse sources as Haitian folk music, Caribbean rhythms, and American jazz and big band music. Many consider the *meringue* Haiti's national music. The meringue has a fast, five-beat base like Dominican merengue, but differs in its gentler progression. Early piano versions bore some similarity to ragtime. The greatest recent influence upon the tradition came from American jazz bands.

Currently the most popular Haitian music is *compas*, meaning "beat." Compas started as a big-band style of meringue, to which were added such diverse musical elements as jazz, Vodoun rhythms, Creole lyrics, vaccines, and Cuban brass instrumentation. The Ensemble Nemours Jean-Baptiste popularized the new style in the 1950s. The next decade brought influences from rock and rhythm and blues, as younger bands began to play compas. A more recent ingredient is West African-style electric guitar playing. Contemporary compas bands generally include trumpet, trombone, sax, guitar, base, conga, drum, keyboard, and

vocals. The total effect resembles salsa, but has its own distinctive, driving sound and rhythm.

Miami has spawned several successful compas bands, including The Islanders, Top Vice, Magnum Band, Skandal, and others. In order to make themselves commercially viable to a larger audience, many Haitian groups have learned such Caribbean musical styles as soca, reggae, salsa, or calypso. With this wide repertoire, they can easily play to Spanish or English-speaking audiences in addition to the Haitian community. Like many other Miami bands, Haitian compas groups frequently shuttle between Miami, New York, and their homeland to make club dates or recordings.

As with many dances keyed to Latin and Caribbean rhythms, Haitian popular dance consists of fluid, contrasting motions. In this polyrhythmic dance style, the feet move fast, the head slow, and the torso even slower. Thus, rather than imitating the beat, the dances provide a counterpoint. Numerous clubs feature Haitian music and dance.

Konbo Guinen International performing Haitian *Rara* music (Photo by Brent Cantrell/Courtesy of HASF)

Material Arts   Haitian culture has sustained myriad art forms
that express a Caribbean synthesis of African and European elements.
The *fanal*, or Christmas lantern, experienced a revival in Miami thanks
to an annual contest sponsored by the Haitian American Community
Association of Dade County. The Haitian fanal can be linked directly to
West Africa, where items of the same name appear in late-December
lantern festivals in Senegambia and Sierra Leone. African fanals are
large, intricate lanterns shaped like houses or ships.

Haitians cut cardboard in intricate patterns to create fanals in the
shape of churches, houses, stars, or birds. Perhaps the most popular
form is that of the distinctive, brightly colored, gingerbread-decorated
Haitian houses. Artists glue brilliant, jewel-toned tissue paper inside the
structure, then insert a candle in the bottom. At night they place the
lanterns in windows, so passersby may glimpse the beautiful, stained-
glass effect.

A few Miamians create traditional Haitian Carnival masks. They first
build a mold from clay or plaster. When it dries, they glue several layers
of paper over the mold. After a few hours, they remove the mask and
paint it with bold colors symbolizing a particular character or spirit.
Some apply Spanish moss to form a beard or other facial hair.

Nicaraguan and West Indian cultures survive in Miami through the
continuation of traditional arts. Festivals, food, music, dance, verbal
arts, sports, folk medicine, architecture, and material arts exhibit the
contributions of Nicas, Creoles, Miskito, Bahamians, Jamaicans, and
Trinidadians to the Miami area.

CHAPTER

Land and Sea: Traditional Skills and Occupations

Miami's many cultural groups find a common bond in the environment. In the regions surrounding Miami, the abundant natural resources of land and sea provide both the materials and the impetus for a wide variety of traditional skills and occupations distinctive to the region. In conjunction with the people, these traditional activities define Miami's unique character.

MARITIME ARTS

Water seems omnipresent in southernmost Florida. Homes and business districts embrace the shoreline and trickle through the string of tiny islands that is the Keys. Pastel hues of waves and clouds find their reflection in the local use of color, and the brilliant white heat of the sky is mirrored in the water and marks the faces of residents with the imprint of the sun. But most residents have an even closer relationship with the water. For them, it provides a constant source of sustenance and recreation.

Saltwater marine environments such as beaches, mangrove swamps, and coral reefs yield a variety of edible treasures: fish, conch, lobsters, oysters, and shrimp. South Florida residents have developed many traditional skills and occupations that reap the rich maritime harvest or facilitate enjoyment of its recreational possibilities. Local craftspeople supply equipment necessary to those activities, while others process the harvest.

The Harvest

When you approach any of the myriad bodies of water in South Florida, you are immediately struck by the numbers of people pursuing marine creatures. Traditional practices range from hobbyists angling off bridges to commercial operations with fleets of boats, fish packing plants, and markets for distribution. Commercial fishermen undoubtedly haul in the largest catch, but the legions of private anglers provide fierce competition.

In southeast Florida, there is often little distinction between private and commercial fishing. Commercial fishermen may also fish privately and, depending on the season or other employment opportunities, private fishermen sometimes fish commercially. Moreover, fishermen must obtain commercial licenses if they expect to catch over a certain regulated poundage, whether or not it is intended for personal consumption. There are thousands of noncommercial fishermen in southeast Florida. Indeed, such a large portion of the population engages in this activity that it is almost a regional obsession. Fishermen come from all ethnic backgrounds and socioeconomic levels. While some bring techniques and preferences from their ethnic backgrounds, for the most part they share similar methods and seek the same prey.

Fishing   Although fish, shrimp, oysters, and other seafood were an important food source for early settlers, they were not commercially important until the railroads brought fast transportation and improved handling methods in the late nineteenth century. Before the railroads, commercial fishermen supplied the local populace and developed trade in salted mullets and fresh groupers with Cuba. In the early twentieth century they continued to net mullet, sea trout, and other fish. Some fishermen also turtled on the capes near Flamingo, in the southernmost regions of the state. They lobstered on a more limited scale than today because they hauled in the traps manually. Two hundred traps per boat was considered a large quantity.

Today, commercial fishermen catch large quantities of fish and sell them to fish houses on shore. Many local fishermen belong to families that have fished for generations. Boat captains often hire regular crews, then fish in small fleets. Captains acquire extensive traditional knowledge concerning weather, sea beds, fish behavior, and equipment through years of experience and apprenticeship. Although fishermen compete with each other, they often develop comradeship and respect for others' abilities. Within this context they share information about successful locations, techniques, and tackle, and they help each other at sea.

Some commercial fishermen still seine net in the bays from Miami south to the Keys. They bring their boats close to the shoreline, while a fisherman on the boat holds one end of the net and another walks along the surf with the other end. In this way, they scoop up the abundant schools of pompano and permit that feed near the shore. Native Miamian Randy Reed has been fishing the waters from Biscayne Bay through the

Keys both privately and commercially for over forty years. He explains the technique:

There are two types of seine nets and one would be like a ribbon. And the other would be the same ribbon, except right dead center in the net . . . would be what looks like the cod of a shrimp net. So when they pulled the net together and closed it up, all the catch would go into what they called—instead of a seine net then they call it a purse seine. So the catch would go into the purse. Yeah, I've done that.

A lot of Cubans do it now. They do it in the bays. They do it on the beach when they can get away with it. Mainly because of the hotel owners and what not. There's one section off of Miami Beach, that the land goes a little bit further eastward. There's a lot of pompano and permit there in November, December. A lot of the commercial boys go out there with gill nets and purse seines, which can be worked from a boat also. They'll drop one end of the net off and then they'll run the boat and it will pull the net out of the boat as the boat moves through the water. And they have kept a line on the first part of the net that they have let out first. And after they get the whole net off of the boat, then they would turn ninety degrees to the net and run away from the net, and then they would be letting out the last part of the net, which would also have long rope on it. And when they got where they were somewhat perpendicular to the net, then they would tie off the net ropes—lead ropes, pleats, and they would pull forward on it. And that would make everything go to the back of the net on a purse seine. And we use those to catch ballyhoo. We use a straight seine or gill net—it's what I call them, for catching ballyhoo. . . .

And they work them in the bays. . . . On the north side of the 36th St. Causeway, on the west side of the bridge up by Miami. Those guys will walk out in the shallow waters there. And they usually do it with two people. One will stay with the staked end of the net and one man will walk off short and walk it around in a big half-moon shape and bring it back to shore. And on the beaches when you use those, the bottom of the net is weighted and the top has floats on it. They'll use nets that will be deeper than the water depth that they're working in. So that the fish isn't smart enough normally to jump over the net or go under it. And they'll walk that net all the way back up to the beach. And as they're coming up to the beach, of course the net will get a big bag in it. And the fish get trapped in it. And they'll pull it right up on the beach and the catch is up on the sand. Whereas these guys down here, they're doing it from the seawall. I don't know how they keep the fish in it. We used those for catching little tropical fishes off of Key Biscayne . . . used to have a lot of fun doing that.

Sport fishermen with access to boats fish on the bays, along the Keys, and sometimes farther out in the Atlantic. They usually catch fish by trolling—dragging bait from a line as the boat moves slowly ahead, or by dropping baited lines into areas where fish gather. Kiting is a less common method reserved for sailfish. Fishermen attach live bait to a kite, which keeps the bait fish near the surface and pulls it behind the boat. This causes the bait to jump like an injured fish and thus attract sailfish.

Many South Floridians of all ages and ethnic groups fish off the numerous bridges that span the canals, rivers, and intracoastal waterways. Most fish because they find it relaxing and enjoyable. Junior Ellis of Junior's Bait and Tackle in Miami Beach divides bridge fishers into three categories: the near-professionals who fish from around two in the morning until dawn; those who come out after sunset and leave earlier than the first type; and those who work the bridges during the day. Miami's most popular fishing bridges are the Venetian and MacArthur causeways.

One of the advantages of bridge fishing is that the equipment is relatively cheap and little technical knowledge is required to bait a hook and wait. Anglers use bait such as ballyhoo, mullet, shrimp, sardines, pilchards, or glass minnows to catch saltwater fish, and earthworms, crickets, grasshoppers, minnows, or caterpillars to land freshwater fish. With luck and determination, they may carry away a pinfish, grunt, snapper, spotted sea trout, perch, chain pickerel, bass, or other prize.

Mullet, a saltwater fish, thrives in the brackish water of southeast Florida's many canals. Although fishermen savor mullet in Flamingo and the Keys, most in Dade County use them only for bait. Since mullet subsist almost exclusively on algae, their mouths are very small and soft; thus people usually gig, snag, or net them. One exception involves the use of a line baited with compressed balls of white bread.

Once or twice a year, thousands of mullet school as they spawn in the canals. Local boys sometimes seize the opportunity to gig them for sport. They may buy a three-pronged steel gig at a hardware store, and attach it to an old broom handle. Then they drill a hole at the end of the handle, slide a rope through the hole, and tie the ends together. As schools swim down the canals, the boys stand motionless on the canals or sea walls, then spear the mullet when they swim below. As they spear the fish, the boys put their arms through the rope so they can easily retrieve the gig.

Residents "snag" mullet by using a large three-pronged hook. If the fish are not badly hurt in the process, fishermen use them as live bait for shark, tarpon, or snook. Fishermen walk along canal banks looking for schools of mullet, cast over them with snag hook, then pull the line and hook into the school. If lucky, they hook a mullet and reel it in.

Shrimping   Not many decades ago, offshore commercial shrimpers based in southwest Florida regularly followed a seasonal run from

Corpus Christi, Texas, around the Gulf Coast, down Florida's west coast, and to the Keys. At the Dry Tortugas or the Keys, the fleet would divide. Some boats proceeded to the northeast coast of South America and others up Florida's Atlantic coast. The shrimpers would remain in pursuit thirty to sixty days at a stretch.

Although their numbers have diminished, shrimpers still follow the same path and use much of the same equipment. To sample the waters, shrimpers use small try nets. If there are sufficient shrimp, they lower large trawl nets attached to a central boom in the stern. Trawl nets for shrimping are essentially long, tapering bags. Many have flaps, or "wings," that extend from each side, and each wing has a wooden panel, or "door," that attaches to cables from the boat. When the boat cruises through the water, pulling the net, water pressure holds the doors open so that the net collects anything in its path. At the end of the net is heavier mesh netting, called a cod or tail bag, which holds the catch. Many shrimpers attach tickler chains to the front of the nets to force the shrimp up as the nets run along the ocean floor. When the net is full, they pull in the cod with the center boom, close it, and dump the load onto the boat. From there the shrimp are either taken directly below deck and iced down in the hold or stored in modern refrigeration units. Shrimp fleets may also have mother ships that collect the catch and bring it into port.

Although there was more commercial shrimping in the past, many shrimp boats still operate in Dade County's Biscayne Bay, south of Rickenbacker Causeway, or in the Keys. Stock Island in the Keys is the only regional port of call with a large dock and other facilities equipped to handle shrimpers. The shrimping season in the Keys lasts from late November to the end of December, then shifts north to Biscayne Bay from December to January.

About a dozen Biscayne Bay shrimpers dock their boats at Virginia Key and about two dozen dock at Dinner Key just south of Miami. Many shrimpers come from old Miami families, who have passed on intimate knowledge of the grounds and how to work them. Their equipment usually consists of roller nets with a spool. Boats generally use two nets, one port and one starboard, which are lowered to the bay floor from a single boom. While the offshore trawl nets may measure fifty to sixty feet across and are held open by booms and doors, bay shrimp nets are only twelve to sixteen feet across, about five feet high, and have a rigid rectangular frame. A spool stretches across the lower end of the frame and rolls on the bottom of the bay. In conjunction with a tickler chain on the front of the net, this causes the shrimp to rise up into the net. Bay shrimpers generally truck the live shrimp to the bait stores in large containers of water and sell them by the pound. Fishermen buy the shrimp by the can.

Randy Reed's father ran shrimp boats from Florida to Texas. As Reed grew up, fishing, crabbing, shrimping, and even building boats were second nature to him. He started shrimping in Biscayne Bay around 1969 as a commercial endeavor, then later pursued it noncommercially. Reed explains some of the local practices:

In this area they primarily run on an outgoing tide. And we used to do it, we used to start it five days before the moon. I mean the full moon. And the particular place we went to was three and a half hours after Government Cut's high tide. And it was like clockwork. We could hit it within about thirty minutes before the vein of shrimp. . . . When the shrimp first start running, they're scattered all over the area just in general. And when there are not a lot of boats there, that would close down into a vein that may only be a couple hundred feet wide going through Rickenbacker Causeway. And you could set the boat right up into that stream of shrimp and fill the nets very quickly. It wasn't uncommon for us to pull in ten gallons of shrimp in each net, and we had two nets. . . .

They're all called trawl nets because of their shape. These were on rigid frames. The ones we ran on the side of the boat, I think they were four and a half feet deep and nine feet wide. And they'd go right along side the boat, about mid-ship, and the cod would troll back behind the boat. So you could be running the boat, one person would be running the boat, and another person—while the boat's still in motion, could bring the cod aboard, dump the shrimp into a holding tank, then put the net back out. Because these veins . . . would last forty-five minutes to an hour and fifteen minutes. And then it was all over. So if you could keep the boat in motion, you could collect a lot more shrimp. . . . You're getting all my secrets!

In the last few decades there has been a dramatic increase in the number of noncommercial shrimpers and the different methods they employ. One of the most common methods involves the dipnet, a large net with fine mesh attached to a ten-to-fifteen-foot pole. Like other shrimpers, dippers seek places with particularly strong tidal movements, such as Haulover Cut, Government Cut, Bear Cut, and the waterways leading into the southern bay. When dipping from bridges or banks, they hang Coleman lanterns or other light sources so they can see the shrimp in the water. Some also dip from boats equipped with lanterns. Bridge shrimping employs equipment created within the last fifteen years: a rectangular frame of PVC pipe from which a twelve-to-eighteen-foot net bag tapers to a point. Although these nets were formerly made only by shrimpers themselves, they can now be purchased in marine supply stores.

A large, growing segment shrimps from pleasure boats. Certainly they haul in the best catches, since shrimp have difficulty eluding their large moving nets. These shrimpers usually drag trawl nets with rectangular PVC frames from the rear of the boat. The few who plow with nets extending from the sides use nets with steel pipe frames to compensate for the greater strain on the equipment.

Thousands of private shrimpers crowd Biscayne Bay on cool winter nights during the full moon, when tradition has it that the shrimp will rise from the grass beds at the bottom and move out to the sea in the strong tidal flows. Marine radios crackle with anglers discussing the movements of the shrimp. Often they talk in code so that others will not move into their territory. Although shrimpers frequently make large catches at those times, even optimum conditions do not ensure that the shrimp will run. As more people have started shrimping in recent years, the rich veins of shrimp have become rare. Most likely, the commotion made by the hordes of boats disperses the shrimp or drives them to the bottom.

In recent years the Coast Guard has regulated shrimping more closely. Anyone who trawls for shrimp must have a saltwater products license or a noncommercial registration for each net. Noncommercial nets have a corkline measurement of sixteen feet or less. Private shrimpers are not allowed to bring in more than twenty-five pounds. The state also regulates the minimum size of shrimp and restricts shrimping in certain areas. The Coast Guard insists that private vessels trawling for shrimp display the same green-over-white warning lights as commercial trawlers, so that other boats will keep their distance at night. No doubt such lights also assist the authorities in identifying shrimpers so they can go aboard to inspect the catch, lighting, and location.

Lobstering   One of the most sought-after denizens of South Florida's waters is the delicious Caribbean spiny lobster, *Panulirus argus*. Although technically a crawfish because it has no claws, the creature is universally referred to as a lobster. Until recent decades, lobsters were so plentiful that there were no regulations surrounding their capture. Some grew to three or four feet in length, though such giants were difficult to catch and tough to eat.

Many residents make lobster traps for personal or commercial fishing. Most trap makers use cypress, a relatively water-resistant wood. Lobster traps are generally three feet long by two feet wide by two feet high. The bottom is divided into three sections, with the two end sections filled with cement to keep them on the ocean floor. Due to state regulations and the increasing problem of pirated traps, trap makers engrave owner identification numbers in the cement and on the buoy. In this way, stolen traps may be identified and the offender prosecuted.

The lobster goes into the trap through an entrance, or throat, at the top, but cannot exit through the same opening. Depending on the

Building lobster traps
(Photo by Brent Cantrell/
Courtesy of HASF)

client's desires and the size of lobsters where the traps will be used, the entrance may be straight or angled inward. One Cuban trap maker says that his American customers request an extra trapdoor to the side of the mouth. Americans extract the lobster through the trapdoor, whereas Cubans prefer using the throat.

In the past, many residents caught lobster with a bully net. Fishermen would quietly pole a boat into the shallow waters of Biscayne Bay at night, then hang a lantern at the bow. The bully net had a circular frame attached at a right angle to the end of the ten-foot pole, which supported a conical bag of large mesh webbing. When they saw a lobster, fishermen would position the hoop over it and allow the webbing to drift down until the lobster become entangled. Noncommercial fishermen still occasionally use this technique off Key Biscayne, but most now snorkel or scuba dive to catch lobsters by hand.

Lobster season formerly began on August 1. However, commercial lobstermen were allowed to set their traps out a week in advance for "soaking." Since the bulk of the lobster are caught in the first three or four weeks of the season, sport divers did not really have the same opportunities as commercial lobstermen. Thus, the state and federal governments created a two-day sport season preceding the general season in order to afford sport divers a better chance and to encourage Keys tourism during the slow summer season. By 1991, the sport season had become so popular that thirty-three thousand divers annually descended on the Keys in late July.

Currently, lobster season is strictly regulated by federal and state governments. The federal government controls the number of lobsters that can be collected more than three miles off the Atlantic Coast and nine miles off the Gulf Coast, while the state regulates the number within those limits. In 1992, the federal limit was six lobsters per day. The state imposed a bag limit of twelve lobsters outside the Keys and six lobsters within the Keys in an attempt to stem the overwhelming influx of tourists.

After the sport season closes, commercial lobstermen bait their traps with leather or meat, then dump lines of traps into the ocean with a buoy marking their location. A commercial lobster fisherman may set out dozens to hundreds of traps at a time. They haul up the traps about a week after the sport season ends, unload the catch, rebait the traps, and repeat the process until the end of lobster season. Although the season runs eight months, the lobsters depart for deeper waters within a month or two.

Crabbing   Commercial crabbers use different techniques to catch the two kinds of edible crabs found in South Florida—the blue crab and the stone crab. Stone crabs (*Menippe mercenaria*) are unique to the coasts of South Florida. For the most part, they remain in the area as a local treat, and many residents adamantly insist that they are the most delicious of all crabs. Stone crabs possess large, meaty claws, which are the only part eaten. Crabbers usually break off one claw from each crab, then throw them back. The claws eventually grow back for another possible harvest.

Fishermen in both southeast and southwest Florida catch stone crabs during the season from October 15 to May 15. Most use traps strung in lines, for which they must purchase a commercial license. Crab traps resemble lobster traps, but are slightly smaller. Most are made of wood, but a few are plastic. The opening is a short tunnel, or throat, and is tapered so that the crabs cannot exit. The trap has a lid that opens, allowing the crabbers to extract their catch. Crabbers secure a brick in the base so that the trap will land upright and stay on the ocean floor. They also write their license number on the throat, since all commercial fishing equipment must carry the owner's number. If the marine patrol finds a crabber with traps not imprinted this way, they fine him for not properly identifying his equipment or for stealing a trap.

Today the largest numbers of stone crabs are caught on the southwest coast, especially near Everglades City and Chokoluskee. Until the 1960s, crabbing was not a commercial operation there—most locals used to catch stone crabs by hand for personal consumption. West coast crabbers put together lines that may include as few as twenty or as many as eight hundred traps. Some have six lines and work six days per week, checking a line each day for crabs. Those with fewer traps may drop them off one day, then check them the next day.

On the east coast, some crabbers still use trot lines in Biscayne Bay. Former commercial crabber Randy Reed elucidates:

We would work it in a grid. We would keep moving the traps and moving the traps, until it started getting productive. And then we would work that area until we started getting the crabs back in the traps that had no claws, and then we'd keep on going. . . .

Depending on the area you would get no crabs at all or three or four crabs per trap. . . . Some would be too short to take and you'd have to throw them back. Or they'd be a female that you would throw back, especially if she was carrying eggs. And we worked traps different ways. Either we would individually buoy the traps, or we would take a trot line that was sixteen hundred feet long and we'd put eighteen to twenty traps on the trot line. And we'd work three or four trot lines every three or four days. And then of course your biggest problem was catching enough bait for traps. . . . We would go out to catch mullet. We would set nets to catch garbage fish. Go to the fish house and get them to save the debris from cleaning fish. When somebody buys a fish at a store and it gets cleaned, they'd put the debris in a container. And we'd freeze it and take it out and use some of it that night. And we'd keep a couple of freezers. Garbage fish—we'd get a shark or an amberjack or something like that, and we'd chop them up into chunks and freeze them in quantities of what was on that trot line. If we'd have eighty traps, we'd freeze eighty baits. . . .

If you're in a productive area, you have to pull them on the third or fourth day, otherwise they start destroying one another.

When crabbers set out trot lines, they are supposed to have a buoy on each individual trap. Unfortunately, it is common for others to pirate marked crab and lobster traps. Reed and his partner once started a season with two hundred traps, but had only sixteen by the end. Over time, they found many of them abandoned on seawalls, private docks, and islands in the bay.

At the end of a day, crabbers deliver their catch to fish houses where workers pile the claws into baskets, boil them, then chill them in cold water. If they do not boil the claws prior to refrigeration, the meat sticks to the shells. Finally, they load claws onto grading tables and sort them into different sizes before sale, packing, and shipment.

During the summer months after the stone crab season ends and before lobster season opens, crabbers set traps for blue crabs in Biscayne Bay. Blue crabs used to be abundant before they cleared the mangroves and filled in the land around Haulover Cut. Since they are relatively scarce, most fishermen catch blue crabs for personal consumption. Crabbers make blue crab traps from large-grade wire mesh, or chicken wire, bait them with old chicken parts, and cast them into the shallow waters of the bay. Most leave the traps out for relatively short periods before checking them.

Sponges   Florida's coastal waters are the only habitat in the United States where sponges grow. Sponge gathering and processing is not new to South Florida. By the 1890s, hundreds of sponge boats operated by Americans, Conchs, and Bahamians were active from Miami south through the Keys. Key West competed with Tarpon Springs for the position of the chief sponge market. However, with the sponge blight from 1938 to 1952, sponging activity diminished.

The Arellano brothers' sponge packing warehouse lies next to the Miami River near downtown. Here sponge fishermen from Biscayne Bay and the Keys bring the different types of sponges they harvest to be processed, packed, and shipped. It was largely through the efforts of the Arellano brothers that the sponge industry was revitalized in the early 1960s. The Arellano family operated a sponge business in Cuba, then established a packing and processing enterprise in Miami in 1962. During the first years, the brothers made weekly trips down to Key West to buy sponges from fishermen along the way, and they sometimes helped the sponge fishermen establish themselves through loans of money or equipment. Today Miami is the commercial sponge center of Florida.

Sponges are collected by two methods: in the shallower waters they are hooked by fishermen with a four-pronged rake attached to a pole up to forty feet long, and in deeper waters, they are cut by divers who wear

Cubans trimming sponges in the Arellano brothers' warehouse on the Miami River (Photo by Michele Edelson/Courtesy of HASF)

an airhose and diving suit. After they harvest the sponges, the fishermen dump them into crawls, or wooden enclosures at the water's edge. Two or three days later, the fishermen beat the sponges with a piece of wood to remove the black outer skins, then dry them so that they will keep until sold to the processor.

At the warehouse the sponges are dampened, then cut into standard sizes. A few sponges of medium size and good shape are left whole. Next, the sponges are trimmed to a round, even shape, sorted into five grades, and dried in the sun. Sponges for cosmetic or decorative purposes are cleaned chemically to lighten their color. Finally, the sponges are counted into lots, stuffed into burlap sacks, and pressed into bails for shipping.

Equipment

Maritime skills and occupations require a wide array of equipment. In Miami and its environs, innumerable craftspeople and lay people create accoutrements ranging from the largest boats to the smallest fishing flies.

Boat Building With the immediate proximity of the ocean, rivers, canals, lakes, and marshes, Florida ranks fourth in the nation in the number of boats. Each year, South Floridians build thousands of boats ranging from rowboats to large commercial vessels and yachts. Although most vessels are made commercially, individuals often use their own skills to create their personal craft. In many Miami neighborhoods, passersby can glimpse householders building small boats in backyard lots.

At the other extreme is Broward Marine, the largest national producer of custom motor yachts that are between 80 and 120 feet. Since prices for the enormous boats can climb as high as $6 million, clients come from a very small segment of the population. Nevertheless, there has been increased interest in large yachts during the last decade, and business is good.

For twenty-five years, Broward Marine has conducted business on the New River in Ft. Lauderdale. The business began when Frank Denison bought the old Dooley Yacht Basin and started a repair shop. After building navy minesweepers for the Korean War, he switched to private yachts in 1956. Denison's son, Ken, still manages Broward Marine as a family business: "Just in the last five years it's become a glitzy business. There are a lot of people getting into the business for that reason now. But Dad's a boat builder. His saying is 'Don't look at what the other guy is doing. Just keep your head down and keep sawing wood.'"

Since each yacht requires about one year to build, the company produces no more than ten each year. Broward Marine employs about 250 workers, many of whom have learned their skills traditionally. For example, Mario Raus has been creating marine woodwork at Broward Marine since he emigrated from Italy thirty years ago. He points out that it takes at least three or four years for new employees to learn how to do simple carpentry jobs, not to mention the more specialized items he creates.

Sails The craft of sailmaking is ancient. In prehistoric times, sailmakers used skins to catch the sea breeze; colonial-era craftspeople fashioned sails from linen; and nineteenth-century sailmakers made cotton sails. Although some contemporary sailmakers still use cotton, many prefer synthetics such as Dacron, Mylar, or the more recent laminated materials. Dacron is one of the most popular materials because of its low price, strength, and durability. Dedicated sailboat racers use Mylar and laminate sails because of their lightness and rigidity.

There is very little handwork left in sailmaking, and few companies make their own sails. Many, if not most, sails are designed by computer and executed entirely by machine. Since sails can be manufactured relatively inexpensively, it is often difficult for custom sailmakers to stay in business.

Among the many small sailmaking enterprises in southeast Florida, and one of the oldest, is Bremen and Sons Sailmakers. Fred Bremen, Sr., has been making sails for over forty-five years. Although officially retired, he continues to make a few sails, especially for dinghies. Fred Jr. and Tom Bremen now run the family business assisted by Rita Gomes, their seamstress for almost thirty years. Now in his early forties, Fred Jr. developed an early interest in sailboat racing and learned the business. His brother Tom does much of the handwork necessary to finish sails. The Bremens have earned a national reputation for doing fine work at fair prices and for finishing orders on schedule.

Bremen and Sons makes sails for boats ranging from small dinghies to windsurfers to large sailboats, always following a certain process. First, they locate an appropriate pattern in their extensive files. The Bremens examine the particular sail plan, then chalk it onto the floor of their spacious workshop. Next they lay down fabric panels a yard in width and mask the sail's length and shape onto the cloth. Rita then sews the panels together on a sewing machine. Dinghy sails require three and one half hours, while larger sails for racing yachts take several days to complete.

Tom Bremen completing some aspects of sailmaking by hand (Photo by Tina Bucuvalas/Courtesy of HASF)

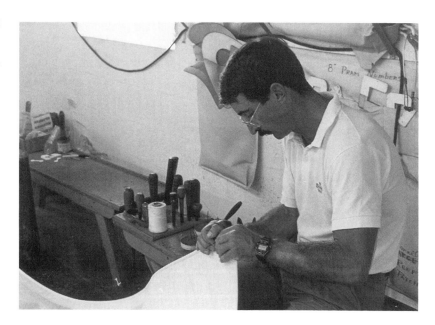

Fishing Rods   Like sails, most fishing rods are mass-produced, but Miami does support a number of establishments that make fine custom rods. Ken Carmon, a sister, and two brothers manage Biscayne Rod Manufacturing Co., a business started in 1948 by their father and grandfather. Ken learned rod-building from them and now teaches all employees the necessary skills.

Unlike companies that manufacture thousands of rods each day, Biscayne Rod builds fifty to seventy-five custom rods per day. The Carmons view their product as the Rolls Royce of fishing rods, and sell them to serious anglers throughout the nation. The fishing rods are based on customer specifications as to size, usage, and materials. The types of rods they make are almost unlimited: spinning, glove, trolling, fly, snook, and many others. Each type may employ up to 130-pound test line, though the use of certain kinds of line may require radically different parts, spacing, or other treatment.

The Carmon method of building a rod begins with a detailed understanding of the customer's needs. Armed with that information, they select an appropriate blank and add materials that may be either ready-made or built to customer specifications. First, they attach grips and a reel seat. They mark the rod for guide spacing to hold the line in place, with the type and number of guides dependent on the proposed use of the pole. Next, thread is wrapped up and over the guides to hold them in place. Using different colors of thread, the wrapper creates patterns that are not only functional but are also aesthetically pleasing. Finally, a worker finishes the rod by applying coats of two-part polymer epoxy. While the actual building process is not complicated, it requires a great deal of knowledge about rods, fishing, and temperatures to calculate the number and placement of the guides and to determine the best materials.

Although the method of building fishing rods has not changed significantly in the last few decades, the quality of materials and the parts themselves have changed drastically with the application of new scientific knowledge. Back in 1948, rod blanks were made of bamboo or Calcutta sticks. The early rods weighed at least five pounds, whereas modern rods built of synthetic materials such as fiberglass are literally light as a feather. Recently, the Carmons have created woven graphite glass rods, which are extremely lightweight, of high quality, and costly.

Nets   Most South Florida fishermen buy nets readymade at marine supply stores, but a few craftspeople still make or modify nets for a variety of purposes. Hugo Fernandez, who runs a small family business called The Castnet Maker, is reputed by locals to be among the best netmakers. As a young boy, Fernandez learned how to make fishing nets from the old fishermen in Las Esmereldas, Cuba, just to satisfy his curiosity. When he emigrated to Miami in 1962, Fernandez started making nets in order to earn a living. Through the years, he mastered many different types to accommodate the needs of southeast Florida fishermen: glass minnow, sardine, shrimp, trawl, mullet, black mullet, seine, throw, bully hoop, pilcher frames, pilcher rings, all purpose bags, scoop, and other nets.

At first Fernandez wove cotton nets by hand, treated the knots so that they did not become slippery and stretch the net, and sold them for ten dollars each. Although he still believes that handmade nets are best, the method proved too time consuming to be financially rewarding. Consequently, Fernandez started to buy manufactured netting, which he cut and sewed into special shapes to satisfy his customers' needs. In the late 1960s, he began using nylon netting. By 1972, Fernandez switched to monofilament netting and reserved nylon for such special purposes as catching lobster. Fernandez is credited with several innovations in local netmaking.

Processing

Most of South Florida's maritime products are eaten locally or distributed throughout the state and the nation while fresh. However, many residents engage in processes designed to preserve fish for future consumption or for decorative purposes.

Smoking   For millennia, people have smoked, pickled, or dried fish in order to preserve them for future consumption. A number of South Florida businesses continue these practices. One of the oldest is the Blue Marlin Smoke House. From the outside, the old Blue Marlin Smoke House near the Oleta River in North Miami looks like a dilapidated fisherman's shack, but inside there is a treasure of delicious smoked fish. Dan Diefenback, who homesteaded the property, started the smokehouse in 1938. Several years ago he sold it to Denver Connelly, who now runs the Blue Marlin with the help of his wife and children. Connelly himself was reared on the water in Coconut Grove, where he learned maritime folklife from the old fishermen. Among the things they taught him were recipes for smoked fish from the West Indies and Louisiana. When he acquired the Blue Marlin, Connelly apprenticed himself to Diefenback in order to learn his methods.

The Blue Marlin obtains most of its fish from local commercial fishermen. Private fishermen and restaurants from the area also bring in fish, and fishermen from throughout the country sometimes ship their catch for smoking. The Connelly family smokes primarily amberjack, sailfish, mackerel, and wahoo.

The smoking process requires both time and attention to ensure success. First, the Connellys butcher the fish in their skins, then filet and bone them. Next, they cure the fish by salting them in a tank with eleven pounds of salt brine and eighty to one hundred gallons of water. The fish remain there for eight hours before the Connellys place them on racks to allow excess water to drain.

To begin the smoking, the Connellys build a fire with hard Australian pine. The bark of the pine imparts a flavorful seasoning during the smoking process. Australian pine is considered a pest plant in South Florida, so the wood is widely available in disposal piles at construction sites. The Blue Marlin formerly burned black mangrove, but it is no longer available. The Connellys must maintain the fire throughout the eight-hour process, constantly adding logs to increase the heat and flavor. They fire the oven to 110 degrees for the first two and one-half to three hours, then increase the temperature to 125 to 130 degrees for another three and one-half hours. During the final hour, they increase the temperature to 140 to 145 degrees to ensure that any extra moisture is drawn from the heavy fish steaks. At the end, the fish should be meaty but not dehydrated.

Marine Taxidermy Fishermen are proud of their skills, and many seek to preserve prize catches through taxidermy. There are several formal and informal marine taxidermy enterprises in the Miami area, but in 1926 Al Pflueger, Sr., established what has become the world's largest and most renowned marine taxidermy business. Fishermen from all over the world send their fish to be mounted at Pflueger's in southern Broward County.

There are two types of taxidermy: the older style utilizes the original skin and the newer style uses replicas. Taxidermists usually process mammals the old way, with a molded foam base or blank fitted to the original dried skin. Most marine taxidermy involves the replica method, but Pflueger's is one of the few that utilizes both methods for fish.

Pflueger's originally employed a few workers who each processed a fish from start to finish. Due to the vast number of orders in recent decades, the business was restructured into discrete areas staffed by specialists in a given process. No schools teach the craft, so experienced taxidermists teach new employees.

Mounting a fish is a long and complicated process. When a fish is received, employees record the size and species, then attach an identification tag to its tail. They remove the skin, scrape it to remove any remaining meat, and place it in a degreasing tank. After that, the skin is dried in the sun and then soaked in a special solution that preserves it and makes it pliable. Next, it is placed facedown in a mold, covered with a plaster inner-skin, and stuffed with sawdust. When the taxidermist removes it, he or she smooths the skin over a lifelike form, repairs any major flaws, stretches the fins into an open position, and sets the fish aside to dry on the form.

In the next phase, the fish is hung upside down so that the sawdust can be removed. The taxidermist covers the seam on the back of the fish, attaches a hanger, and inserts the mouth. Subsequently, the tag is removed from the fish, and both are stapled to a mounting board. An employee backs the fins with large pieces of cardboard, then fills in missing pieces of skin and blends them to match the surrounding area. Next, a worker replaces missing details, removes small flaws, and inserts the eyes. In the finishing department, taxidermists go over the fish with primers and putties to remove remaining flaws. Finally, artists airbrush each fish to re-create the underwater colors, apply a clear gloss coat, and hang the finished fish in a special drying room.

THE LAND

The region surrounding Miami includes extensive rural tracts where people still raise crops, tend livestock, and practice a variety of folk arts based on the natural resources. Some of the traditions maintained here occur in no other region of the country.

Tropical Agriculture

Few realize that agriculture is almost as important an industry as tourism in South Florida.★ In this southernmost agricultural region in the continental United States, the most important growing area is the southern Dade County district known as the Redland, so named by early pioneers because of the red soil common in parts of the region. Local residents generally agree that it includes farming areas from Goulds and Naranja south to Homestead and Florida City, where eighty thousand acres of land are annually put into agricultural production. Although the Redland yields a wide variety of common vegetables and fruits, it is the production of tropical crops that distinguishes it from other agricultural regions.

As the sole subtropical zone in the continental United States, South Florida provides the only environment in which a wide variety of tropical fruits can be grown. Settlers raised crops of mangos, guavas, pineapples,

★This section was written before Hurricane Andrew struck in August 1992. Although the tropical agriculture industry will eventually recover, the hurricane devastated production for 1993 and many years to come.

Label for a grapefruit/ lemon jelly from the Miami area (Photo courtesy of HASF)

coconuts, papayas, and other tropical fruits as early as the 1890s. By the twentieth century, they were even importing improved stock, such as the Haden mango. Tropical crops have grown in importance during this century. By the mid-1900s there were sizable pineapple plantations in the northeast section of Dade County. Until Hawaii started cultivation, Dade County and the Keys were the major pineapple suppliers for the nation. Large growers in south and west Dade continued to harvest substantial avocado, mango, and lime crops during that period.

Although farms and orchards produce the largest portion of tropical crops, backyard trees have always provided a substantial source of tropical fruits for personal consumption and commercial distribution. In fact, since the late nineteenth century families have commonly planted a variety of citrus and other fruit trees in their yards to supply their own needs. Native son David Teems remembers the food his family ate during the 1940s and 1950s:

Guava is a big one. I love guava jelly. And sea grape jelly. You know the seagrape trees, we've got a bunch of them around here. If you let them grow big, these trees, they get grapes on them. It's a funny kind of a fruit, they're not good to eat unless you make jelly. Yeah, they boil it and all that. That came from the Bahamas. And of course everybody canned. You'd put up everything you could—store it, and can it, and make it last.... When I was growing up of course, most of the things, if you really needed them you could buy at the store, but ... mother and my grandmother particularly, they would can things because it was cheaper.

We grew grapefruit, oranges, lime, mangos, bananas, avocados.... It wasn't uncommon—still isn't in most Florida families, I think, to have sliced mango on a plate just as part of the meal. And the avocados here—you're familiar with them, they're not like California avocados, these are real ones. . . . Always had lime pie. Now there is a difference between Key lime and lime. . . . The fruit itself is different—much tarter. Most of what you get today is not Key lime, because they just don't have any. But there used to be groves of them in the Keys, actual lime groves on Key Largo. The only ones that are really left are in people's yards.

Mangos are one of southeast Florida's most plentiful and popular tropical crops. The region produces 36 million mangos per year, about 12 to 20 percent of all mangos eaten in the United States. First introduced to Florida in 1833, they were common by the end of the century. Mangos ripen in June and disappear by July. Since many people have household trees, the season is a mad rush of messy, drippy, delicious mango consumption. Most residential areas sprout tiny mango stands as young-sters sell the excess produce. Tree owners produce a crush of mango breads, cakes, cookies, candy, jam, jelly, chutney, and relish.

Many recent immigrants seek coconuts for their milk and fruit. Although there used to be coconut plantations in South Florida, most of the trees were killed by a blight decades ago. The majority of coconuts marketed today are imported from the Dominican Republic and Costa Rica. However, there are bands of harvesters that gather the coconuts on remaining backyard trees from Okeechobee south to the Keys, then sell them to distributors. In this way, they harvest more than fifteen thou-sand coconuts per week.

Since the late 1970s, there has been an explosion in both the production and variety of tropical crops in southeast Florida. The region now has about twenty-two thousand acres planted in tropical fruit crops and thirteen thousand acres in tropical vegetables. Longtime southeast Florida resident Bill Schaefer is marketing director for J. R. Brooks & Son, the largest producer and handler of tropical fruit in the country. He cites three reasons for the explosion:

Well, there's a combination of factors. The ethnic population is one. The demand for fresh as an overall general trend is the second. And the third is the combination of the health consciousness as well as—in conjunction with, if you're health conscious you eat fresh fruits and vegetables. And the secondary corollary is, if you eat fresh fruits and vegetables, after a period of time you're going to get sick of only apples and oranges and peaches and pears and plums. And as a consequence it all dovetails into "Give me something strange or different or unique." And then you have the added impetus to the tropical items which are lesser known, but very, very tasty. In many cases more flavorful and sweeter than some of the commercialized traditional crops.

In addition to the preeminent mangos, limes, and avocados, southeast Florida now also produces star fruit (carambola), lichee, longan, kumquats, atamoyas, mamey, and passion fruit. Both Hispanic and Anglo growers cultivate the tropical fruit crops on farms that range in size from very large to very small. The lesser known tropical vegetables include malanga, yuca, and boniato. Most vegetable crops are produced on small- to medium-sized Cuban-owned farms for local consumption.

In 1927, J. R. Brooks founded a small vegetable farm in Homestead. Over the years it grew steadily. His son, Neal, bought it in 1967, and recently one of Neal's sons joined the company. The Brooks philosophy is to produce and distribute a large volume of tropical fruits. In this way they hope to provide consumers with good products at a low price, while maintaining a substantial profit margin. Brooks now raises an enormous share of southeast Florida's tropical produce: 70 to 75 percent of mangos, 40 to 65 percent of avocados, 55 percent of limes, and 80 percent of star fruit. There are no percentages available for the lesser known tropicals. The amount of production is also astonishing. The Brooks Company grows about 27 million mangos each year. In 1991 they produced 4 million pounds of star fruit, and they anticipate 10 million pounds in a few years. Brooks employs a year-round work force of about 250, which is supplemented by migrant laborers during the heaviest harvest times.

The company currently imports about 20 percent to 25 percent of the produce they distribute. This practice enables them to provide stores with fruit on a year-round or extended seasonal basis, and thus continue to educate consumers and create a permanent market for tropicals. Although Brooks does not produce abroad, they form partnerships with reputable growers and packers in Costa Rica, Brazil, Peru, Ecuador, the Bahamas, Haiti, and Belize. Currently, they ship 75 percent of their production to large out-of-state supermarket chains.

Horses

The Spanish brought horses to Florida as early as 1527, and until the 1850s they were the primary means of land transportation. Moreover, horse racing and hunting using horses were popular sports from the sixteenth through nineteenth centuries. Today, horses are still big business. In 1987 the United States Equine Marketing Association estimated Florida's horse population at over 314,000, with a $6.8 billion capital investment generating a cash flow of over $600 million per year.

Southeast Floridians raise and maintain horses for a variety of purposes: ranching, showing, pleasure-riding, and racing. There are significant numbers of most recognized breeds. Thoroughbreds predominate, but there are also quarter horses, Appaloosas, Arabians, Standard-breds, Tennessee walkers, Paso Finos, and Paints. Horsebreeders from around the country have established themselves in Florida because the mild winter weather provides greater training and racing opportunities. Many South Floridians practice a variety of crafts designed to equip and maintain the horses.

Saddle Making   Contemporary Florida cowmen often use saddles made in western factories, but a number of excellent craftspeople create saddles fitted to the size and preferences of customers. Saddle makers generally learn their skills by apprenticing themselves with master craftspeople. There are at least three basic elements of saddle making: the handskills, the artistic ability, and the understanding of what is needed for comfort in a good saddle. It is the rare saddle maker who excels in all areas.

Most saddle makers order wooden saddletrees from the western manufacturers, then apply and tool the many layers of leather that form the saddle proper. A western saddle has sixty-odd pieces of leather, with many overlapping layers that should result in a certain smoothness and continuity. Although it requires only forty to fifty-five hours to make a saddle, the process occurs over two weeks because of the wetting and drying necessary to produce some parts. A plain saddle might cost around fifteen hundred dollars, but a beautifully engraved one could cost between three thousand dollars and five thousand dollars. A good handmade saddle lasts thirty or forty years, while a good manufactured one lasts only ten to fifteen years.

The McLelland Saddlery enjoys a national reputation for beautifully tooled, custom products. Born in 1956, Perry McLelland is the youngest to carry on the long family tradition of fine craftsmanship. His great-grandfather started making saddles back in Virginia during the 1870s, and the family has been in the business ever since. Perry's father, James D. McLelland, moved the family to Lake Worth in Palm Beach County when Perry was only a year old. As Perry explains, "My brother and sister and I grew up in the business. We all work in the business nowadays; we each have a different function in the business.... My brother is more in the sales and marketing of the business, my sister is office manager and personnel manager and head bookkeeper. And I ... and my father are still making the saddles and the bridle work and the other leather work that you see here." In addition to family, McLelland's Saddlery employs about fifteen craftspeople who each specialize in a separate aspect: tooling, strap work, gluing, cutting, refining, stitching, coloring, chapmaking, neckties, and clothing. The elder McLelland also writes up orders and assigns tasks.

Although the McLellands used to make English saddles, they now make western saddles exclusively. The saddletree, or foundation, of the saddle is western pine, which provides strength and flexibility. Perry describes the various saddle parts: "In our saddles they're wood and they're covered with rawhide, which is the natural state of leather after it's skinned off the animal. That's where you get the shape of the seat, its strength, and where everything is hung off the saddle. From there you just begin building up the desired shape of the seat that each individual rider wants for their comfort and purpose. And then you start fitting the different parts—we have basic patterns that we work off to get the basic styles."

In order to fit a customer with a saddle, the McLellands encourage them to test various styles and sizes:

Well, we let them look at our basic styles that we have. In our store we try to keep about twelve different designs on hand all the time that they can get an idea of what's available. Then they start sitting on . . . we've got about three or four different trees. I guess it's like an easy chair—whichever one feels the best to you. They'll fit in those, they'll pick out the basic style of the tree they want. And then they'll start adding their design: what kind of tooling pattern they want, whether they want an oakleaf or a flower design, or a woven design. And they pick out their silver design, whether they want something fancy or more refined and simple.

A customer ordering a saddle from McLelland's Saddlery makes out a workorder using a comprehensive form covering a wide variety of possible types, weights, sizes, materials, and other attributes in the categories of style, tree, seat, swell, cantle, horn, tooling, rigging, silver, fenders, stirrups, stirrup leather, and accessories. McLelland's takes about two to three weeks to make the actual saddle, but a backlog of orders makes delivery time closer to three months. Some clients visit frequently to follow the progress of their saddle.

Perry learned handtooling when he was eleven years old because his father needed someone to fill the position. He enjoys creating detailed tooling patterns, and the complex process has become second nature to him:

When you first start out you have your piece of leather that has been fitted to whatever part of the saddle that it's supposed to be. We mark an outline to show the area we will work in. We dampen the leather, and as it begins to dry, it goes through a kind of process called "casing." And that just . . . when the leather becomes really ripe for tooling and cutting—that's when you start working on it.

You draw your pattern on. You take a knife . . . and it's called a swivel knife. You cut your pattern in by hand then you have a series of about twelve to eighteen tools that you use and emboss—and when I say "emboss," this is not done like a machine would . . . but you begin creating this relief by hand with the different tools and a rawhide mallet. So it's all done by hand.

In Miami, the Torres family makes and repairs a wide variety of saddles and other leather goods in their small shop. Beginning at the age of seven, Felix T. Torres learned leatherwork from a Frenchman who owned a neighborhood shop in Havana, Cuba. Torres taught the craft to his son, Felix G. Torres, when he was also very young. Although the Torreses are modest about their abilities, their saddles are internationally famous and have been sold in Spain, Puerto Rico, Venezuela, Panama, and other countries.

The Torreses most often build western saddles, which became popular in Cuba during the 1950s and 1960s. They purchase leather from Texas and decorative silverwork from craftspeople in Montana and California. A few years ago, they made a saddle with extensive silver fittings that sold for fifteen thousand dollars in Panama.

In addition to saddles, the Torreses make tooled halters, belts, custom holsters for police officers, hunting equipment—any leather object that cannot be purchased ready-made. Felix G.'s mother sometimes sews leather outfits for motorcycle races. Also, a large portion of the Torreses' work involves repairs, as is often the case with modern craftspeople.

Racing Crafts   Starting in the 1920s and continuing into the present, the sunny climate of South Florida has attracted a variety of horse racing establishments. Currently there are three racetracks in Broward and Dade Counties: Calder, Gulfstream, and Hialeah. The tracks stagger their seasons, with Gulfstream open during the height of tourist season from mid-January to April, Calder during the summer months from May to November, and Hialeah from November through mid-January. The quality of the horses draws sizable crowds to the tracks, ranging from ten thousand or twelve thousand on weekend days during the summer to twenty thousand during the winter.

Horse racing requires a good deal of specialized equipment. Although most racing gear is manufactured today, a few small workshops continue to produce custom merchandise. At Merlano's Saddle Shop in southern Broward County, you can usually find Eric Merlano making saddles, boots, and other equipment especially for racing. Merlano is the only racing-saddle maker in South Florida and one of the few in the country. Consequently, most of his orders are shipped to individual clients and shops in other states.

Merlano became interested in making saddles when he worked as a jockey in the 1950s and 1960s. Back then, he learned to fix racing

equipment by taking apart saddles and questioning the craftspeople who worked around the racetrack. When he retired from racing, Merlano learned the fine points of saddle and boot making from such masters as the late Tyckoscham Trocholoski of New York City; then he opened his own shop.

Merlano has taught a few employees to cut, stretch, sew, and finish racing boots and saddles. They make the upper portion of the boots from colored leather or patent leather. The inside is leather particle board, and a rubber sole is applied to the bottom. The craftspeople sew both boots and saddles by machine. The shop includes a line of heavy old Singer sewing machines, each of which does a different type of sewing. Although making a pair of boots takes only a few hours, completion time is actually much longer because various parts must dry before the process can be resumed.

Merlano usually works from existing saddle designs. but sometimes creates his own innovative patterns or details. The size of the saddle depends on the dimensions of the owner, and Merlano creates a custom

An employee preparing the soles of a jockey's racing boots at Merlano's Saddle Shop (Photo by Tina Bucuvalas/Courtesy of HASF)

pattern for each saddle. Merlano and his employees use a small fiberglass saddle tree for the base, apply foam backing, then sew leather to it. Instead of leather, they sometimes use clorina, a light, strong, synthetic material that resembles patent leather. The tiny, streamlined racing saddles require a little less time to make than the boots.

Merlano also fashions leather riding whips with a popper on the end. Each whip is wrapped with decorative multi-colored plastic strips. Like the saddles and boots, the whip bears the distinctive colors of the jockey.

Creating Beauty from Nature: Cypress Furniture

The abundant natural resources of southeast Florida provide the raw materials for cypress furniture making. Once a common craft in Florida and other deep southern states, cypress furniture making is less common now than a generation ago. This is due, in part, to the disappearance of large cypress hammocks from South Florida.

Robert James Rudd is a cypress furniture maker from Lake Worth in western Palm Beach County. Born in 1926, Rudd grew up working his father's cattle, fishing, and hunting frogs. As a child, he also helped his father pull cypress and mangrove from the swamps in order to make

Cypress chair built by Robert Rudd (Photo by Michele Edelson/Courtesy of HASF)

chairs, swings, love seats, and small tables. After World War II, Rudd did construction work and lathing, but began to lose his hearing after working in noisy environments for many years. Consequently, he decided to build cypress furniture to support his family.

The curving shapes found in Rudd's furniture are made possible by the combination of strength and flexibility found in young cypress trees. Although he used to collect his materials near his home, Rudd must now drive 220 miles north to cut cypress every six weeks or so. He selects small cypress trees for the "poles" that form the legs and support structure of the furniture, and long, skinny shoots for the "benders" that made the curving seat and outer frame of his chairs and chaises longues.

Through his own invention and customers' suggestions, Rudd has expanded his repertoire of furniture styles to include chairs, chaises longues, bedframes, tables, and stools. Before starting a chair, he strips the bark off the cypress with a knife or machete, then rounds off the ends with a jackknife. He puts the benders in a clamp to curve them for the back or arm sections before he starts the chair; then he nails the frame together and adds the arms and back. Bending switches into the chair to create the seat and the backing, Rudd nails them into place with brads. Finally, he burns off loose cypress strands with an acetylene torch and brands his name into the chair. The result is a product that is beautiful, functional, and very much in demand.

Miami's broad expanse of beach and inland rural tracts encourage farming of sea and land resources. The area is rich in unique crops of sponges, seafood, and tropical fruits and vegetables. The diversity of all of these occupations and those necessary to maintain them, such as sail and saddle making, boat building, horse raising, and taxidermy, allow the equally varied Florida population to find common interests and employment.

Key West and
the Keys

Florida's Tropical Islands

The Florida Keys, a chain of coral islands curving from the mainland south of Miami to Key West one hundred miles to the southwest, comprise the southernmost land in the continental United States. Keys residents have historically made their livelihood through the harvest of the land and especially the sea, sometimes supplemented by tourism or smuggling. The isolated nature of the Keys, combined with the mixture of American, Bahamian, and Cuban settlers, has produced a traditional life unique to the area and an exceptional atmosphere of tolerance.

Journeying south from Key Largo to Key West, the cultural influence of the mainland gradually diminishes and the character of the Keys increasingly asserts itself. The island of Key West, which is four miles long and two miles wide, has a fascinating history. As the only real urban center in the Keys, this remote spit of land has always attracted adventurers and opportunists and is now one of the nation's top tourist destinations.

The lifeblood of Key West has traditionally been the sea. Lying between the Atlantic Ocean and the Gulf of Mexico, the island is home to commercial fishermen, recreational divers, treasure-hunters and shipwreck salvagers. Even the land has been affected by the surrounding waters, for much of its vegetation, including sapodilla, frangipani, East Indian palm, tamarind and banyan, has been brought to the island by seafarers from far-off parts of the world.

Spanish explorers who discovered the island in the sixteenth century named it *Cayo Hueso*, or Bone Key. Legend has it that they found piles of human bones littering the beaches. These sun-bleached remains were reported to be the skeletons of a losing tribe in an early Native American conflict. It is said that the Arawak, Carib and Calusa tribes had all lived on the island. Key West was soon after inhabited by a succession of pirate bands, and then by fishermen who supplied Cuba with the abundant catch from surrounding waters.

When Florida came under British rule in 1763, the small Spanish outpost of Key West was abandoned. Twenty years later, with another

Spanish rule in Florida, the island was again seen as a resource, and permanent settlers were sought. However, for several decades Key West remained a maritime haven for outlaws. In 1823, Commodore David Porter and his fleet were sent to the island to rid the place of buccaneers. Following Porter's successful mission, families from New England, Virginia and South Carolina, as well as British Bahamians settled in the tropical frontier.

Despite attempts to "civilize" the island, the presence of permanent residents did not stop the adventurous from exploiting Key West's assets. As early as 1828, the American government felt it was necessary to issue salvage licenses to mediate disputes among the many competing treasure-hunters off the coast. The treacherous reefs and waters off the Keys had claimed ships for centuries, and it was said that some had been deliberately lured to disaster by false beacons set by eager salvagers. Professional wreckers now maintained a headquarters in Key West where buyers could bid on merchandise and treasure recovered from the hapless ships. To this day, the waters off the Florida Keys remain a lure for treasure-hunters, and the state maintains an office to regulate the salvaging of shipwrecks in state waters.

Early exploration and decades of pirating had little impact upon Key West as we know it today. Key West culture has been shaped by the people who ventured to the island and settled there in the nineteenth century—mainly people of British descent from the Bahamas (but including a sprinkling of seafarers and others from the American mainland), Hispanics (principally Cubans and a few Spanish "peninsulares"), and groups of African descent from both the Caribbean and the mainland. Collectively Keys residents became known as "Conchs," after the shellfish native to the crystal waters.

The rich folklife of the Key Westers was first documented and promoted during the years of the Great Depression and the bold experimental programs of the Works Progress Administration, part of Franklin D. Roosevelt's New Deal. Like other states in the country, Florida discovered her heritage and culture largely through the efforts of federal workers who were charged with the task of writing a state guidebook. One of the writers employed by the Florida Writers' Project (FWP) was Stetson Kennedy.

In 1936 Stetson Kennedy was a freshman at the University of Florida in Gainesville, beginning his career as a writer and observing the catastrophic political events that were occurring around the world. Convinced that the university academic program was politically, socially and intellectually irrelevant to the world situation, which was "on fire," Kennedy decided to leave the academy to write and work for social change. As he explains it:

It looked like the world was going to explode and the university seemed totally unaware of it . . . . So, I had a cold beer on a cold night and had a cold chill and looked at the map to see how far south you could go without money, by hitchhiking, and Key West was it. . . . I packed a trunkload of books and shipped it by water, and hitchhiked to Key West to spend time writing for a year or two.

Stetson Kennedy and photographer Robert Cook recording Cuban folk songs for the Federal Writers' Project in 1938 (Photo courtesy of Stetson Kennedy)

Kennedy would spend the next two years in this island city, gathering material for his literary career, which put him in the unintended role of folklorist. With greatly restricted finances, Kennedy lived the life of a starving artist. He would sleep late "to minimize the hunger" and rise to have a five-cent box of gingersnaps and water for breakfast, then a twenty-five-cent bowl of soup for dinner, with a loaf of Cuban bread covered in guava paste. More important to him than food was the wonderful cultural mix that formed Key West life:

I lived in the Cuban quarter and it was my first exposure to any culture other than the black and Cracker southern cultures. So, to find myself in a Cuban, Spanish-speaking community was quite an eye-opener. In spite of all the hardships [of the Depression], they were having a ball. They were really enjoying life in a way that I'd never seen anybody enjoying life. . . . It had something to do with the Creole outlook on life, making the most of it, wine, women and song and making music. You can't beat it. . . . It was all new to me. I've never gotten over it. I probably never should have left.

Stetson Kennedy remembers that the whole city was saturated in folk tradition and folklife—British/Bahamian (Conch), Cuban, and Afro-Caribbean. He recounts that "everything they [Key Westers] did was folklore, the entire community." Kennedy began to collect diligently—nicknames, stories, songs, foodways, dances, and occupational lore. All of this observation and record-keeping preceded the work that he would soon do on the Florida Writers' Project and was accomplished to be used "as raw material for my own writing."

Kennedy's talents were tapped in 1937 when he was hired by the FWP as a junior interviewer. Kennedy produced the "Key West Tour" section of the *Florida: A guide to the Southernmost State* and compiled an "Inventory of Key West Conch and Cuban Folklore." In December 1938, upon the recommendation of Benjamin A. Botkin, director of the folklore section of the Federal Writers' Project in Washington, D.C., Stetson Kennedy became the director of the Folklore, Life History and Social/Ethnic Studies Units of the Florida Writers' Project. He was twenty-two years old and had already compiled what still stands as the most significant body of Conch and Cuban folklore from the Keys. He wrote descriptions of the singing street musicians known as *cantantes callejeros* and roving marimba bands. He interviewed Abelardo Boza, who organized and led the island's only comparsa dancers. He gathered local legends about "Monkey Man" and other Key West characters, while recording in his notebooks the beliefs, songs and rituals of the black Bahamian *obeah* and Afro-Cuban *ñañigo* religious groups. He continued to pursue his primary interest, folk idiom, documenting the speech of both Cuban and Conch residents of the island community.

Stetson Kennedy has continued to visit and document Key West life over the years, most recently in 1992 to do research for this book. What follows are his observations, reflections, and a rare sampling of his Key West folklife collection.

FOLKLIFE DOWN ON THE KEYS

Like one of Darwin's Galapagos finches, a unique species of folklife and culture evolved in the splendid isolation afforded by the Florida Keys archipelago during the nineteenth and first half of the twentieth centuries.

This string of uplifted coral isles, stretching 108 miles from the tip of the Florida peninsula to Key West and beyond through the Marquesas and Dry Tortugas, was settled in the main by peoples representing three disparate cultures: Anglo via the Bahamas, Hispanic via Cuba, and African from both of those islands and the American mainland as well. Needless to say, a great deal of acculturation had already taken place between the Africans and their "host" cultures prior to their arrival on the Keys, and the process continued despite the constraints of the legally imposed system of racial segregation that was part of the process of Americanization throughout the South.

Given the geographic dimensions of the Keys, where even in Key West you can see water in all directions from atop any two-story edifice, separatism of any nature was a physical impossibility. Intimate coexistence and shared environment, resources, and experiences were all dictated by the geography of the islands.

It was this isolation, especially during the long period when the only communication was by sea, that gave rise to the in vitro birth of a distinct Florida Keys culture. In those halcyon days, the Keys were Mother Nature's laboratory, in which she demonstrated that different peoples not only could get along but that they could share cultures and actually enjoy one another's company. This is not to say that there were never any disputes, but overall, life on the Keys was about as Arcadian as it could get here on earth. It was one of those places where everybody knew everybody, by sight if not by nickname.

By far the most densely populated of the islands, Key West has always set the tone, for better or worse, for the folks on the other Keys. There was probably no more absolute route for going "back to nature" than to establish residence anywhere between Florida City on the mainland and Key West. The absence of the amenities of "civilization" there was well-nigh total. Key West itself, on the other hand, by virtue of being a deep-water maritime port and strategically located naval base (and in earlier years a world capital of shipwreck salvage and auction) has always manifested a pronounced cosmopolitan flavor.

Key West's standing as a cultural oasis in the feudal South was second only to that of New Orleans. The island's status was markedly enhanced during the latter part of the nineteenth century by the coming of the handrolled cigar industry from Havana. By 1870, Key West had become the world's largest cigar manufacturing center, and it remained such until the great fire of 1886, which destroyed half of the city, including the large cigar factory of Vicente Martinez Ybor. However, while it flourished, the cigar business made Key West the largest city in Florida and the most affluent city per capita in the United States. The

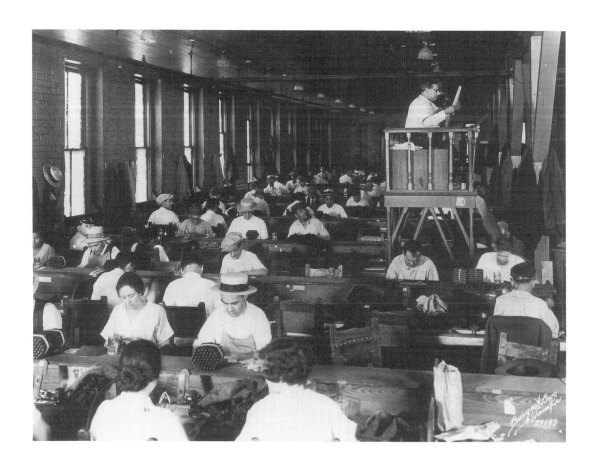

Cigar rollers being read
to by a *lector* in Key West
(Photo courtesy of FSA)

cigar industry also brought with it a certain level of erudition uncommon to working-class life in the South.

In the days before radio, television, or Muzak, the Cuban cigarmakers hired *lectores* (readers) to sit upon a platform and read to them all day. The rollers listened not only to newspapers and magazines, but to classics such as those by Cervantes, Hugo, and Tolstoy. In addition, opera, theater, and dance groups were imported from Europe and Latin America. Thus the folklife of a cigar-roller was urban, not rural, and sophisticated rather than provincial.

In such a free-for-all cultural give-and-take atmosphere as that found on "The Rock," there was still a tendency for one group or another to predominate in certain areas of folklife; Cubans were often cigar-rollers and white Bahamians spongers, for example. However, biological amalgamation tended to keep pace with cultural creolization, so that nowadays you cannot predict the ethnicity of a native by family name alone—Mrs. Curry may have been a Moreno, or vice versa.

In time, the sense of common identity that came to embrace all the peoples on the Keys found expression in their adoption of the appellation "Conch." Originally a title proudly worn by Anglo-Bahamians, it came to be a generic label for any and all natives of the Keys, regardless of race or culture of origin. No comparable degree of solidarity has ever been achieved on the mainland, where the name "Cracker" continues to be reserved for whites only. (An exception to this, in the days of segregated sports, was the Negro League counterpart to Atlanta's white baseball team, the Crackers, calling themselves the "Black Crackers.")

Conch identity, on the other hand, has reached such a stage that, whenever Tallahassee or Washington promulgates something distasteful to Keys folk, they threaten to secede and form a "Conch Republic." This predilection for self-government goes all the way back to 1822 when Florida became a territory of the United States. At that time, Key Westers decided to designate their leader not "mayor" but "president."

Although Key West cannot claim, like its north Florida coastal counterpart, Fernandina, to have lived under seven flags, it has seen flags enough, including the Jolly Roger. Key Westers still like to tell how, during the Civil War when The Rock remained in Union hands, Caroline Lowe periodically unfurled the Stars and Bars of the Confederacy from the balcony of her home at Duval and Caroline streets. It always disappeared before irate Union soldiers could climb the stairs, and only after the war was its hiding place—a hollowed-out rail—discovered.

During that war any number of Conchs became engaged in smuggling goods to the Confederacy through the Union blockade. On one occasion when a boatload of blockade-runners was halted out in the Gulf Stream by a Union gunboat demanding to know their nationality, the men on board hoisted a conch shell on an oar and replied "Conch." The navy men, not being well-versed on the nations in the Caribbean, let it pass.

During the year 1860, on the eve of the Civil War, United States gunboats brought into Key West a total of 1,432 slaves who had been confiscated from slaving ships because of the illegality of the trade. The slave ships *Williams* and *Wildfire* each had carried 450 of these and had each lost 100 at sea. Key Westers hastily constructed a frame "barracoon" on Whitehead Point. While housed there, 294 more slaves died and were buried in a trench on the beach, where their skeletons are occasionally unearthed by construction crews. The remaining survivors were turned over to the American Colonization Society for "repatriation" to Liberia. Another 194 were said to have expired on the journey back to Africa.

While the war was still in progress, without waiting for Lincoln to issue his Emancipation Proclamation, the Union commander in Key West, a Colonel Morgan, proclaimed in 1862 that thenceforth he was going to pay wages to the forty-odd slaves he had leased from their Key

West owners to work on the construction of Fort Taylor. Until then, the United States had been paying the slave owners a total of twelve hundred dollars per month for their collective labors. Some of the black Union troops stationed in Key West, of which there was a considerable number, also hired themselves out to work on the fort at forty cents per day.

In both the Bahamas and Cuba, the "color line" was far more flexible than in America, and was mostly a matter of social practice. Segregation imposed by law was something entirely new to the immigrants who came to the Keys from the islands. Unfortunately, much more than segregation was involved in the system of white supremacy that prevailed throughout the South—the Keys included. Gross discriminations were imposed against blacks in the educational, vocational, political, and social spheres.

Newcomers to the Keys sorted themselves out racially with what grace they could muster, and there were few, if any, instances of laws being invoked to diagnose anyone's racial identity. So it was that all blacks, without any regard to whether their cultural background was Bahamian, Cuban, or American were compressed into a "Colored Town" on the eastern end of Key West, west of Whitehead Street, in what might be described as compulsory acculturation.

The situation was somewhat different in the white community, where the Bahamian, Cuban, and American cultures coexisted, despite some juggling for status, in a more or less egalitarian relationship. The divisions along occupational lines already noted were not rigid, and no absolute monopolies existed. Furthermore, when it came to rum-running and alien-smuggling, everyone got a piece of the action.

As to all of the various elements that constitute Key West folklife and culture, people kept what they wanted and borrowed what they desired. Since the Bahamians shared with Americans the heritage of language and such oral traditions as "London Bridge," they felt that, unlike the Cubans, they didn't need any Americanization. So they clung to their out-island Bahamian dialect, while the Cubans, especially those attending school at the Canadian-operated Convent of Mary Immaculate, learned the "King's English." Although Spanish was discouraged on the public school grounds, it was as prevalent as English, with the *Conchos* speaking it too, when they were of a mind. Key West was a bilingual community par excellence.

It is a striking and significant fact that the blacks having Bahamian or Cuban backgrounds who came to Key West were able to conserve far more of their African cultures than had those coming from the American mainland. One such survival is the practice of black magic, and the casting/uncasting of spells, which the Bahamians refer to as *obeah*, the Cubans as *brujeria*, and the Americans as hoodoo. A hoodoo practitioner, "Chucker" Edwards, was quoted in the *Key West Citizen* before World

War II as saying he had a *mojo* idol that was "so tough it ate steel wool for breakfast."

While the African culture survived in religious beliefs, music and *obeah* practices, in the culinary realm it was the creole Cuban cuisine that captured the island. Everybody on The Rock is hooked on Cuban bread and sandwiches, Cuban coffee, yellow rice, black beans, garbanzo soup, paella, and for dessert, flan (a caramelized egg custard cup) or guava shells with cream cheese. If an after-dinner demitasse is served, it might well have in it a splash of Bacardi rum.

Among snacks, too, it is the Cuban *bollos caliente* (hot balls) that dominate the Key West scene. Made of blackeyed-pea meal and heavily seasoned with garlic and black pepper, they are fried in olive oil. The bollo is a cousin of the Cracker hushpuppy and the Arabic falafel. The aroma of their cooking once wafted over the entire island and the trade winds never smelled so good!

The Bahamian Conchs still fondly remember their traditional dish of pigeon-peas and rice with loggerhead fin. However, since loggerhead turtles are on the endangered species list, they are happy with the Cuban chicken and rice substitute. Whatever their respective cultural backgrounds, Key Westers know just what to do with such tubers as malanga, yuca, and llame, which are usually boiled, sliced, and served cold like a potato salad, perhaps accompanied by a bottled mojo dressing consisting mainly of oil, vinegar and liquified garlic. For such tropical fruits as guanabana, anon, soursop, Spanish limes, tamarind, avocado, papaya, and mango, recipes abound for beverages and sherbets.

One cherished recipe is to Key West what the Sazerac is to New Orleans. You simply insert a jigger or two of rum into a coconut and leave it out in the sun until it boils over. Another Key West liquid concoction, a bit more complex, is *compuesta*. It calls for pouring anisette over rock sugar crystals, adding a twist of orange peel, and stirring with a stick of cinnamon.

A Conch contribution to the lingua franca of The Rock is "sour belly," which everyone understood to mean the red table wine you once could buy for fifty cents a gallon if you took your own glass jug to be filled. Also popular was the Cuban idea of the cantina, where you could buy such staples as black beans, yellow rice, and fried plantains for takeout, plus a *plat de jour* such as *arroz con pollo*, though you had to take your own pot or platter.

A unique aspect of Keys foodways is the reliance on sweetened condensed milk. Sweetening and canning milk was one of the first methods devised for its preservation and storage. Use of condensed milk became popular in the Keys, where the scarcity of pasture and fresh water made fresh milk a rarity. Key lime pie is one of the most famous condensed milk recipes; others include queen of all puddings, a bread pudding with guava paste; and custards.

Another shared culinary institution on the Keys, no doubt of Bahamian origin, is known to all as "sour." It is simply a Coke bottle of pure Key lime juice, preserved with a teaspoon of salt. A bottle of sour is *de rigueur* on every table, whether in household or cafe, in much the way ketchup is ubiquitous on the mainland. Diners shake it on just about everything, including salads (especially conch salad), fish, and meats.

The custom of sour survives, but many another traditional foodway lives only in memory—such as the cow that walked from door to door for custom milking, and the loaves of hot Cuban bread that were left on one's doorstep each morning. Also now gone, but not forgotten, is the *Brazo Fuerte* (Strong Arm) brand of coffee, dark-roasted over native buttonwood fires.

On all the upper, middle and lower Keys firewood was abundant, but on Key West the ratio of people to trees was such that the latter were soon exhausted. Buttonwood was the fuel of choice, both as logs for burning and when reduced to charcoal. On the South Florida mainland, gathering firewood and making charcoal for delivery by boat to Key West was an important occupation. A traveller in 1885 reported seeing, in a single day, eight outbound sloops bent upon fetching firewood and charcoal for the island City. An attorney named William Hackley had recorded two years earlier that his household alone consumed three cords of firewood per month. This dependence upon imported wood continued in Key West long after kerosene and electricity became available on the Florida mainland.

The census of 1870 recorded that the sole resident of Big Pine Key, George Wilson, was the only maker of charcoal on the Keys. The next census, in 1880, listed thirteen charcoal makers on the Lower Keys, three of them black. By the turn of the century there were said to be over twenty-two makers living between No Name and Cudjoe Keys.

In 1939, I was fortunate in being able to document two white-Conch charcoal makers at work, and photographed their kiln, which they said was "the largest ever stood up on the Keys." It measured twenty-five feet in diameter, was twelve feet high, and would produce two hundred sacks of charcoal at a firing. The last reported charcoal-making on the Keys occurred in 1960, the work of Bertram Cash, a black Bahamian who had been in the business for over forty years.

Aside from a reliance upon firewood and charcoal, the lack of electricity on the Keys fostered other adaptations to place. Generations lived and died on the Keys without benefit of refrigeration. For years, the only ice arrived at great intervals aboard sailing schooners, having been cut from fresh-water ponds in Maine. This fact of life contributed to the popularity of such dishes as Cuban ropa vieja (Spanish for "old clothes"), which includes beef jerky that has been dried and cured on racks beneath the hot Keys sun.

During the root-hog-or-die days of the Great Depression, various "hard times specials" appeared on Key West tables, such as *montadella*, spiced ham luncheon meat that was fried and dumped (grease and all) over hot grits. Another hard times treat was "Twenty Grand Cigarettes," which could be purchased for two cents each wherever you went on the Keys.

The rarity of fresh water on the Keys presented another challenge for the inhabitants. Up until the completion in 1937 of an overseas aqueduct bringing potable water from the mainland, almost everyone had to rely upon rainwater drained from rooftops and collected in cisterns. Tight covers were a must to keep cats, rats, lizards, and other animals from falling in.

Another nearly universal institution dictated by the absence of running water and inside plumbing was the *cursao* (literally, "frequented place"), complete with a Sears catalogue in lieu of toilet tissue, which cost money. Flies abounded, but the brilliant sun evidently sterilized them en route from outhouse to kitchen. Many Key Westers, impatient for progress, made periodic pilgrimages to Miami where they bought a ticket to the movies—not to see the movie, but to use a flush toilet.

The water shortage also caused pioneer methods of bathing to persist on the Keys long after they had been superceded on the mainland. Bathrooms were equipped with pitcher and bowl, with a tin washtub for bathing the whole body. All water for household usage was drawn from the cistern by a hand pump on the back porch.

For those Conchs engaged in maritime pursuits, Mother Nature dictates many daily activities. Everyone on the Keys knows that the only time to go fishing is "when the wind is walking right and the water is crystal as gin." What's more, every Key Wester knows that only a damnfool stranger (mainlander) would go swimming after a big blow has made the water milky. Anyone who does gets the seven-day itch.

Maritime occupations predominate on the Keys, with fishing, sponging and trapping all common pursuits. Even those residents who have little to do with the water recognize the preeminence of the fishing captains and others who harvest the sea. There are two distinct types of professional fishermen in the Keys—commercial fishermen and fishing guides. The former make their living by catching fish or crustaceans in large quantities and selling them at the local fish houses. Guides take sport fishermen to likely spots and instruct them on the techniques of deep sea fishing. The most capable fishermen are from families who have been fishing in the Keys for several generations. Techniques and knowl-

A commercial fisherman hauling in an amberjack off Islamorada (Photo by Brent Cantrell/Courtesy of HASF)

edge are passed from one generation to another, and at any given time there may be several family members earning a living by fishing.

Commercial fishing as practiced in the Keys may be ending. The recent influx of new residents has brought pressures on the environment that have in turn resulted in new laws governing fishing and boating. These regulations are forcing men whose families have fished the Keys for generations to give up the profession. Sport fishing, on the other hand, is doing well. Sport fishing guides rely upon the thriving tourist industry, which seems in no danger of collapse.

There are many other occupations related to the sea besides fishing. Boatbuilding, sailmaking, ropeknotting, netmaking, trapmaking (for turtles, crabs, and Florida lobster), sponging, shelling, and scavenging are all Keys professions that continue to provide livelihoods on the island chain. Moreover, those who practice maritime occupations are not indifferent to the possibilities inherent in their materials and techniques. Like other folk artists, they sometimes use them to create aesthetic objects which reflect aspects of their lives. Such is the case with Richard Blaes, who utilized knowledge acquired as a fisherman, boat builder, and boat repairman to create a monumental scale model of a Florida lobster. Using a real lobster as a model, Blaes graphed his design in the manner of boat construction drawings. Over a period of five years, he assembled the thirty-eight foot long, eighteen foot high giant from $65,000 worth of steel, resin, and fiberglass boatbuilding materials.

After work, Key Westers are ready to play. Anytime there are some thirty thousand people on a rock only a few miles in diameter, with little more in the way of commercial diversion than Sloppy Joe's Saloon, Pepe's Cafe, the Monroe Theater, and the Delmonico and Ramonin restaurants, folkways are bound to flourish. For Key Westers, these traditionally included baseball, boxing, cock fighting, "meeting the boat," and the promenade.

In 1873 the Mallory Steamship line began regular service between New York, Key West, and Galveston. In addition, there were many other regular callers at the Trumbo Island Docks, such as the *Mascotte* and *Olivette*, which did a thriving business transporting Key West and Tampa Cubans back and forth to visit relatives.

Meeting the boat was an event that drew large crowds of Key Westers, regardless of whether they knew anyone on board or not. The reception included boys diving for coins, and there was always the bustle of passengers and crew who had dropped contraband overboard out in the harbor with floating markers attached arranging to retrieve their caches before customs agents beat them to it.

Retired fisherman and netmaker Popeye Thompson demonstrating his casting technique with one of his handmade nets (Photo by Brent Cantrell/ Courtesy of HASF)

One meeting-the-boat tale that is still told on the island relates how Jose Martí, the Cuban liberator, arrived at Key West from Tampa and shunned the flower-adorned carriage that awaited him. Noting the large crowd that had gathered to greet his arrival, he declared, "I prefer to walk with my friends."

Payday at the cigar factories was for generations a highly festive affair. Wages were paid entirely in silver dollars. "Brrrr..., across the counter, just like that," a veteran of those days recalled. Waiting outside the factory gates was a crowd anxious to do business—the union agent to collect dues, the *bolita* salesman selling lottery tickets, the *piruli* man with the Cuban equivalent of an all-day sucker. "In those days, when people had plenty money, they would buy anything," the veteran explained, "even a chickenhead on a stick."

Another Key West celebratory custom is the promenade. This twilight stroll up and down Duval Street, from Atlantic to Gulf, is a Key West institution that bids fair to go on forever. In the good old days, the twilight promenade was a sedate affair that provided a chance to see and be seen. The *muchachas Cubanas* (single Cuban girls), trailed by aunts acting as chaperons, envied their Conch counterparts, who had no such encumbrance. The *buscanovia*, or "looking for a sweetheart" curl over the forehead, was a device used by the Cuban girls to send a green-light signal to admirers. The promenade still happens every evening, beginning about five o'clock. It is especially crowded on Saturday nights, which in recent decades has turned into a mob scene that scares off many locals. Today, the promenade is the pedestrian equivalent of "cruising."

A celebratory contribution to black folklife on The Rock, perhaps inspired by similar events in New Orleans, is the resplendent funeral procession preceded by a cornet band in colorful uniforms and white gloves. The first of these musical ensembles, organized in 1874, was the Key West Cornet Band, with seventeen pieces. This band was succeeded at the turn of the century by Welters' Cornet Band, founded by Frank Welters. Still active today, the Welters band marches and plays in funeral processions as mourners accompany the casket to the old city graveyard. In times past, Key Westers followed the old-world custom of closing shop doors and residential shutters as a funeral procession passed by. This custom has been lost, but the music lives on.

Another musical treat on the island is Bahamian junkanoo music. The Island Junkanoo Band of Key West is composed of seven young Afro-Bahamian musicians. They perform spirited renditions of traditional Junkanoo and calypso music, as well as popular rhythm and blues and original songs adopted to the junkanoo style. The band's repertoire includes not only Bahamian songs enjoyed by their parents, such as

Welters Cornet Band, by Mario Sanchez (Photo courtesy of the Key West Art & Historical Society)

"Sponger Money," "Bellamena," and "Hoist Up the John B. Sail," but also many other songs that refer to maritime activities and Key West.

Most of the band members in the Island Junkanoo Band learned their music as children from friends and relatives in Key West. As teenagers, they used to beat pots and pans, saws, and other household objects to create the infectious, percussive sounds of a Bahamian Junkanoo celebration. The homemade instruments have gradually been replaced with congas, maracas, cowbell, timbales, bongos, and a musical saw.

Boza's Comparsa Dancers is the name of the Key West Cuban comparsa group founded by Abelardo Boza in 1938. Under Boza's leadership, the group performed traditional comparsa line dances with colorful costumes and *farolas* (decorated towers) in the streets of Key West for many years. Although the tradition lapsed after Boza's death, it was revived several years ago and a new generation is now participating in this festival dancing tradition.

A series of "invasions" to the island—to some extent concurrent—began in the wake of World War II, and have continued to this day. These intrusions are radically modifying, and even threatening, the continued existence of the unique folklife that has evolved in the Keys. The influx consists of three distinct elements—tourists, "hippies," and gays. All three groups have brought their respective lifestyles with them, and the indigenous Conch culture has been hard put to accommodate them and still preserve its own identity.

The Key West hippie colony may be the largest surviving aggregation of individuals who adopted the philosophy and lifestyle of the 1960s counterculture. The folklife of this movement is well represented by its disciples on The Rock—dress, drugs, and all. Its most conspicuous contribution to Key West has been the inauguration of a Sunset Ceremony paying homage to the life-giving orb as it sinks beneath the horizon on the Gulf of Mexico. Daily the shops along Duval Street provide the public service of posting signs advising "Sunset Today: 5:56." The counter culture clan, accompanied by an almost equal number of tourists, gathers in Mallory Square and spreads out along the adjacent waterfront. Sunset on the Keys is rarely less than spectacular, and so its worshippers are seldom disappointed. In full regalia, they make music, sing, dance, chant, smoke, meditate, and do anything else they can think of short of self-immolation. As the last rays dissolve into the long Keys twilight there is reverent silence. It is all very good business for Sloppy Joe's and other area drinking establishments, and tourists burn up rolls of film, finding the spectacle to be one of the most fascinating of the island's cultural attractions.

History informs us that the Keys have always been a mecca for nonconformists of every known description. After the counter-culture invasion came a huge influx of gay men. As this new population increased, it fostered and supported many specialized entrepreneurs, who opened restaurants, shops, bars and motels that cater to a gay clientele. Gays have organized a Key West business guild of their own, with a membership at this time of over two hundred. Besides playing prominent roles in commerce, politics, and other facets of Key West life, the community has brought a new genre of folklife to the island.

Celebrations are important to gay life, and the Sunset Ceremony is marked by the participation of many in the community. Key West gays also stage a skating party every Tuesday night, and produce a gala party on both the Fourth of July and Halloween. These events have become gay traditions and function to bind the community together by providing a shared culture.

While the impact of the hippie and gay subcultures upon traditional Conch folklife has at times seemed to reach hurricane force, Key Westers, having a long record of nonconformity of their own, have been taking it in stride—much as they do the regular "big blows." The tourist invasion, however, with its concomitant "development," has been an entirely different matter and threatens to put the indigenous Keys folklife on the endangered cultures list.

Thanks in good part to the Historic Florida Keys Preservation Board, much of the renovation and new construction that has taken place has actually served to perpetuate the traditional Key West architecture. When the Keys were first settled, the fishermen and pirates built homes of salvaged wood or of cedar from Cuba and the upper Keys. The typical

A recently renovated
Key West Conch house
(Photo by Tina Bucuvalas)

Key West residence has roots in Bahamian culture. It consists of a
one-and-a-half-story frame anchored deep in the coral rock. The roofs of
older homes had two or three combs that were fitted with pipes leading to
the backyard cistern. Most houses feature slatted shutters (also known as
Bahama shutters), which can remain closed to eliminate glaring sunlight
while permitting breezes to cool the house. In the past, most Conchs left
their homes unpainted, for paint was a luxury and was ephemeral in the
hot tropical sun. Today, Key West houses are much the same, although
paint often covers the weathered wooden boards of the exterior.

Although the structures are being preserved, the same cannot be said
of Key Westers themselves. Native Conchs are rapidly being taxed off the
island by skyrocketing real estate values. Residents may find themselves
informed by the tax assessor that the frame cottage they purchased for
$4,500 has been reassessed at $120,000, and that they should feel lucky,
for the cottage next door has just sold for $159,000. The annual tax in
this particular instance comes to $1,685, which many Key Westers on
modest fixed incomes cannot afford.

The bottom-line result of development and restoration in the old city has been a veritable Conch diaspora, a forced exile in which the native-born are obliged to sell their homes, pack their belongings and memories, and leave their family graveyards behind. For the most part, these exiles have settled on the South Florida mainland, although a few have crossed the border into Georgia and Alabama.

For some reason there has come to be a certain concentration of Key West emigrés in and around Ocala, Florida. Some say it is because one can still acquire a home there for about thirty thousand dollars. It is not at all easy for a native of the Keys to live happily anywhere else. Homesickness is so pervasive that Conch reunions are held, not annually, but three times each year—Labor Day, Memorial Day, and the Fourth of July—at a marina on the outskirts of Ocala. There emigré Conchs and charter busloads of relatives from back home congregate to eat Key West food, listen to Key West music and reminisce about their former life on the Keys. For some, the nostalgia is too much, so they sell out a second time and return to The Rock to live out the rest of their days, often in a retirement complex.

A KEYS FOLKLIFE SAMPLER

Stretching It Some

Talk About Mosquitoes   Wherever you go in the world where there are mosquitoes, you can hear tall tales about how big the local ones are, how ferocious and bloodthirsty. However, the mosquitoes of the Florida Keys are in a class by themselves. For generations, Key Westers could not keep a cow, goat, dog, cat, or chickens because mosquitoes would eat them alive. The only way the Keys deer have managed to survive is by wading out on the windward side of the islands until only their noses are sticking up above the water. People still talk about a sailor on leave who got drunk and passed out on the waterfront. The mosquitoes got so much of his blood he never woke up.

Before mosquito spray was invented, Conchs went around with leafy twigs in their hands, which they kept waving around their heads, arms, and legs. If you got a small boat and went to pick tamarind on one of the outlying Keys, you had to wear not only a face net, but gloves and two or three thick shirts. The mosquitoes would come at you in black clouds, taking the shortest route possible to your skin, and they could penetrate any shield. Key Westers who had to stay up there ten days or so at a time, making charcoal for sale, found that the only way they could foil the insects was to brad their beaks when they were stuck through the wooden doors.

Any time you started up the Keys for the mainland by auto, you had to make sure you had plenty of gas, since gas pumps were scarce as hen's teeth after you left Key West island. If you ran out of gas after dark, sometimes the mosquitoes would be so bad that rolling up the windows would not do you any good—they would come through the clutch and brake pedal holes in the floorboard. You would have to escape by wading into the water like the deer, and pray that someone would come by in a car before the night was over.

You don't have to believe any of this if you don't want. Just be glad it's not the way it was back then, when folks had to be sure to set their alarm clocks so they could get to work on time, as otherwise the clouds of mosquitoes would be so thick that everyone would think it was still dark, long after the sun was up.

Cats, Ten Cents Apiece.   Everyone knows about Ernest Hemingway's penchant for six-toed alley cats, and that the Hemingway premises in Key West are still overrun by descendants of those he befriended. What people don't know is that on at least one occasion, Key West cats were an export item, worth ten cents apiece on the hoof, delivered at the dock.

It happened in 1908, a couple of years before the Big Blow of 1910. By the turn of the century a few Conchs had settled on the islands and coast of the Cape Sable area, and they were engaged in growing sugarcane. The cane juice they would boil down in cast iron kettles made blackstrap molasses ("long sweetnin'") and sugar, both brown and white. The 1910 hurricane blew away thousands of cans of their syrup, after which the folks up there went back to fishing.

In 1908, however, they were still growing sugarcane in a big way, their chief problem being hordes of rats that ate up an awful lot of the cane. One day, Gene Roberts had an idea. Calling all the Conchs of Cape Sable together, he said, "Boys, we've done everything we could think of to get rid of the rats, but it ain't doin' no good. No use in us spending any more money on poison—these rats would rather eat our sugarcane. These few cats we got here has done the best they could, but they can only eat so many rats. So I say we ought to chip in and make a run down to Key West and buy up a whole bunch of cats and bring them here!"

At first the men all laughed, but the more they thought about it, the more they began to take the idea seriously. Finally they decided to give it a trial, and Gene set sail for Key West. As soon as he got there he stuck up a sign—"Will pay 10 cents apiece for every cat delivered to this dock!" In no time at all, there was a steady stream of children with cats to sell. When Gene had four hundred of them, all that his boat could hold, he cast off for Cape Sable. "That ninety-mile trip was the worst I ever made!" he said. "Those durn cats fought and yowled the whole way. Many a time I thought I would have to jump overboard to keep 'em from eating me alive!"

As soon as the cats could jump ashore, they did, and took off in all directions. They got to be so wild, folks said they were breeding with the bobcats. But Cape Sable hasn't had a rat problem since, and after awhile, the mosquitoes killed off all the cats.

Quevedo   It is rare to hear Quevedo tales today, but they were popular in Key West as late as the 1930s. Quevedo's reputation was so well-known that during the 1930s Hispanic students at the University of Florida banded together as "Los Picaros de Quevedo," or "The Rascals of Quevedo."

Quevedo was born Francisco Gomez de Quevedo y Villegas, in Madrid about 1580. The Quevedo family was one of the most influential in Spain, with close ties to the royal family. Although Quevedo was born into privilege, he elected to leave the royal court and live among the common people. He became a prolific writer of satiric essays and verse critical of the government and nobility. For this he was frequently thrown into prison, where he wrote some of his best work. In modern times, Quevedo has been ranked with Seneca and Cervantes in giving literary distinction to the Castillian language and instigating a cultural renaissance in Spain.

The folk hero Quevedo has been highly vulgarized, and tales of his life are both exaggerated and legendary. Prior to the regime of Castro in Cuba, numerous collections of the tales of *Quevedo* were published. Many of the stories were risque and offended sedate sensibilities. The books were smuggled into Key West and other Florida Latin communities, where the tales live on. Quevedo often appears as the Latin equivalent of the trickster hero found in many cultures. Here are two typical tales, collected from Key West Cubans during the 1930s:

Once upon a time, the king decided that he would tolerate Quevedo no longer, and he ordered that the rascal be executed. So Quevedo was thrown into prison. The last day before his execution, Quevedo asked that the king allow him to choose the manner in which he should die. The king replied that, since he would die one way or another, he would grant Quevedo his last wish. Quevedo requested that he be allowed to die of old age. The king had given his word, so he had to let Quevedo go free.

Once Quevedo happened to see the princess riding by in her carriage. He immediately fell in love with her, and resolved to meet her. Having heard that she was very fond of *frijolitos* (black beans), he went to the royal palace and wangled an introduction to the princess. "Just call me Frijolito," he told her. Then some time later, he invited her to have some frijolitos, which he said were exceptionally good, and she accepted. So, Quevedo, who was a womanizer and natural-born rascal, entered her room, which adjoined that of the queen. Without a moment's hesitation, Quevedo made advances to the princess, and she cried to her mother, "Mama, Frijolito is hurting me terribly!" Her mother, not knowing what was taking place, called back to her daughter, "You certainly deserve it! I've told you many times not to eat frijolitos!"

Gone, But Not Forgotten

Key West's Last Pirate   When on rare occasions some Key Wester would display signs of sudden affluence, everyone's first thought would be, not that they had inherited a fortune, or robbed the bank, or won the Cuban lottery, but that they had stumbled upon some buried pirate treasure. It did happen, but not often. Legend and history alike attest that the Keys long served as a major base for both piracy and wrecking.

What may have been one of the last live Key West references to piracy was recorded in 1935 at 525 United Street. This two-story frame house is now a glistening white, but then (like virtually every wooden structure on the Keys) it was unpainted and displayed a grey patina as thick and soft as moleskin. Number 525 was a rooming house owned and operated by "Miss Mamie," age ninety-one. Miss Mamie spent her days gently rocking and moaning softly, "I'm dying...." Every so often, undertaker Pritchard would stop by and ask, "Miss Mamie, you ain't dead yet?" And she would shoo him off the porch and go on moaning, louder than ever.

Among Miss Mamie's boarders was a man named Raoul, who said that his father had been the last pirate in Key West. According to Raoul, one day his father was walking down Duval Street, as Key Westers will, when some Conch gave him a "Bronx cheer," as some Key Westers will. On this occasion, the retired pirate whirled and splattered the man's brains with the diamond-studded cane he carried. "After that, he just kept on walking down Duval Street," Raoul concluded. "Nobody ever said nothing to him about it."

Manungo, the Last of the Ñáñigos   Manungo was the last of the ñáñigos in Key West. Manungo's last street dance was in 1923. In Cuba, the ñáñigos were a secret society, started by the slaves, something like the crocodile clan back in Africa. They even had their own language, *las palabras de ñáñigo*. Ñáñigo groups became quite popular in Cuba, until the government put a stop to it since people were turning up dead after the dances.

Manungo had a *bodego* (grocery) on the southeast corner of White-head and Catherine streets. On Nochebuena (Christmas Eve), after everyone had finished feasting on pork roast, black beans, rice and sweets, Manungo would come out in the street in front of his shop and start tuning his drum. Soon, other people would come out with their bongos, tumba, and quinto drums and tune them up, sometimes burning a piece of newspaper or a can of Sterno under them to rid the goatskin drumheads of moisture and tighten them into tune.

The drummers would all be dressed up in African costumes, and when everyone was ready they would start off down the street, winding all over the island, drumming and dancing. Everyone would come out to watch them, but you had to be ready to jump, because every now and then the *diablito* would take a whack at someone with his stick.

Monkey Man   Frank Mastragani ran what was probably the first self-serve grocery in America. It was located in the 700 block of Duval Street, near Petronia Street, next door to the Cave Inn bar. The reason that it was self-serve is that Frankie, or "Monkey Man" as we called him, weighed all of seven hundred pounds. It was hard for him to get up on his feet, or to stay up for long, so he would sit in a straightback chair, tilted back, on the sidewalk out in front of his store, and you would go in and get what you wanted and pay him on your way out.

Monkey Man kept his fruit and vegetables on a rack sticking out over the sidewalk, and he spent a lot of time sleeping in his chair. As boys, we used to saunter by with a fish-hook on a line and snag a watermelon with it; then when we got out of sight around the corner of Petronia, we would start pulling on the line. The melon would inch around the corner without disturbing Monkey Man's slumbers in the least.

In addition to produce, Monkey Man had chickens for sale, alive in cages, which is the way that they were kept fresh in those days. He also had a clerk called Pelluso who developed a lucrative habit. When nobody was looking, he would take a hatpin and stick the chicken of his choice in the head. As soon as the bird began to droop (which didn't take long), Pelluso would take it out of the pen. Rousing Monkey Man from his slumbers, he would say, "Look here, Frankie, this one looks awful sick." "Throw it out quick, before it infects the others!" Monkey Man would order, and fall back asleep.

Pelluso would then take the chicken inside, give its neck a twist, and toss it over the back fence, where, by prearrangement, some member of his family would be waiting to catch it and take it home for dinner.

Pepe's Café   Pepe's Café was located on Duval Street across from Sloppy Joe's bar. It was the place where everybody who was anybody and many who weren't took their morning coffee. Pepe served Cuban *cafe con leche,* of course, and you could choose between the cans of *condensada* and *evaporada* that were to be found on every table. With the coffee would come slabs of Cuban bread, toasted and buttered. It was a good way to start a day in Key West.

Some say that during the 1930s, more city and county business was transacted in Pepe's Café than in the halls of government. Once ensconced in Pepe's, the city fathers tended to dawdle indefinitely, gossiping, swapping tales, threshing out public issues, and taking votes. There are even those who say that it was in Pepe's Café that the fateful decision was reached to give the city and county away during the desperate days of the Depression. It is further said that Governor Dave Scholtz came to town and accepted Key West and Monroe County on behalf of the state of Florida, at Pepe's. He promptly passed them on to the Florida administrator of the Federal Emergency Relief Administration, who also had made the trip to Pepe's to claim jurisdiction over the archipelago on behalf of Uncle Sam.

Looking for Pena's Liquor Cellar   For those generations of Key Westers who were interested in nightlife during the days of prohibition and beyond, Pena's Garden of Roses was a focal point. A native of Spain, Pena did not personally smuggle in his own contraband liquor, but, like most of the other nightclub proprietors, he bankrolled others to bring it in for him. Where Pena stashed his liquor has always been one of Key West's great mysteries. None but Pena and a black man he had working for him at the Garden of Roses knew where it was hidden—and they are both dead. Whenever the Garden of Roses started to run low on something, Pena would send that man to get it. It didn't take him long, so everyone figured it was in a cave somewhere.

Pena didn't just bring in what he needed for the Garden of Roses, he filled orders from all over the country. A call would come in from some speakeasy or big shot in, say, Chicago. "Okay," Pena would tell him, "send me some trunks." When the next steamship arrived from Havana there would be on board some touristy-type traveller with any number of large trunks. Upon being inspected by U.S. Customs, the trunks would be found to contain nothing but old clothing, maracas, and junk. Emblazoned with large "Cleared" labels from Customs, the trunks would then be turned over to Pena, who would throw away the contents and refill them with liquor, each bottle carefully packed in shavings from the Key West sponge dock. The trunks would be taken to the Overseas

A monumental sculpture of a conch adorns the grounds at Key West High School. (Photo by Brent Cantrell. Courtesy of HASF)

Railroad, where the handsomely tipped station master and baggage master would accept the trunks without questioning their clearance status. Once the train was on its way, the baggage master would affix new labels for the Chicago consignee, and that was that.

Pena and other rum-runners had an arrangement with the Overseas Railroad conductors. They would wire ahead to the island City whenever a revenuer boarded the train headed for Key West. By the time the train arrived, not a bottle could be found anywhere on The Rock. It was common in those days for everyone—revenuers, customs agents, Coast Guard, and even conservation agents—to exact bribes from the rum-runners. "I remember one time my man got stopped three times out in the Gulf Stream, and paid off three times. I still made ten thousand dollars on the trip," Pena boasted.

Had it not been for the Key West connection, America would probably have died of thirst. Entrepreneurs like Pena became legendary on The Rock. When World War II came along, the navy decided it needed the land where Pena's Garden of Roses stood, and they offered him twenty thousand dollars for all of his property. Pena made such a fuss that they finally paid him thirty-nine thousand dollars, but he was still so mad he went to Spain and never came back.

When word went around the island that the navy was about to bulldoze Pena's buildings, the whole island turned out to watch, hoping that the dozers would uncover Pena's secret liquor-hiding place. They never did find it, though, and people are still looking.

Mario No spot on earth has had its folklife so lovingly and brilliantly immortalized as Key West, thanks to its native son, Mario Sanchez. His bas-relief carved and painted murals of the island's street scenes during the decade leading up to World War II have won him world renown. Today, Sanchez's paintings, when available at all, are auctioned by satellite, with opening bids pegged at ten thousand dollars.

Mario was born in the upstairs of his family's *bodega*, at the corner of Duval and Louisa streets, in 1908. The shop was in the heart of the Cuban quarter, known as "Gato's Village," and was situated across the street from the Sociedad Cuba and Jesus Carmona's El Anon ice cream parlor. Gato's Village was named for the most prosperous local cigar manufacturer and employer of most of the village residents—Eduardo Hidalgo Gato.

In the mid-1930s, Sanchez acted upon his urge to carve and paint life-sized wooden replicas of some of the spectacular fish that inhabited the Keys waters. He did so with incredible accuracy, working entirely from memory, with no models in sight. He sold his fish through Thompson's Hardware Store, at prices ranging from $1.50 to $3.00 retail.

It was Mario's mother who suggested that he switch from fish to street scenes. After first sketching on paper, Sanchez proceeded to trace a scene onto a wooden panel, usually two inches thick, a foot and a half high, and three feet long. Using ordinary chisels, a mallet, razorblade, and a piece of glass, he created detailed bas-relief works that he then painted in vivid colors. His first such creation, *Manungo's Diablito Street Dancers*, was purchased by the manager of a Duval Street clothing store for $250.

Every scene that Mario has created has been truly a representation of

Key West folklife. The buildings, people, vehicles, and even the cats and dogs that appear in his works are never generic, but are readily recognizable by name to Key Westers. Although Mario was depicting the root-hog-or-die days of the Great Depression, every scene he painted—even the funeral processions—exudes *joie de vivre*, and a commingling of dignity, whimsy, and fantasy.

Tearoll   A star performer in the Afro-Conch community of Key West was Theodore Rolle, better known as "Tearoll." A native of the Bahamas, Tearoll was in great demand as a singer after he settled on The Rock. He was one of the most prolific singers documented by the Federal Writers' Project and other WPA cultural programs during the 1930s. After his repertoire of traditional Bahamian songs had been exhausted at a 1939 WPA recording session that took place at the AME Church, he was asked if he knew any "dirty songs." He replied that he knew plenty, but could not sing any so long as there were ladies present. The session was therefore adjourned and a "men only" audition was set for the following morning.

Long before the appointed hour, the windows of the church were all filled with the heads of women, who, having been barred from entry, were determined to hear Tearoll's dirty songs anyway. Gentleman that he was, Tearoll went on with the show. One original composition, which received much laughter from the windows, was titled "Tearoll's Idea." The song was punctuated by sotto voce lines such as: "Baby, you wanna run around with me, You gotta wear your drawers half down." Reliable sources say that this and other "dirty songs" recorded by the WPA workers may be found in an obscure corner of the National Archives in a file labeled "Delta."

Grits and Grunts

Eat More Conch   The conch has emerged as the symbol of traditional Keys life. No matter how you spell it, or what language you speak, if you want to be understood in the Keys, you should pronounce it "konk." The word is derived from the Greek *konche*, meaning a variety of spiral-shaped gastropod marine mollusk. The Romans, who didn't learn their Greek very well, spelled it *concha*, and applied it to mussels, a bivalve creature.

All Keys and Caribbean natives know their "conchology" well enough to know that the Greeks were right. Even tourists know the conch for what it is, having seen piles of them stacked in front of roadside shell shops up and down the Florida coasts. As late as the 1950s, the signs atop those piles read "Five Cents Each" or "Free," which almost made the conch an endangered species.

Long before Europeans and Africans came to the Western Hemisphere, the Native Americans were making good use of conch shells as bowls, scrapers, and digging tools. The shells were also used as horns for blowing messages. This form of communication was also employed by peoples from other continents.

Despite these early uses, it has been the culinary use of the conch that has endeared the mollusk to the peoples of the Florida Keys. Both the elongated king conch and the more common queen conch are relished raw and prepared in a variety of forms. They are not only a taste treat, but reportedly have aphrodisiac powers. Perhaps for both reasons, tourists also have acquired a taste for conch, and their demand for conch dishes is in evidence on restaurant menus throughout the South Florida region.

In Miami, a flourishing chain of lunchrooms developed during the 1930s under the name He-Man Conch Chowder, with claims posted such as "It has What You Lack—Gives You Vim, Vigor & Viggle!" Conch is said to do the most for your sexuality when it is eaten raw—alive and kicking.

On days "when the wind is walking right" and the waters are "crystal as gin," Key Westers equipped with glass-bottomed buckets used to peer into the ocean to find conchs lying on the sea bottom. These buckets, a traditional tool, were also used by the spongers, who harvested their catch from the ocean floor. A conch fisherman carried a long pole with hooks attached to one end, in order to locate and snag the mollusk in depths up to sixty feet. Lacking a pole, Key Westers who spotted a conch on the ocean floor while on a fishing trip could seldom resist diving for it.

Once the conch was on the boat, the fisherman extricated the flesh from the shell by piercing the third spiral from the tip with a screwdriver, then severing the attaching muscle with a deft twist of a knife inserted into the slot. When the flesh was freed, it was often sliced into strips, dipped into the salty sea water, and eaten raw. Some fishermen would spit chewed conch portions into the water as chum, drawing all the fish in the area. These folkways have disappeared since conch fishing became illegal in the 1980s. Today conch is imported in order to fulfill local demand.

To a Key Wester, the next step down the culinary ladder is conch salad. Prior to the refinements aimed at the tourist palate, the traditional Key West conch salad was simply diced conch marinated in a dressing of Key lime juice, wine vinegar, salt and pepper.

Conch is also cooked in a variety of ways. When fried, conch strips are marinated in this same dressing (minus the vinegar) and dipped in a batter of choice. The traditional Key West recipe for making conch chowder is as follows: Four conchs, coarse ground; four potatoes, diced; 1/2 stick of butter; 1/4 pound of salt bacon, diced; one onion, diced; one green pepper, diced; one tablespoon Worcestershire; salt and pepper; two quarts of water. Simmer conch and potatoes in water. Saute onion and green pepper with bacon and butter. Add other ingredients to sauce, simmer, then combine with liquid containing conch and potatoes. Simmer to desired thickness.

Back when wrecking, sponging, and cigarmaking made Key West the most affluent community per capita in America, a deluxe "cream of conch" was in vogue. This recipe went out of favor during the Great Depression, but it has enjoyed a comeback since. If strangers only knew what they were missing, they would demand this version in Keys restaurants, at any cost! Here is the recipe for Conch Puree Supreme: Six conchs, ground; one onion; celery; three quarts of milk; one quart cream; 1/2 stick butter; salt and pepper. Boil conch, onion, celery in 3/4 quart of water for twenty minutes. Heat (but do not boil) milk, cream, and butter. Combine both liquid mixtures, let stand, strain, stir in six crumbled soda crackers. Serve in bowls topped with whipped cream.

After feasting on conch, one can recite the Key West jingle that goes:

> In all my mother's children,
> I loves myself the best;
> And 'til I gets my stomach full,
> God help the rest!

One last word about the conch. Although the conch is important to all Key Westers, they will warn that you should never bring a conch shell into the house—it is nothing but bad luck. However, if kept in the garden, the conch shell is a decorative and harmless object.

Florida Keys Songbag

A la Bahama   The Anglo and Afro-Bahamians who settled in Key West and elsewhere on the archipelago brought an abundance of cultural riches with them, including an overflowing songbag. Some songs harken back all the way in to the British Isles, others to the African mainland, and still more were created from the two groups' shared experiences in the Bahama Islands. The Bahamians engaged in maritime pursuits such as fishing, sponging, turtling, rum-running, wrecking and boat building. It was much the same in the Florida Keys, and their songs reflect these Conch occupations.

Conchy Joes

Conchy Joes, all they know
Is after supper to the crawls they go;
Talking 'bout fish and turtle too,
Mark my word, you'll find it true.

I went a-fishin', fished all night,
My grapple got hooked, fish won't bite;
Hard times, nothin' to do,
I lost my grapple and mainsail too!

Another classic of the Bahamian waterfront, known wherever Bahamians have gone in South Florida, is "Bellamena." This version, recorded in Key West during the 1930s, includes a number of verses not found in the recorded version by Harry Belafonte. The significance of black paint lies in the fact that, during Prohibition, Bahamian boats were heavily engaged in smuggling contraband liquor into South Florida. Black boats were more difficult for the Customs agents to spot at night.

Bellamena

Bellamena, Bellamena,
Bellamena in the harbor;
Mena, Mena, Mena in the harbor,
Gonna put Bellamena on the dock,
Gonna paint her bottom black, black!

Oh, the Mystery, oh, the Mystery,
That boat she tote the whiskey;
Gonna put the Mystery on the dock,
Gonna paint her bottom black, black!

Oh, the Maisie, oh, the Maisie,
That boat she drive me crazy;
Gonna put Maisie on the dock,
Gonna paint her bottom black, black!
Now I ain't talking 'bout her backsides—
Gonna paint her *be-hind* black, black!

A la Cubana   One of the most venerable musical institutions in Key West's Cuban community was the *cantante callejero*, or "strolling troubadour." Usually teenagers with guitars, they did much to enliven street corners, cafes, and moonlight swimming parties on South Beach. The last two *cantante callejeros* within living memory were the brothers

Matique and Oswaldo Alphonso, who made music with a marimba fashioned from a large olive oil can. They made their exit from the Key West scene in the early 1930s.

Singing musical ensembles like the cantante callejeros played an important role in enlivening the street scene in Key West. One of the last of these was the marimba group that played for the first incoming planeloads of tourists from Miami during 1935. The Septeto Encanto was hired by Julius F. Stone, the federal administrator who had charge of Key West during 1935–36, when the island had declared bankruptcy and was under federal rule. The ensemble consisted of marimba, bass, two guitars, bongos, drum, and claves. When they were not meeting planes, the Septeto Encanto was apt to turn up almost anywhere—day or night—with renditions of Cuban traditional and popular songs. They also sang improvisations about such Key West characters as Monkey Man and Pena. Many of these songs were recorded by the WPA Florida Writers' Project and are available today in cassette form at the Monroe County Library, the Florida Folklife Archives in White Springs, and the Archive of American Folk Culture at the Library of Congress.

A typical song by Septeto Encanto is the Key West version (with improvised verses) of "La Cucaracha," translated here from the Spanish:

La Cucaracha

The cockroach, the cockroach,
Already cannot walk,
Because he has no,
Because he lacks
Marijuana to smoke.

The girls of Key West
Use much rouge;
They don't put it on with the puff,
They put it on by the package.

The girls of Ybor City
Are pretty and dance well;
But they have one defect—
They do not wash their feet.

The girls of West Tampa
Have much personality;
They wear many fine clothes,
With their stomachs empty.

On the beach of Key West,
They caught a shark;

And from its stomach they took
A "Monkey Man" in a gown.

The Florida Keys persist as both a tropical fantasy for tourists and adventurers, and an island home to people who are uniquely tied to the sea. Like the mainland of South Florida, the Keys are both isolated and cosmopolitan, nurturing a wealth of traditional folklife while adopting new expressions of popular culture. The Conch and Cuban communities that have created a unique Key West lifestyle are now joined by newer groups who are attracted by the island's environmental and cultural charms. There have been many changes since Stetson Kennedy first documented the traditional culture of the Keys. Although the rapid development and influx of outsiders in recent years has altered life on The Rock, many aspects of Keys folklife remain and will live on for future generations, to be joined by the newer cultural offerings of recent residents. Together, all Key Westers will redefine the meaning of their folklife.

Tourism

Tourist Traditions

Florida is the state that tourism built. Florida historian Gloria Jahoda has written that "whatever else it is and has been, the state of Florida is the Great American Escape. . . . Florida is the place to go when you want to get away at a price you can afford, from life in the rest of the United States." The fact that tourism is, and always has been, the state's premier industry is perhaps due to the paradoxical nature of Florida's culture. Florida is a wilderness with sophistication, a place that remains exotic despite its taming by humans. It draws visitors by offering a dizzying array of extraordinary attractions in an ordinary place: wax museums, circus concessions, western towns, Spanish jails, aquatic zoos, parrot and monkey jungles, orchid and tropical gardens, "mermaid" and water-ski performances, alligator farms, reptile ranches, African safari parks, Seminole villages, and urban ethnic enclaves such as Little Havana in Miami or the Greek presence in Tarpon Springs. And, of course, Florida is best known as the home of the world's largest theme park complex, which is in Orlando; this megapolis of fantasy alone has made Florida the most sought-after destination for domestic and international tourists in the United States.

Government statistics bear out the astounding impact that visitors have had upon the state of Florida as a whole, and particularly on the lower half of the peninsula. In 1926 the state already was hosting over 1.8 million tourists. Ten years later, during the height of the Great Depression, Florida saw 2 million tourists spend over 224 million hard-to-find dollars. By 1958, 7 million people were visiting, with 45 percent going to southeast Florida. In 1965 16 million tourists came to the state, with nine hundred thousand of them headed for the city of Miami. The most recent figures available reveal that in 1991 40 million tourists flooded into Florida, spending an astronomical $28.9 billion, yielding $1.72 billion in state sales taxes and employing seven hundred thousand in the tourism industry. Of these visitors, 40 percent were headed for South Florida, perhaps contributing to the 30 percent increase in the region's population between 1980 and 1990. In 1874, thirty-three thousand tourists visited Florida; in 1992 that number was surpassed each morning at the state's airports.

Obviously, an industry of this magnitude has had profound effects upon the culture of South Florida. Unlike other southern states, Florida has a tourism industry that is larger than its agricultural complex, which is vast in and of itself. Tourism has created a multicultural, multidimensional playground for both rich and working-class Americans. It has shaped people's views of what the region is and has contributed to the paradoxical stereotypes in their minds concerning Florida and Floridians.

The word "tourism" was coined as recently as the early nineteenth century, in conjunction with the new concept of leisure time for an emerging affluent middle class. The three conditions necessary for tourism to become part of the American scene—money, time and transportation—would be met, for a few, starting in the mid-1800s. From the inception of American touring, Florida has been a mecca for those looking for exotic nature, culture, and recreation. With more and more people achieving the American dream of leisure time and money, the state, trying to attract those wishing to "get away from it all," has worked to create and maintain its image as a tropical paradise.

As the number of tourists who tell their stories back home has increased, this image of Florida has become part of American folklore. South Florida promotes the notion of a regional fantasy land, selectively showcasing some aspects of the region, while burying others. Nineteenth-century Florida was touted as a tropical paradise, but the insects and oppressive heat were never mentioned; during the Florida boom of the 1920s, promoters waxed poetic about the "moon over Miami" while ignoring the muck fires on the Everglades. Today it is much the same; South Florida's tourism revolves around sunshine and sand, while officials downplay the migrant labor camps of U.S. Sugar or the Krome Avenue detention camp where hundreds of Haitian refugees are interred. As early as the 1930s, Floridians were admitting that attempts to romanticize the state's playground features had resulted in an elaborate gilding of the lily.

The story of how this image-making and the tourism agenda have affected South Florida's folk culture is essential to an understanding of this complex and varied region. More than in any other place, South Florida's folk include seasonal residents and ephemeral visitors who have contributed to the multicultural nature of the area and constitute a viable folk group in and of themselves. Moreover, South Florida has developed new social institutions that arose from the tourism industry. These institutions, including retirement centers, timeshare condominiums, camping complexes, and theme parks, have entered American culture and are now firmly a part of our heritage. Finally, tourism has shaped the folklife and culture of native South Floridians—Crackers, the Seminole, the Miccosukee and others—who live on the commerce that these temporary residents bring to the region.

HISTORY

The first American tourists were wealthy industrialists and their families who had made millions in the free enterprise system that blossomed in the nineteenth century. These pioneering tourists were seeking to ogle scenic wonders, enjoy recreational diversions, and, most importantly, relax on a health-restoring sojourn. Two men would make this dream possible.

In 1893 Henry Flagler secured a charter to extend his rail lines to South Florida. His Florida East Coast Railway would open the "Gold Coast" to tourism, and his vision of an exotic paradise has been felt throughout the region to the present day. In 1894, when the railway reached Palm Beach, the community had one thousand residents and was unincorporated. Flagler built the Royal Poinciana Hotel to accommodate fifteen hundred guests, already indicating an expectation that the tourists would outnumber the residents in South Florida.

While Palm Beach rapidly grew as a tourist mecca for the wealthy, Miamians wanted to be sure that the railway would continue to Miami. Two principal land owners, Julia D. Tuttle and William B. Brickell, offered Flagler half of their land holdings to extend his railway. By April 1896 the first trains reached Miami, and the next January Flagler opened his Royal Palm Hotel in downtown Miami. Flagler's investments paid off as tourism boomed during the early 1900s. By 1908 the Flagler hotels could accommodate over forty thousand guests on the South Florida east coast.

Meanwhile, Henry Bradley Plant, owner of the Atlantic Coast Line which ran from Savannah to Jacksonville, capitalized on the tourism and transportation opportunities for Florida's west coast. In the 1890s, Plant extended his system of rail lines from Richmond, Virginia, to Tampa, where he built what is perhaps Florida's most fantastic structure—the Tampa Bay Hotel. Designed to resemble a fantasy Moorish castle, the hotel features silver minarets and uses decoratively the horseshoe-and-crescent motif of Islam. When asked why, Plant allowed that the Tampa Bay Hotel was his version of the Alhambra.

Although Henry Plant died in 1899, his company continued to thrive, extending the railway down Florida's gulf coast and building luxury hotels in the central Florida cities of Ocala, Winter Park and Kissimmee, as well as in the "Sunshine Coast" cities of Clearwater, Fort Myers and Punta Gorda—all to house the flood of tourists who travelled on the Plant system of railroads. Henry Flagler, who had been Plant's friend, died in 1913, a year after his dream of opening the "overseas railway" to Key West became a reality.

Without the entrepreneurial impetus provided by these two tourism

Camp at Stuart Florida.
Florida East Coast - 5/10-1929

The Miller family of Toledo, Ohio, "getting away from it all" in 1929 (Photo courtesy of FSA)

magnates, Florida would likely have remained a tropical wilderness that was virtually inaccessible to development for many more years. With the advent of the Flagler/Plant system of transportation and accommodations for visitors came the need for workers to fill service industry jobs and the desire for settlement. The frontier of South Florida was about to be tamed forever.

With the completion of "Dixie Highway" (U.S. Route 1 from Maine to Miami in 1915, the American highway asserted its undeniable dominance over the nation's transportation, opening up tourism to a wider variety of citizens. The automobile democratized tourism, allowing middle-income families the mobility to "get away from it all." These new tourists were attracted by the same Florida features as their aristocratic predecessors—sun, sand, relaxation, and healthy air, all in an exotic setting. The end of World War I came at a time when travel was popular and automobiles were affordable to many. The 1910 move of major league baseball teams to spring training camps in South Florida may also have been a drawing card for the middle-class visitor.

This grassroots tourism fostered a response from the natives on the same scale. There began to appear many small "roadside attractions" and sales booths set up by resident Floridians anxious to turn a profit from the steady stream of visitors motoring down Florida's highways. The *WPA's Florida: Guide to the Southernmost State* noted that an enterprising Cracker could "set up a vegetable display, then install gasoline pumps and a barbecue stand, and finally with the addition of overnight cabins he was in the tourist business."

In the 1920s working Americans enjoyed paid vacations and retirement benefits for the first time, and it was as well a time of new spending and unprecedented wealth for their employers. Both groups journeyed to Florida to fulfill their vacation and retirement dreams. Miami developer Addison Mizner was soon followed by other enterprising real estate tycoons who fed the boom-time capitalists' appetites for opulence and display. South Florida was rapidly becoming the country's "Never-Never Land." Carl Fisher transformed Miami Beach from an isolated barrier island into an Art Deco wonderland that is today the nation's largest National Historic Register district; Boca Raton became a planned paradise city; and George Merrick envisioned "an enclave of Spanish perfection" to be known as Coral Gables.

Land speculation in South Florida broke wide open in the late summer of 1925, when assessed value of Miami property increased 560 percent and there were 5,917 registered real estate brokers operating. Unsuspecting tourists who were lured into development schemes would pay over one hundred times the value of property in America's new playground. At the same time, unscrupulous "swampboomers" traveled north to sell acres of flooded Everglades "farmland" to gullible Yankees. This activity could not last forever—the old adage "what goes up, must come down" would prove to be true.

The decline of the great Florida land boom began in 1926, when a shortage of housing and a breakdown of transportation in Miami made potential investors wary. As the inflated prices of land began to dip, Florida was for the first time receiving negative press in the North. Although human disaster would have struck, it was nature that literally washed away the Florida boom. South Florida had not experienced a tropical storm since 1910, when it was virtually unpopulated. On Labor Day in 1926, a hurricane hit the lower east coast of Florida at Miami and streaked northwest across the Everglades to Lake Okeechobee. The storm blew the water out of the southwest end of the lake, overtopped and washed out a low earthen dike, and flooded the city of Moore Haven. Three hundred and ninety-two people died in this disaster and seven thousand were wounded. The city that had hugged Lake Okeechobee was flooded for weeks, while over twelve hundred refugees from Moore Haven had to be evacuated from the eighteen-foot floodwaters.

Governor John Martin and the newspapers of South Florida, motivated by a concern for the coming tourist season, tried to play down the devastation, making matters worse, as the Red Cross could not get the supplies and food needed to help victims. The damage in Miami was equally grim. Twenty years of building was destroyed, and many tourists and new residents, unfamiliar with hurricane behavior, were killed when they went outdoors as the eye of the storm passed over.

During the 1930s, Stetson Kennedy collected this song, composed by a black migratory worker in the Everglades to commemorate the 1926 "Big Blow":

Miami Hurricane

The rich white folks and the well-to-do
Was playin five-up and pool;
God-Almighty got angry, and glory—
They forgot each other's move.

Some was floatin' on the ocean,
And some was floatin' on the sea;
And some was cryin' on bended knee,
"Lord, have mercy on me!"

Ships swam down that ocean,
It was 'most too sad to tell,
Ten thousand people got drownded,
And all but twelve went to hell.

And the lady left Miami,
She left in lightnin' speed;
Every time the lightnin' flashed,
She think about her dirty deeds.

Yon stands a lady,
Standin' in the back door cryin',
If I can ever git back to Georgy,
I won't go to Floridy no more!

(Chorus:)

Great God Amighty did mo-o-ove out on the water,
And all the peoples in Miami run.

Just as South Florida was dispelling the negative impressions left from that great hurricane and was attracting its seasonal visitors for the 1928 season, tragedy struck again, and this time it was even worse. On September 16, a fierce hurricane slammed into West Palm Beach with wind gusts of up to 130 miles per hour. The storm again moved inland to Lake Okeechobee, with greater fury and magnitude than the previous one. When it reached the lake, winds drove the water against a weak, eight-foot dike on the eastern and southeastern shores, overtopped it, and swept most of it away. The lake waters rushed out, completely drowning the settlements of Pelican Bay, Pahokee, Canal Point, Belle Glade, South Bay, and other vegetable-growing centers. The water in the Glades rose four to eight feet in one hour and eventually flooded the towns to a depth of twenty-five feet. More than twenty-four hundred people lost their lives in the flood, three-quarters of whom were black seasonal laborers, in South Florida to harvest vegetable crops. Two hundred people were said to be drowned as they raced down the road from Belle Glade to search for safety.

As a result of this disaster, Governor Doyle Carleton sought aid from President Hoover to build the thirty-eight-foot-high levees that contain Lake Okeechobee's waters to this day. South Florida natives vividly recall this hurricane, and almost all survivors have a tale to tell. This storm also inspired folklorist Zora Neale Hurston to write *Their Eyes Were Watching God*, and it has been the subject of many poems and songs. The late Florida songwriter, Will McLean, is perhaps best known for his composition "Hold Back The Waters," which ends in an apt prayer: "Lord, hold back the waters of Lake Okeechobee, for Lake Okeechobee's deep waters run cold."

The Great Depression hit Florida early and hard, as the tourist market shrank. Following the 1928 hurricane and the subsequent collapse of the real estate boom, Florida came to be thought of as a dangerous place, a playland that had lost much of its charm.

In South Florida, the city that was most destitute during the Depression years was Key West. In 1936, having lost their two major industries (cigars to Tampa and sponging to Tarpon Springs), Key West officials found themselves without funds to pay for basic city services—even fire and police protection. The city fathers declared a state of emergency and passed a resolution in 1934 giving jurisdiction of the town to the federal government. This decision made Key West a national experiment in tourism development. The New Deal government accepted the challenge presented by the island city and assigned a Federal Emergency Relief Administration (FERA) administrator to develop Key West into a profit-making tourist attraction, using WPA labor.

Stetson Kennedy remembers that these early New Deal projects were a lifeline for the residents, 80 percent of whom were on relief. When he was interviewed in 1988, he recalled that "one of the jobs of the WPA (FERA) workers in Key West consisted of raking up the seaweed, which conveniently came in every six hours with the tide. They were raking it up for the benefit of the tourists, who never came."

Despite the work done on the island, tourism developed slowly on

Key West. In 1935 a hurricane destroyed Flagler's Overseas Railroad and the island was fairly isolated until 1938, when the Dixie Highway was opened all the way to Key West. By this time the federal government had already printed tourist brochures listing forty-eight attractions on the island, including Ernest Hemingway's house. Hemingway was livid that he was used as a tourist draw and complained bitterly about the unauthorized use of his name. In a 1935 *Esquire* he wrote that he "had hired an old man to stand at the gate and pretend to be Hemingway." As the story goes, some tourists asked him one day why he always wrote in the first person, and the old man was stumped for a moment, but finally answered, "No, sir, you're wrong, sir. I don't write in the first person at all. I write direct on the typewriter."

Aside from the Key West experiment, Roosevelt's New Deal was exploring the value of tourism for economic recovery in many other venues. One of the most successful and lasting legacies of the WPA is the series of state guidebooks that emerged from the Federal Writers' Project offices of almost every state in the union. A major purpose of this series was to encourage tourism in the United States. A recent reprint of the WPA guide to Florida, originally printed in 1939, has an introduction by John I. McCollum. McCollum describes the guide as "an instrument of seduction," with over half of its pages devoted to outlining auto tours that are a "must" for visitors and residents alike. The complex nature of life and culture in Florida, especially in burgeoning South Florida, was barely hinted at in the 1939 guide. In an effort to foster economic recovery through tourism, the WPA editors made no apologies for using the guide as a government-sponsored public relations tool.

After World War II, two factors revolutionized the tourist industry in South Florida and made the traditional "season" an obsolete idea: the interstate highway system was launched, providing faster and more convenient access, and air conditioning became affordable. Thus visitors could travel to this steamy, tropical land, enjoy the sun and sand, and retire in the cool comfort of air conditioning. South Floridians now saw two major onslaughts of visitors—a winter crowd and a summer crowd—as well as a steady flow of tourists at any time of the year.

By the 1950s, South Floridians were several generations into a traditional lifestyle that revolved around serving and entertaining visitors. To attract customers, billboards were ubiquitous, marketing everything from citrus fruit to suntan lotion to retirement homes. Out-of-state advertising blossomed as Governor Farris Bryant increased spending to bring in tourists. The governor saw tourism as a way to raise revenue without raising taxes. The Florida government still uses this strategy, and the state is one of only four without a state income tax.

The early South Florida pioneers would be shocked to see the area today, for tourism has proven to be almost *too* successful in attracting residents to the region. The southeast and southwest coasts of Florida are completely developed, with the area from Palm Beach to Miami being a fifty-five-mile megapolis. Tourism is now both a private industry and a government objective. The Florida Department of Commerce (DOC) maintains five official welcome stations on the interstate highways coming into the state where tourists can get travel brochures, advice on accommodations, and a free glass of orange juice. The DOC Annual Visitors' Survey states that the department's major objective is "to contribute to the state's image as an ideal travel destination."

Miami is still a playground, with horse and dog tracks, miles of luxury hotels along the beach, and exotic restaurants for every taste. Dade County, home to over 3 million people, continues to be one of the fastest-growing areas of the country and is increasingly diverse demographically. The influx of Cuban refugees in the 1950s and the 1980s has created a new tourist draw. Little Havana is just one of the ethnic enclaves of South Florida that has marketed a unique cultural heritage to the tourist population. The proliferation of festivals throughout the local communities means that on any weekend during the year, there is a festival or tourist event planned in at least one South Florida city.

As for Key West, the WPA experiment has paid off royally, for the island is one of the most popular tourist destinations in the state. Ernest Hemingway would be appalled to know that fifty years after he left the island, his home still ranks as a top attraction in the city, and even his cats are featured on postcards. Sad to say, many of Hemingway's fears have come to pass, as real estate taxes and new zoning to accommodate the tourism industry have largely displaced the native Conchs who settled in Key West when it was a sleepy fishing village.

Hurricanes continue to be a serious concern, but South Florida's tourism officials have developed strategies for combatting any negative impact on the region's major industry. In a recent article in the Atlanta *Journal-Constitution*, the Tourist Development Council announced its plans in the event of a hurricane, saying that it would "balance the 'overblown' damage reports by letting travel magazines know what hotels and attractions are still open [through] an emergency advertising campaign, aimed at keeping people from unnecessarily changing their travel plans." After the devastation of Hurricane Andrew in 1992, this battle plan was used most effectively, and tourists were kept along the relatively untouched beaches.

Tourists leave home for varied reasons—some want to rest and recreate (the beach set); some want fantasy (Disney enthusiasts); some want to enjoy nature (the Everglades adventurers); and some want to experience another culture. South Florida, in addition to offering elaborate theme parks to thrill fantasy-seekers, miles of beach for recreational visitors, and a unique tropical environment to attract nature lovers, also has a tradition of providing cultural tourism. Cultural tourism, the most complex of the forms of visitation, has been a topic of intense debate for folklorists, anthropologists, sociologists, and cultural brokers in recent years.

CULTURAL TOURISM—THE SEMINOLE CASE

"Cultural tourism" is the marketing of local human resources to outside visitors. These resources include festivals, handicrafts, foodways, music and dance, storytelling, representations of local color, customs and ceremonies, historical reconstructions, monuments and shrines, archaeological sites, museums and other products of human endeavor. In short, cultural tourism is the presentation of a local lifestyle to a visiting public. Although much excitement has been generated in recent years concerning the potentials and pitfalls of cultural tourism, it remains the rarest form of visitation. In South Florida this is particularly true, where the 1991 figures show that of the top ten activities enjoyed by visitors in that year, "rest and relaxation" ranked number one, while "dancing and night life" and "historical sites" ranked seven and eight respectively. The most popular form of cultural tourism was eating in restaurants (number two on the survey).

Tourists who travel to experience a different culture, or to rediscover their own cultural heritage, are searching for "authenticity"—interaction with what they perceive to be "real people" in a natural setting. Cultural tourism has been seen by some to be a means for instilling an appreciation of cultural differences, while providing economic opportunity to local communities. However, cultural tourism may actually worsen cross-cultural understanding by transforming those "real people" into exotic attractions. The divisions between tourists and locals are thereby intensified as each group exploits the other for its own ends—the hosts for economic gain and the guests for entertainment. More to the point, a brief encounter with another culture rarely affords enough exposure to give a tourist true understanding; it merely provides a brief and superficial look into another lifestyle.

Anthropologist Davydd J. Greenwood, in his essay titled "Culture by the Pound," cautions that cultural tourism is "the commodification of local culture," with local culture being "altered and often destroyed by the treatment of it as a tourist attraction." By selling the essence of its culture to outsiders, this argument goes, the local community changes the meaning behind their own beliefs, ceremonies, and customs. Other scholars have observed that art forms change dramatically to serve a tourist market, that new ideas, materials and techniques from other cultures bring an outside aesthetic resulting in alterations in traditional forms.

With or without such worries, however, culture is a process that is forever changing. Whether or not tourism is a factor, local cultures evolve and reform—otherwise they would die. Most people in the United States have grown up with the false notion that tradition and modernity are opposites. Americans have not recognized the common elements found in both traditional and contemporary societies. Most importantly, their notion of what constitutes a "traditional" society (i.e., rural communities, ethnic enclaves, Native American reservations) is a stereotype. Such notions are shaped by one's own experience, which is often influenced by a media-dominated, mainstream, modern society. To complicate matters, tourists' experience with other cultures is limited to what those "other people" present to them. Each culture selectively picks aspects of its lifestyle, folk arts and heritage to show to the outside visitor. What is selected not only forms the visitor's view of the culture, but begins to alter the community's self-image.

Many times, people invent "traditions" for the benefit of the outside visitor, giving tourists what they expect and want to see. This phenomenon has been labeled *folklorismus* by European observers who decry the staging of "unauthentic" folk events and festivals for tourists. American folklorist Richard M. Dorson labeled this activity "fakelore." However, despite the outcry by folklorists, local communities have shown remarkable resilience in the face of increased cultural tourism, actually using *folklorismus* to satisfy the tourists while maintaining control of their culture. Certain events are staged for an outside audience so that other private ones can remain private. Thus traditions are invented both for a group's economic gain and to affirm its local and national cultural identity in the face of seasonal tourist invasions.

In South Florida, cultural tourism was part of the region's appeal from the time of its first visitors. Not only were tourists interested in the healthy air, the tropical climate, and the jungle flora and fauna—they were fascinated by the "untamed Seminole." These mysterious Native Americans have figured prominently in the imaginations of South Florida's tourists for over two hundred years, and they continue to play a major role in the region's tourism industry today. A look at the Seminole/Miccosukee peoples and their role in South Florida provides us with a fascinating case study of cultural tourism at work.

The Seminole living in the Everglades wilderness began to trade with white people early in the nineteenth century, providing hides, plumes, pelts and furs in exchange for beads, coins, fabric and other manufac-

Ted Smallwood and
Charley Tiger Tail (Photo
courtesy of HASF)

tured goods. The first whites to visit were adventurers and nature lovers.
In 1883, when President Chester A. Arthur made a steamboat trip on the
Kissimmee River to go fishing, he concluded his adventure with a
ceremonial greeting given him by Tom Tiger Tail. Also along the
Kissimmee River, it was reported in Alfred Hanna's Lake Okeechobee

history, when the enormous *Bertha Lee* made her ill-fated journey up the river "Indians cautiously approached the river banks to gaze with wonder on the magnificent 'Bertha Lee' and to sell her crew wild turkeys at twenty-five cents each."

The first white settlers in South Florida quickly entered into commerce with the Seminole. George M. Storter, a native of Alabama, became one of the earliest pioneers when he moved to Allen's River in 1887 and opened a store and trading post for the Miccosukee-speaking Indians living in the Big Cypress Swamp. On the east coast, Frank Stranahan of Ohio moved to the New River in what is now Fort Lauderdale and established an Indian trading post in 1893. Before the turn of the century, Charley Tiger Tail's Store was open for business, selling trade goods and whiskey in the undeveloped region around the western Tamiami Trail. Charlie did regular business with Ted Smallwood, a pioneer and general store operator in the tiny community of Chokoloskee. This early trading resulted in the Seminole becoming dependent upon manufactured goods and United States currency as early as 1900.

In 1906, the federal government began its program to drain the Everglades, which was to be the single most disruptive force in the traditional Seminole lifestyle. By draining the fragile ecosystem of wetlands and swamps, the government endangered traditional Seminole hunting, fishing, and transportation. Canals were cut through the Everglades from Lake Okeechobee to the lower east coast, reducing the water table and causing regular droughts. Game and fish were drastically reduced and shallow swamp waterways disappeared overnight. New government regulations, aimed at conservation, forbade hunting of exotic birds and alligators, thereby taking away a major source of Seminole income. Compounding these environmental changes, the early Florida land boom was bringing record numbers of white visitors to South Florida. The Seminole, in their need to find a new source of income for survival, were forced once more to adapt, and the influx of tourists became their new means of livelihood. The lifeblood of the Seminole, and later the Miccosukee, tribes has been and continues to be tourism.

Traditional crafts of the Seminole Indians (basketry, doll making, patchwork clothing, beadwork, and woodwork) have survived largely due to the tourist market; however, such items have evolved from being functional items for personal use to being souvenirs that evoke a South Florida experience.

The introduction of the Singer sewing machine in the late 1880s dramatically changed Seminole traditional dress and its craft sales potential. By 1892, Everglades explorer J. E. Ingraham reported that he observed "sewing machines in all Seminole lodges." It was this imported technology that made possible the evolution of the distinctive patchwork sewing for which the Seminole and Miccosukee are best known today.

The evolution of patchwork from the simple bands and appliqué work of the late 1800s was a direct result of the white tourist market and a new aesthetic, as well as the introduction of new materials and technologies. By the 1950s, Seminole women were spending less time sewing for their own use and more time turning out clothing and other sewn articles for the tourist market.

This market had the effect of standardizing design and limiting complexity. Patchwork sewers quickly noticed that outsiders were not willing to pay high prices for a souvenir Seminole skirt or jacket. As a result, today the most complex and expensive designs are made for Indian use, while less time-consuming designs are sold to outsiders.

Seminole basketry has also evolved to serve an outside market. The palmetto grain sifter is virtually a lost Seminole craft. As early as 1965, only one elderly woman on the Big Cypress Reservation knew how to make the rims of these once-ubiquitous Seminole baskets. Merwyn Garbarino, an anthropologist who studied the Big Cypress Reservation during the 1960s, observed that "no one uses the [grain sifter] baskets any longer, and the baskets which the old woman made were all sold to tourists." Basketry itself would most probably have been a lost Seminole craft had it not been for one woman's vision of marketing to an ever-growing tourist population.

Deaconess Harriet M. Bedell, a missionary in the Episcopal church, came to the Everglades in 1932 and established Glades Cross Mission to help the Seminole and Miccosukee become self-supporting through their traditional arts and crafts. Bedell, who worked among the Seminole for twenty-seven years, is credited not only with reviving native palmetto basketry as a marketable skill, but with profoundly influencing the Seminole craft repertoire. The deaconess encouraged craftswomen to make items that were in demand from the white market and also functioned as a broker to outlets in major cities. She was said to have introduced coiled sweetgrass basketry to the tribe, but this most likely was a borrowing from African American tradition. Whether this form of basketry was introduced by whites or blacks, clearly it emerged as a Seminole craft item in the 1930s solely to be a sales item for tourists.

Everglades trader George Storter is sometimes cited as being the first to promote the making of Seminole palmetto dolls for the tourist market. By 1900, Seminole women and girls were making wooden dolls dressed in the traditional Seminole patchwork. Presumably, these early dolls were made for young Seminole girls as playthings. However, early on, dolls became one of the best-selling Seminole souvenirs and were in great demand from the white market.

Mary Billie, who lives on the Big Cypress Reservation, tells of her own family history of doll making, explaining how intimately linked it is to the tourist market. Her daughter, Claudia, translates:

They were for the kids to play with at first. That's what they were making it for, for the kids to play with. She says she really don't know how they really started selling them to the tourists. But she said her great-grandmother said that she wanted tourists to look at it. So they started taking it out in the boat with them when they were going out. . . . She says some white person brought the tourists down the canal because that's where they used to live, in a chickee. That's my grandmother's grandmother. That's where that white person asked her to, I guess, bring the dolls out so the tourists can look at them. . . . That's when they started selling the dolls.

Doll making has continued to provide a steady income for many Seminole craftswomen. As Mary B. Billie states about her own situation in a recent interview: "Since I was seventeen, my main support for my family has come from the dolls. . . . If I don't make any dolls, there is no income." Patchwork clothing, baskets, dolls, and beadwork are all made by Seminole women for the tourists who visit arts and crafts centers at the reservations, as well as other retail outlets. In addition, women of the Miccosukee Tribe make and sell these items from stores and the Miccosukee Center on the Tamiami Trail. Recently, men of the tribes have been making items for sale out of wood, such as sofkee spoons, stickball rackets, and miniature canoes.

Seminole and Miccosukee craftspeople have always altered their styles and repertoire to suit the tourism industry in South Florida—traditional crafts that sell well are kept alive, while new items are added and duplicated if they prove popular in the marketplace. The Seminole and Miccosukee craftsmen who sell their wares at virtually all festivals in South Florida today display an eclectic mix of genuine and spurious culture. Traditional patchwork is found in dozens of items, from eyeglass cases to zippered jackets. Beadwork jewelry has evolved to incorporate the latest styles for both children and adults. Palmetto dolls come in all sizes, from twelve inches tall to a tiny version that can be pinned to a blouse, while the coiled sweetgrass baskets appear in new shapes and with more colorful threads to entice buyers. In addition to featuring these traditional crafts, most Native American craft booths also contain wooden carved guns, bows and arrows, feather headresses, toy spears, models of dugout canoes, rubber tomahawks, bamboo peace pipes and an array of items that sell as souvenirs. For better and worse, the tourism industry has been an important factor in both retaining and changing Seminole and Miccosukee craftwork.

As the South Florida Indians began to understand their new white neighbors, they realized that the Seminole way of life was of great interest to outsiders, that they themselves were attractions to the tourists from the north. A new form of cultural tourism arose that would prove to be a controversial source of income. As early as the 1870s, tourist expeditions were being led into the Everglades to visit Seminole camps and view these exotic people in their "natural habitat." Like rare birds, alligators, tropical orchids, and poisonous snakes, the Seminoles were seen as part of the jungle environment; exotic and mysterious, they could provide tourists with an "authentic" adventure.

Bus drivers from Miami would take sightseers west of town to view the camps along the still-unpaved Tamiami Trail. The only problem was that the Seminole families frequently moved, and one could never be sure to find a camp in the same location. By the turn of the century, Seminole people were visiting the tourist centers of Miami and Fort Lauderdale during the winter season to sell their crafts. Tourist center operators began encouraging them to stay for several days as a draw for their fascinated customers. The Seminole soon became a featured attraction at parades, on the Miami pier to greet cruise ships, and as added "color" at established tourist outlets.

At Coppinger's Tropical Gardens, an "attraction" developed for tourists, 1934 (Photo courtesy of HASF)

In 1917, Henry Coppinger, Jr., became the first to institutionalize the idea of presenting the Seminole way of life as a tourist attraction. In that year, he hired two Miccosukee-Seminole families to set up a chickee camp at his tourist business. Located at NW 20th Avenue near the Miami River, Coppinger's Tropical Gardens was already a thriving citrus fruit outlet and popular tourist attraction. Each Seminole family was paid twenty dollars per week, plus food and yard goods (for craftwork), to let curious tourists watch them as they ate, slept, made crafts, and generally did everyday chores. The families would spend the tourist season (January 1 to April 30) at Coppinger's, then canoe back into the Glades to spend the off-season with enough trade goods and money to make it through the summer.

The Seminole families who settled into the attractions were presided over by a "headman" who was responsible for all conduct and commerce between his people and the outside world. These men would locate families to live at the attraction for each season, negotiate wages and craft prices with the owners, and keep order within the Seminole camp. Jack Tiger Tail, who was one of the first headmen to live at Coppinger's, became so popular with the white settlers and tourists that his image was chosen to be the emblem of the new city of Hialeah. Tiger Tail was a good negotiator with the boomtime businessmen, and he was thought to be honest and strong—the stereotype of the "noble savage." By the time Jack died in 1922, his face was emblazoned on billboards, city signs, and advertising brochures throughout the region.

In 1919, the owners of Musa Isle Grove, a fruit-shipping business established in 1907, convinced Seminole headman Willie Willie to move his camp onto their property and open it for the tourists. Willie Willie and his father, Charley Willie, had been selling crafts directly to the tourists and also serving as middlemen for a number of Seminole craftspeople still living in the Everglades. This enterprising Seminole family was said to have turned a handy profit for over two generations. When the Willie family moved to Musa Isle, tourists could board a boat in downtown Miami and take a "jungle cruise" up the Miami River to see the Indian village.

Musa Isle came to gross over fifty thousand dollars per year in the 1920s, offering an array of sights for the curious—rows of snakes, monkeys, owls, wildcats, and other "wild and sensational creatures of the jungle" joined the Seminole families as part of a living diorama of exotica. James L. Glenn, the federal Indian agent during the 1930s, was appalled by the spectacle of Musa Isle, where, as he reported in a letter, "a human family may be pawed over, gazed at, and made the butt of rude and coarse humor. . . . This kind of living degenerates the heirs of the heritage which that strong man, Osceola, gave these heroic people."

However unnatural the situation seems, by the 1930s over half the Seminole living in South Florida (about two hundred people) were employed in commercial tourist villages. Some families would spend an entire season at a camp, while others would live on display for one or two weeks while they did their trading in town. Scholar Patsy West has said that the tourist attraction villages provided South Florida's Seminole and Miccosukee with an effective economic transition between traditional life and the modern lifestyles of mainstream society. This transition was accelerated when the completion of the Tamiami Trail in 1928 created an ecological watershed in the lives of the Miccosukee living south of the road. As drainage was completely cut off by the elevated roadway, these isolated peoples were forced to change their way of life. Many of the Miccosukee followed the lead of their white neighbors and established businesses to attract tourists. They did this by simply moving their camps to the side of the highway, erecting fences and charging the motoring public admission to view them as they went about their daily lives.

The 1939 WPA guide to Florida remarked on the Miccosukee camps that had proliferated along the Tamiami Trail in the decade since the highway was completed. The tribe had "set up their palm thatched villages . . . hoisted tribal flags as a lure to passing motorists, and they sell souvenirs and pose for photos." By the 1950s, the Miccosukee living along the trail had opened the Miccosukee Restaurant at Seven Mile Tower, and many had added alligator wrestling to their activities, as well as offering airboat rides into the Everglades wilderness. It was during this time that Cory Osceola established a large chickee gift shop along the trail south of Fort Myers, with a huge road sign proclaiming "This is Cory Osceola's Seminole Indian Village, one of the finest in Florida."

At both the Tamiami Trail camps and the camps set into city tourist attractions, women made patchwork clothing and other crafts, cooked over the traditional open fire, cared for the small children, did the washing, pounded corn into sofkee, and generally were busy throughout the day. While men occasionally carved miniature canoes and made other wooden crafts, their hunting and fishing skills could not easily be presented within an attraction setting. Their apparent lack of industry began to worry the camp operators, as well as to baffle the tourists, so a solution was found that has changed Seminole tradition.

Henry Coppinger, Jr., is credited with starting the spectacle of "alligator wrestling," which has become indelibly linked in the American mind with the Seminole Indians. This "sport" pits a man against a wild alligator, seemingly locked in mortal combat for the benefit of an audience. Alligator wrestling and snake handling, both crowd-pleasers at

Tourists watching recent performance of alligator wrestling at the Miccosukee Indian Village (Photo by Michele Edelson/ Courtesy of HASF)

the Miami attractions, were never part of Seminole culture. In fact, a renowned alligator wrestler of today, Allen Jumper of Hollywood Reservation, has admitted that the practice was against tribal custom, but the extra money derived from tips overcame the traditional taboo.

Until 1925, Henry Coppinger did his own alligator wrestling, but Seminole men who had observed him in action began to present shows at Musa Isle. The sport is dangerous, but a knowledgable wrestler knows how to do it: keep the gator well fed, grab it by the snout so it can't open its jaws, flip it on its back and stroke it to sleep—then pretend to be struggling valiantly with the beast for a long time so as to earn big tips. The Seminole and Miccosukee became so adept at alligator wrestling that it has become part of their public display of culture to this day. Modern Seminole attractions and festivals present this unusual skill as a major part of Seminole life, and most outsiders believe it to be a unique South Florida Indian tradition. Even the Seminole have come to think of alligator wrestling as a traditional part of their own folklife.

Although evidence indicates that life at the tourist attractions and life on the reservations were fairly similar and "authentic" from the tourist point of view, several changes were necessary. For the attraction Indians, many of the Seminole rites and customs had to be kept private, in spite of their fishbowl existence. The training of a medicine man, tribal council meetings, the coming-of-age and purification rituals of the Green

Corn Dance, and many pre-Christian religious practices were never presented to the tourist audiences who sought to know the most intimate details of traditional Indian life.

Taking the place of authentic rites of passage, which still held power within the Seminole and Miccosukee community, new staged rituals were adopted to assuage the tourists' curiosity. These invented traditions combined familiar elements of white culture with exotic touches that fit the stereotype of what Seminole culture "should" be. A prime example of this was a series of "Indian weddings" that were held at Musa Isle during the 1930s. In Seminole tradition, marriage is not marked by ceremony—certainly not by a wedding in the western sense. However, these profitable shows, which combined Christian ritual with staged drama to create the appearance of authenticity, drew capacity crowds. The weddings were viewed with horror by federal Indian agent James Glenn. He describes one nuptial occasion:

As the time draws near, the buses from downtown [Miami] pour out excited and strange people from every part of the nation. The stage has been well set; the show is already going strong. The cash register sings its wildest symphony. . . . The "medicine man," who here is acting, leads the riotously dressed Indian man and girl before the crowd. In the name of matrimony he invokes a solemn pledge from each, only the girl may be giggling in the meantime. And then to ascend to the seventh heaven, or pure, undiluted farce the "groom" wraps his arm about the "bride" and plants a pair of saliva-coated lips on her face. They both shudder, and she grabs her dress or cape and wipes away the residue of this filthy habit.

Although the invented tradition is "fakelore" in every sense of the word, it serves a very real function, allowing the native culture to maintain its true rites of passage while satisfying a curious public with a spectacle that does not alter folk culture. This type of activity occurs in all cultural tourism, where the host society determines what and how much of authentic culture will be presented to an outside public.

A recent example of controlled presentation of culture is the Green Corn Dance. This annual festival is powerful in Seminole and Miccosukee culture to this day. As tourists have demanded access to this most private event, Seminoles have created a series of public "field days" at the major reservations that incorporate the non-religious, non-sacred elements of the Green Corn Dance. The Seminole Field Days and Festival at Hollywood Reservation provides tourists with a weekend where they can buy Seminole crafts, eat Seminole frybread and sofkee, help judge a Seminole beauty contest and patchwork clothing contest, see a Seminole rodeo and stickball game, and view a demonstration dance that is labeled the Green Corn Dance.

Events like field days, the Seminole Heritage Festival, and a series of regular "pow-wows" provide the tourist audience with activities and spectacles that satisfy their need to glimpse Native American life. At the same time, the Seminole and Miccosukee keep control of the truly powerful and sacred rituals that continue to function within their culture.

The commercial camps that displayed Seminole people drew fire from the very beginning for what was seen (by agent Glenn) as "shoddy tourist shows where Indians were displayed as though they were circus curiosities." Deaconess Bedell started her mission to "exhibit arts and crafts, not people." During the 1930s, James Glenn and other government officials decried the practice of hiring Seminole people to display themselves. Glenn found Miami to be a city where tourism had run amok, a place where "artificiality and exhibitionism are sold over the counter of commercialism. . . . To cash in on the curiosity of the tourist sucker has become at least one of the aims of this industry." Many believed that Seminole and Miccosukee culture would be completely degraded and eventually destroyed by frequent contact with the tourism industry.

Another view, taken by historian Patsy West and many leaders in the tribes today, is that the families that were active in the tourist attractions were the most enterprising and yet the most traditional of the tribe. Far from losing their traditions, attraction-dwellers revived many skills and learned useful tactics for dealing with the outside world.

Today, the Seminole Tribe of Florida and the Miccosukee Tribe of Indians, both corporate entities, are firmly in control of their own cultural resources and are major participants in South Florida's tourism industry. In 1992, the Seminole Tribe has five reservations—Brighton, Big Cypress, Hollywood, Immokolee, and the newest one located in the heart of Tampa. Each of these sites has its own arts and crafts shop, along with the ubiquitous cigarette sales trailers. In 1962 the Hollywood Reservation opened a large craft sales outlet as well the Okalee Indian Village, modeled on the earlier attractions that had been run by whites. Ironically, both tourists and the Seminole are aware that the Indians who populate the village chickees during the day go home to suburban-style ranch homes at night. The Okalee Indian Village has become a historical reenactment, a portrayal of life as it once was, a Seminole version of Colonial Williamsburg.

Similarly, the Miccosukee camps along the Tamiami Trail have been incorporated into a long, narrow reservation for the tribe. This reservation which has grown up along the roadside, has been literally shaped by the tourist economy. The centerpiece of the reservation is the Miccosukee Indian Village, which is advertised in a tourist brochure printed in five languages and on large billboards along U.S. Route 41 with the promise "Alligator Wrestling Daily." Located twenty-five miles west of Miami, on the Tamiami Trail, the village features a museum, amphitheater, sewing demonstrations, crafts sales, alligator wrestling, nature trails into the Everglades, a restaurant that has deep-fried frog legs as its specialty (a dish that makes the Miccosukee turn green), a cooking chickee, where "the mystical star-shaped fireplace is important to all Miccosukee families," and a "native island," reached only by airboat ride, where tourists are enticed to "discover a typical hammock village where a Miccosukee family still lives." Airboat rides, offered by the Tiger family, run four dollars for a short ride and eight dollars for the trip to the native island. Without sufficient land, industry, or agriculture, the Miccosukee reservation supports its people solely through tourism.

One of the most controversial, yet lucrative, business ventures for the Seminole, and more recently the Miccosukee, has been high-stakes bingo. Following in the wake of the tourism magnates who instituted gambling through horse and dog racing, as well as jai alai, the Seminole have created a new form of gambling in South Florida. "Seminole Indian Bingo of Hollywood, Florida" is advertised on billboards and in bilingual brochures available at every tourist outlet in the state. Offering a grand prize of thirty-five thousand dollars per night, this is no church basement form of the game. Exempt from the federal laws that govern gambling elsewhere, the reservation has added this unique appeal to tourists, and it brings in hundreds of players each evening. They provide income that finances a health center and a native language program, as well as assuring each man, woman and child in the tribe a monthly stipend.

Both the Seminole and Miccosukee tribes are carrying on traditions that have survived for generations. They are also adding new survival skills as their environment changes—one of those is marketing and tourism. Originally controlled by whites, the sale of Seminole and Miccosukee crafts and culture is now in native hands. Once a new adaptation to a changing world, cultural tourism for the South Florida Indians has become a tradition in itself. It remains to be seen how tourism and development will continue to change the Seminole way of life and what traditions of tourism will be passed along to future generations.

TRADITIONS OF THE TOURIST

A tourist has been defined by anthropologist Valene L. Smith as "a temporarily leisured person who voluntarily visits a place away from home for the purpose of experiencing a change." Tourists, who often seek to experience cultures and traditions other than their own, become a folk group themselves once they leave home. Tourists share a common goal (to experience a change), have a specific material culture (the specialized accoutrements of camping and traveling), develop a jargon with which to communicate, share a common folklore (legends, personal experience narratives, jokes, songs, beliefs), and have an identity that is conferred upon them by non-tourists. Although this identity is a stereotype, it functions to bind the group together, both from within and without the tourist community. At times one may be part of this group, and at other times one may be part of the host community that segregates the tourist from the "real world" of which it is a part.

Why do people become tourists? Tourism is a special form of play that involves travel. Touring is a time away from a rigid work ethic, a time where the moral code gives people license to "turn the world upside down" and engage in playful activities without guilt. Like other festival activities, touring relieves people from their ordinary lives and gives them the chance to be someone else for a short time. In contrast, American folklore demonstrates a mistrust of people who travel for *work*, as the obscene jokes concerning travelling salesmen testify.

When people become tourists, a sort of magical quality accompanies even the most ordinary activities (eating, sleeping, relaxing) when they are undertaken in extraordinary settings (restaurants, motels, camping parks). Florida's *1991 Visitors' Survey* shows tourists admitting that what they enjoyed most while touring in Florida was "eating in restaurants and shopping"—activities they could very well have engaged in at home! The number two favorite activity was "rest and relaxation," goals that could be accomplished (probably more efficiently) without traveling. Obviously, the act of leaving one's everyday setting is a very important part of the appeal of being a tourist—it invokes the magic that makes everything special.

Recently, anthropologists, folklorists, and other scholars have been researching the phenomenon of tourism. They have found that tourists celebrate "difference" in order to define and preserve their own culture. A basic aim of the tourist society is to provide self-discovery through encounters with "the other." In many ways, tourist attractions serve the same function as the sacred shrines of ancient peoples. Like religious pilgrimages, the travels of the tourist are journeys that hold great symbolic power and function to validate a modern American culture and world-view. Tourists travel to visit other cultures and environments that are perceived as being more "pure" and "natural." The unifying consciousness of tourism is this search for naturalness and authenticity, a search for both the exotic and the familiar. By stepping outside of a normal routine to experience another lifestyle briefly, tourists enhance their own understanding of themselves and their lives. Tourism may be play, but it has a serious function in society.

Like any folk group, tourists are stereotyped by non-tourists, and host societies make certain assumptions about the group that sets them apart. By stereotyping tourists, the locals reaffirm their membership within a different group that has its own distinct identity. More often than not, the stereotypes of tourists are comical and negative. South Floridians have been confronted with this group for over one hundred years, and the image of the tourist has become a cliché in Florida folklore. In 1882 George M. Barbour wrote that each tourist season "witnesses an influx of thousands of these visitors, in search of health or on a pleasant bent, usually wealthy and equipped with more prejudices than their well-filled traveling bags would contain."

Part of the reason that tourists are denigrated has to do with their own contradictory existence. Tourists who are seeking exotic adventure still demand familiar comforts. Most touring parties carry a "bubble" of their lifestyle with them and demand the amenities of a contemporary society, even while travelling in remote and undeveloped areas. These unrealistic demands have created a poor image for the tourist, at times instilling resentment and contempt from the host community. In Miami today, rental car agencies have stopped putting their advertising bumper stickers on cars, for fear that the tourists driving them will be fair game to countless con men and hoodwinkers who prey upon the gullible. This love-hate relationships between South Floridians and tourists has been present since the settlement of the state.

Today, it is evident that even *tourists* dislike tourists. The image of the tourist has become fixed as someone who is superficial, selfish, bigoted, and ultimately stupid. For tourists, who themselves are seeking a meaningful experience with "real people," encountering other tourists is the worst luck.

South Floridians express their feelings and value judgments about tourists through folk expression—jokes, rhymes, nicknames, and other oral traditions. "Damn Yankees" and "snowbirds" are mocked by South Floridians who are admittedly dependent upon these interlopers for their income. Northerners who descend upon the beaches in January, plunging into the brisk Atlantic despite the winter chill, and who sport "fish-white" legs in gaudy Bermuda shorts and rolling Winnebago mansions are the stuff of constant derision. Stories of the stupidity or the extravagance of the tourist are most common in the South Florida folk repertoire. Naples resident and long-time newsman, Vernon Lamme, recalled one such incident from the Depression, when most Floridians "didn't have two nickels to rub together":

Money—I have never had a lot of it, but I have seen it actually thrown away and otherwise totally disregarded. One day on the fishing pier at Naples I watched a tourist living at the big hotel attempt to create some action among a group of pelicans perched on some old pilings near the dock. There was nothing to throw from where he stood—no sticks, rocks or anything. He dipped into his pocket and then threw a handful of quarters and half dollars at the lazy fowls. He got action, but not from the birds, as several small boys dove into the clear water to retrieve the coins.

Stories that portray tourists as buffoons continue to be told in South Florida. *Miami Herald* columnist Dave Barry uses the Florida tourists as a regular butt of jokes in his comical column, and the late singer-songwriter and storyteller, Gamble Rogers, was famous for his portrayals of the northern visitor encountering Florida culture for the first time. A bumper sticker proclaiming the driver to be a "Florida Native" began to be popular in the 1970s.

At the same time that the tourist invasion is decried by the residents, South Floridians continue to give the hard sell to their northern neighbors to keep the industry healthy. Weather forecasters have developed ingenious ways of disguising the fact that summers can be violently hot. Some are said to place thermometers far above ground level for a reading of the "official air temperature" on hot days. Euphemisms are common—enormous flying cockroaches are renamed "palmetto bugs," and impending hurricanes are designated "tropical depressions."

The material culture of tourism is particularly fascinating. The word "souvenir" comes from the Latin *subvenire*, meaning "to come to mind." Since the state of being a tourist is, by definition, a temporary and ephemeral one, souvenirs serve as important reminders of another time and place. South Florida, being the most visited region in the country, is a mother lode of such items—objects that help define the tourism experience and function as tangible evidence of the shared and unusual life that was lived away from home. Tourists bring back seashells, snapshots, and Seminole crafts as proof of their encounter with the exotic world of South Florida. More importantly, articles made specifically for the tourist market—rubber flamingo earrings, t-shirts with appropriate messages, coconut shell ashtrays, shell-encrusted handbags, Mickey Mouse slippers, jars of mango jelly and bottles of tangerine wine—all serve as evidence of travel, as well as being icons of our personal values.

Tourists also send home postcards, almost ritualistically, to share the experience with others and to remind those at home that they are living another reality. The magic of tourism is enhanced by the recounting of the experience for others. While many souvenirs are collected as proof of experiencing an "authentic" encounter—shells that were personally collected, crafts that were handmade by the Seminole—"tacky" souvenirs have now become traditional in South Florida. Bringing home a plastic flamingo for the front yard is as much a part of a South Florida vacation

Tin Can Tourists in 1920
(Photo courtesy of FSA)

as bringing home maple syrup from Vermont. Tourists now compete to bring home the tackiest souvenir from the state, or to send the most outrageous postcard—an alligator tearing off the bikini bottom of a voluptuous blond is a favorite. These mementoes say much about how tourists view the host community, indicating a reciprocal negative attitude toward the natives.

Many tourists have formalized their association with each other and have incorporated into societies. The first of these was the Tin Can Tourists of the World, which began in Florida in 1920 and claimed over thirty thousand members by 1938. When Wally Bynam's airstream trailer debuted in 1935, an association formed soon after to bind the owners of this popular camper into a group with a common bond. Other groups that claim tourism as a shared tradition have been formed over the years, including the Winnebago Association, the Good Sam Club, and the American Association of Retired Persons.

In all of these fraternities, a spirit of comradeship is evident as thousands of like-minded vacationers descend upon designated camping parks in annual conventions and reunions. These conventions include many activities that strengthen group identity and solidarity, such as parades featuring members in their airstreams or Winnebagos, displays and sales booths showing the latest models of campers and new accessories for the nomadic life, and contests and social events that bring the group into a cohesive, festive whole. And there are countless informal activities, especially talk sessions where tall tales, "lies," and personal experience stories about the touring life are swapped among the group. No matter what part of the country they hail from, the members of these associations share a common heritage of touring and have formed lasting bonds with fellow campers that derive from the shared traditions of tourism.

FANTASY AND THE FUTURE

The most recent form of tourism in Florida is a direct outgrowth of the quests for adventure and exotica that lured nineteenth-century tourists to South Florida and continues the tradition of establishing ornate and extraordinary resorts for visitors. This phenomenon might be called "fantasy" tourism. In 1971, South Florida's tourism industry would be changed forever as the Disney enterprises opened Phase One of their empire, creating a world of fantasy on twenty-seven thousand acres of what was once a barren wilderness of scrub, rangeland and played-out orange groves.

Walt Disney World was conceived as a self-sufficient vacation community, with motels, hotels, restaurants, shopping, and constant entertainment. It is to date the nation's largest nongovernmental construction project. "The Magic Kingdom," said to have cost $300 million, surpassed its projected annual visitation figure of 8 million during its inaugural year.

Walt Disney World was just the beginning of a complex of tourist facilities and attractions that have constituted a quantum leap in the industry. Soon after the opening of the Magic Kingdom, Disney opened a billion-dollar Experimental Prototype Community of Tomorrow (EPCOT). Originally envisioned as a permanent community for forward-thinking Floridians, EPCOT became instead another tourist attraction—adventure, it seemed, was fine for a temporary existence, but no one was willing to make EPCOT his or her home.

Orlando is now host to hundreds of millions of tourists who make the pilgrimage to a vast entertainment network that stretches from east to west across the center of the state. Major attractions in addition to Walt Disney World and EPCOT include Disney-MGM Studios, Universal

Studios, Busch Gardens, Sea World, Lake Buena Vista Village, and Spaceport USA.

Without a doubt, fantasy tourism has captured the American imagination and has transformed Florida into a maze of separate realities. Walt Disney World is truly the "magic kingdom" in this regard, for it offers several worlds in one: Adventureland, Tomorrowland, Fantasyland, and even the familiar-but-different Main Street USA. Fantasy environments like those offered in Disney World provide Florida with a safe and controlled way to handle the vast numbers of visitors to the state, while directing tourists away from ecologically endangered natural and cultural settings. At the same time, this form of tourism fulfills people's needs to experience new worlds and exotic spaces. By visiting Huck Finn's island, or seeing George Washington speak in the Hall of Presidents, or touring through the Mayan temple at EPCOT, we are treated to a glimpse of other times, other cultures, and other environments in a hyper-clean setting that is perceived to be "safe and healthy."

Although we all know that Disney's "historic" and "cultural" facsimiles are only copies of authentic events and monuments, many tourists prefer this form of visitation. It removes them from the solemn awe and unrelenting reality of experiencing the originals, and they can do it with all of the twentieth-century amenities intact.

Needless to say, most tourists who enjoy the "Dark Continent" at Busch Gardens would never dream of going on a true African safari. Historian David Lowenthal has observed that this form of tourism

Richard Blaes' monumental lobster sculpture in the Keys delights tourists today. (Photo by Brent Cantrell/ Courtesy of HASF)

"jettisons seedy reality for spurious romance." People like to experience other cultures, but only if they are "nicely cleaned up," with no seamy sides on view. Elements of cultures are ignored and at times purposefully misrepresented in fantasy tourism, for the object is to provide a pleasant, not an authentic, experience. The success of this formula is phenomenal—by 1980, Walt Disney World was the *world's* most visited tourist attraction, with over 20 million visitors a year.

Another spin on the fantasy theme is Fantasy Fest in Key West, which is directed toward gay men. Key West, already enjoying a reputation as a bohemian paradise where "anything goes," first promoted Fantasy Fest as a way to draw tourists during a normally slow month. Every October since 1979, the island's business association has produced this ten-day extravaganza that compares with Mardi Gras in New Orleans and Carnival in Rio. This is truly a turning of the world upside down, where people assume other identities for a short time. Featuring parades, elaborate costumes, parties, balls, mask-making workshops, pet masquerades, coronations, and ribald behaviour, Fantasy Fest drew over fifty thousand revelers in 1991. Less "safe" than the Disney attractions, Fantasy Fest is similarly an unreal environment, offering participants an opportunity to live in another reality, if only for a short time.

Tourism in South Florida has become a monolithic industry, affecting every facet of life in the region. Multicultural South Florida will continue to face challenges in hosting the vast numbers of visitors that flood into her cities and countryside. Although there may be some worry over the effects of the tourist economy upon resident South Floridians and the many folk cultures there, the tradition of tourism in the region no doubt means that South Floridians will pass on traditional strategies of dealing with the situation to new generations.

South Florida possesses physical and cultural characteristics that have combined to create a complex of traditional life unlike that of any other American region. One reason for its distinctiveness is its status as the only tropical region in the continental United States. Not only does the tropical environment produce unusual materials for traditional life, but in many cases it also provides the impetus for certain types of activities. In addition many endeavors brought from other American regions, such as ranching or fishing, have developed characteristics quite unlike the parent tradition. Moreover, South Florida's extreme southerly geographical location brings it as much into the Caribbean sphere as the American.

The most important determinant of South Florida folklife is the variety of peoples who have made the region their home. Beginning in the eighteenth century, bands of Creeks and other southeastern native peoples began migrating into Florida. As their folk culture gradually changed in response to the new environmental and historical influences, they became the Seminole and Miccosukee tribes who maintain a strong presence in the region today.

Although most nineteenth-century pioneers pushed westward, some hardy souls ventured to this most southeasterly corner of the continent. Many of the early settlers were Crackers from Alabama, the Carolinas, north Florida, and south Georgia, whose Celtic heritage thrived in the South Florida wilderness. In addition to the Crackers, Bahamians, Cubans, Europeans, and Americans from the north struggled to eke out a living from the land and sea.

The expansion of the railroad into South Florida in the late nineteenth century stimulated tremendous population growth. Many early twentieth-century southeast Floridians were Bahamian and southern blacks who came to trade or work on the railroad. Later, the 1920s land boom attracted both permanent settlers and tourists from the North. During World War II, over six hundred thousand soldiers were trained in military stations, and many returned to South Florida after the war. Large numbers of retirees, many of them Jewish, moved to southeast Florida during the same period.

From the early 1960s through the present there has been substantial immigration from Latin America and the Caribbean. Hispanics, who currently account for about one-half of Dade County's population, have contributed to Miami's emergence as a major Latin American commercial and cultural center. The majority of the Hispanic population is Cuban, but there are large communities of Nicaraguans and other Central Americans, Colombians, Peruvians, Puerto Ricans, and Argentinians. In addition, sizeable non-Hispanic Caribbean communities, such as Haitians, Jamaicans, Bahamians, and Trinidadians, link the region to the myriad island nations of the Caribbean.

In view of the relatively recent settlement and subsequent rapid changes as successive waves of immigrants from divergent directions have settled in South Florida, is it possible to point to any consistent characteristics in the region's history and traditional culture? The answer can only be that change and adaptation within the context of the environment and the confrontation between Anglo, Hispanic, and African cultures have laid the groundwork for life in South Florida. In this regard, it is the land of the future. South Florida was one of the last settled frontiers—a land where even the history of its Native American peoples reaches back only two hundred years. South Florida is now in the vanguard of the new America: a land whose people are no longer predominantly white and West European but increasingly Hispanic and African American, and—perhaps most significantly—a land where the majority have ties to cultures besides their natal culture.

South Florida is continually changing. The rapid influx of peoples from both north and south profoundly affects the way we live. Although there may be tensions when different groups first encounter each other, for the most part old and new residents have become neighbors and friends. We share our food, languages, values, fears, hopes, and children. Through our shared lives, our cultures also are merging to develop new folkways that express a synthesis of traditions. These may be as disparate as Thanksgiving turkeys stuffed with Spanish rice, Martin Luther King on a Bahamian Junkanoo mask, flamingos and Santería shrines adorning a lawn, or conversations routinely conducted in mixtures of Spanish, English, and Creole. When we stop to notice these new forms, they provide us with a source of delight. Not only do they amuse us by their strangeness or incongruity with past forms, but they also prove our ability to embrace each other and face the future together.

THE SEMINOLE AND MICCOSUKEE

William C. Sturtevant is perhaps the preeminent scholar of Florida's Seminole and Miccosukee peoples. His article "Creek Into Seminole" is a thorough analysis of the genesis of these indigenous peoples. Sturtevant also edited *A Seminole Sourcebook*, which brings together many widely scattered articles documenting Seminole and Miccosukee history and culture. Brent Weisman's recent *Like Beads on a String: A Culture History of the Seminole Indians in Northern Peninsular Florida* provides useful information concerning the roots of Seminole culture. Anthropologist Merwyn S. Garbarino studied the Big Cypress Seminole and published her findings in *Big Cypress: A Changing Seminole Community*. She also created an excellent popular overview of Seminole and Miccosukee history and society in *The Seminole*. Although based on data collected in the 1930s, ethnomusicologist Frances Densmore's *Seminole Music* is the only serious exploration of the topic. Scott Thybony's article "The Black Seminole," in *Smithsonian*, examines that group's history and present life.

Most published information about the Seminole and Miccosukee is dispersed in a variety of periodicals. Among the more noteworthy essays are Robert F. Greenlee's "Folktales of the Florida Seminole" and "Medicine and Curing Practices of the Modern Florida Seminoles." The Bureau of Florida Folklife Programs created several excellent slide/tape shows and a video on Seminole and Miccosukee folklife. Topics include but are not limited to patchwork, basketry, and palmetto dolls. Folklorist Ormond Loomis contributed a detailed study of chickee architecture in "The Seminole Family Camp." David Blackard curated an exhibit and published an informative book titled *Patchwork & Palmettos: Seminole/Miccosukee Folk Art Since 1820*. In "Glade Cross Mission: An Influence on Florida Seminole Arts and Crafts," Patsy West examined the influence of missionary Harriet Bedell on Seminole folk arts in the mid-twentieth century.

THE CRACKERS

The history and culture of the Everglades as a region within a region is provided in several works. Alfred and Kathryn Hanna's *Lake Okeechobee:*

Wellspring of the Everglades, written in 1948, gives historical background, occupational lore and collected tales from the upper Glades area. J. P. Paireault and Jeremy Thomas provide extensive background information in their book, *The Everglades: A Timeless Wilderness*, as does Marjorie Stoneman Douglas in both *The Everglades: River of Grass* (1947) and *Florida: The Long Frontier* (1967). Mike Smith looks at the Everglades as an ecosystem within a larger regional context in *South Florida Frontiers*.

Grady McWhiney, in *Cracker Culture: Celtic Ways in the Old South*, sees the unique character of Cracker culture as part of the Celtic heritage of Deep South settlers. The impact of this culture on the South Florida frontier is given in biographical form in Betty Briggs's *Cracker in the Glades: A Portrait of Robert Storter, Fisherman, and His Family*, while Charles W. Pierce gives an overview of early Cracker life in *Pioneer Life in Southeast Florida*. The two best books on the subject are Florida historian Charlton Tebeau's *Man in the Everglades: 2000 years of Human History in the Everglades National Park* (1968) and *The Story of the Chokoloskee Bay Country* (1955). Further insight, concerning the Cracker's low position on the social scale, is provided in the early travel memoirs of George M. Barbour, *Florida: For Tourists, Invalids and Settlers* (1882).

Anecdotal accounts of Cracker Life in South Florida are provided in the works of Gloria Jahoda (*The Other Florida*) and Marjorie Kinnan Rawlings (*Cross Creek* and "Cracker Chidlings—Real Tales From the Florida Interior"), as well as in Burnett's series titled *Florida's Past: People and Events That Shaped the State*, Alex Shoumatoff's *Florida Ramble*, and Vernon Lamme's *Florida Lore Not Found in History Books*. Fictional accounts of Cracker life in South Florida that draw upon folklore and oral history are Theodore Pratt's *The Barefoot Mailman* and Peter Matthiessen's *Killing Mr. Watson*.

Most of the folklore described within the Cracker chapter was collected by Peggy Bulger during her tenure with the Bureau of Florida Folklife Programs. Florida Folk Festival Program Books from 1984 to 1991 give concise reports about the folk culture of Florida, including this research. Especially pertinent to this chapter were the programs from 1984 (ranching); 1986 (Glades skiffs and agriculture); 1987 (fishing and foodways); and 1988 (tourist jokes, occupational lore).

Peggy A. Bulger conducted interviews with Stetson Kennedy (1981–90) and E. A. "Frog" Smith (1978–83) that provided jokes, tall tales, songs, and other oral folklore. Interviews by Tina Bucuvalas with Peter Douthit and David Teems in 1992 give a contemporary account of Cracker life in South Florida.

THE CUBANS

Cuban American culture is, of course, rooted in the history and culture of Cuba. *Cuba, A Country Study* is part of the series of Foreign Area Studies Handbooks written by American University researchers. It supplies a concise and thorough exploration of Cuba's history, society, and demographic development. Cuba expert Wayne S. Smith's recent work, *Portrait of Cuba*, also provides a beautifully illustrated, readable overview of the topics. Miguel A. Bretos's *Cuba & Florida: Exploration of an Historic Connection, 1539–1991* contains detailed information concerning early interchanges.

Most works about Cubans in South Florida address limited political or sociological issues. In the area of culture studies, very little is published except information concerning the topics of music and Santería. An outstanding exception is *The Cuban-American Experience: Culture, Images, and Perspectives* by geographers Thomas D. Boswell and James R. Curtis, which covers a wide range of subjects. Probably the broadest source of information on Cuban traditional culture is the *Miami Herald*, especially articles by Cuban American writers Ana Veciana-Suarez and Liz Balmaseda.

Tina Bucuvalas's "Cuban Folk Arts in the Miami Area" is one of the only surveys of Cuban folk arts in South Florida. In *Palmetto Country*, Stetson Kennedy provides information on the history and folklife of Cubans in Florida through the 1930s. James R. Curtis's essays, "Miami's Little Havana: Yardshrines, Cult Religion, and Landscape" and "Santería: Persistence and Change in Afro-Cuban Cult Religion," discuss various aspects of Santería. Robert A. Friedman's dissertation, "Making an Abstract World Concrete: Knowledge, Competence, and Structural Dimensions of Performance Among *Batá* Drummers in Santería," is perhaps the most profound examination of this influential musical style. *The Latin Tinge: The Impact of Latin American Music on the United States* by John Storm Roberts is an indispensable source of information concerning the nature and history of Cuban music. Laurie Sommers examines the current dimensions of Cuban music in Miami in "Caribbean Music in South Florida." Gisela Lopez-Mata details the remarkable metamorphosis as the Cubans brought their architectural tastes and skills to a Miami neighborhood in "From Riverside to Little Havana: Transformation of a Neighborhood." Interviews by Tina Bucuvalas with Cuban Americans Olga Garay, Maggie Manrara, and many others were important sources of information for this chapter.

THE NEW MIAMI: NICARAGUANS AND ISLANDERS

Since Nicaraguans constitute one of the newest ethnic communities in South Florida, there is as yet little available information about their traditional culture. By far the most extensive work to date results from a project on Nicaraguan folk arts undertaken by the Historical Museum of Southern Florida's Folklife Program and funded in part by the Folk Arts Division of the National Endowment for the Arts. Folklorist/ethnomusicologist Laurie Sommers and folklorist Katherine Borland both conducted research and wrote extensive reports that are available through the museum. In addition, they have each written essays that will be published by the museum in a forthcoming booklet.

Caribbean Festival Arts: Each and Every Bit of Difference, edited by John W. Nunley and Judith Bettelheim, not only furnishes excellent essays on carnival traditions in the West Indies, but also includes a fine introductory overview of the history and cultural development of the islands. Folklorist Joyce M. Jackson examines the history and folklife of West Indians in Miami in her essay "African American and West Indian Folklife in South Florida." Raymond Mohl details the history of South Florida's Bahamian community in "Black Immigrants: Bahamians in Early Twentieth Century Miami." Laurie Sommers reviews the musical traditions of the British West Indies and their current status in Miami in "Caribbean Music in South Florida." In *Folklore From Contemporary Jamaicans*, Daryl Dance provides good background information on some Jamaican verbal traditions.

Information about Haitians in Miami is not easily available. Brent Cantrell has written the sole overview of Haitian folklife in South Florida in "The Folklore of Little Haiti." Dolores Yonker's article, "Rara in Haiti," provides an excellent explanation of Carnival and Rara on the island. Billy Bergman's "Rara" not only deciphers the musical and festival tradition, but also explores other Haitian musical forms. Oral interviews conducted by Brent Cantrell and Joyce M. Jackson also contributed important information.

LAND AND SEA: TRADITIONAL SKILLS AND OCCUPATIONS

Although South Floridians have long relied on the land and sea for sustenance, there are few full-length works concerning traditional occupations. David Shubow's "Sponge Fishing on Florida's East Coast" in *Tequesta* examines the history and practices of sponge fishing in South

Florida. Otherwise, a range of *Miami Herald* articles provide information on fishing traditions, as do the regulations published by the Florida Department of Natural Resources.

Interviews with South Floridians such as Peter Douthit, George Chillag, Randy Reed, Perry McLelland, William Schaefer, and David Teems were essential to understanding maritime, ranching, and agricultural traditions in South Florida. In addition, Carlos Velardi of the Dade County Agricultural Extension Service provided important information on tropical crops.

KEY WEST AND THE KEYS

Contemporary information concerning Keys folklife is limited. Perhaps the best source is the survey undertaken by Brent Cantrell, Remko Jansonius, and Bob Stone for the Historical Museum of Southern Florida's Folklife Program in 1990. Materials such as research reports, informant data sheets, photographs and slides are available in HASF's Research Center. The survey also generated two published articles, Cantrell's "Key Largo to Marathon: A Report on the Folklife of the Upper and Middle Keys" and Jansonius's "Island Fantasies." *Forgotten Legacy: Blacks in Nineteenth Century Key West,* by Sharon Wells, aptly employs a wide variety of historical documents to illuminate the ancestry, experiences, and heritage of blacks on Key West.

TOURISM

The history of Florida's tourism industry is well documented in books by historian Charlton Tebeau (*A History of Florida*), as well as in more anecdotal accounts by Florida writers Gloria Jahoda (*The Other Florida*), Vernon Lamme (*Florida Lore Not Found in History Books*), and Gene Burnett (*Florida's Past: People and Events That Shaped the State*). The pre-railroad history of Florida's tourist industry can be found in several essays contained in *The Steamboat Era in Florida,* edited by Edward Mueller and Barbara Purdy. Early eyewitness touring reports are taken from George M. Barbour's 1882 memoir, *Florida: For Tourists, Invalids and Settlers,* while statistics were gleaned from government publications such as the Florida Development Commission's *Tourism Report of 1958–59, Florida Tourist Study 1965,* and *1991 Florida Visitor Survey.* The *WPA Guide to Florida* compiled by the Federal Writer's Project in the 1930s provides insight into that era and the rise of Florida as a tourist mecca. Interviews with Stetson Kennedy and E. A. "Frog" Smith contributed personal accounts of the effects of tourism on Floridians. Kennedy's collected folklore from his tenure on the Federal Writers' Project is a valuable resource, especially on Key West history and lore. These materials are now deposited in the Bureau of Florida Folklife Programs Archives in White Springs, Florida. Gary Mormino's insightful article, "Roadsides & Broadsides: A History of Florida Tourism," gives a good overview of the "tin can tourism" that transformed the state. A moving fictional account of the 1928 hurricane is found in Zora Neale Hurston's *Their Eyes Were Watching God*, while Will McLean's "Hold Back the Waters" is printed in *Champion-Bellew Memorial Folk Festival 1988 Program*.

An excellent general history of tourism is found in A. J. Burkart and S. Medlik's *Tourism: Past, Present and Future*. Theories on the role of tourism are put forth in John A. Jack's *The Tourist: Travel in Twentieth-Century North America* and Dean MacCannell's *The Tourist: A New Theory of the Leisure Class*. Cultural tourism as a phenomenon has been explored and analyzed by anthropologists (see Valene Smith, ed., *Hosts and Guests: The Anthropology of Tourism*, especially chapters by Perry, Greenwood, Evans-Pritchard and Deitch), historians (David Lowenthal, *The Past is a Foreign Country*), and folklorists (Handler and Linnekin, "Tradition: Genuine or Spurious?"; Regina Bendix, "Tourism and Cultural Displays: Inventing Traditions for Whom?"; Ellen Badone, "Ethnicity, Folklore, and Local Identity in Rural Brittany"; and David Rotenstein, "The Helena Blues: Cultural Tourism and African-American Folk Music"). These studies provide in-depth criticism of the role that tourism plays in shaping culture. A compiled volume that explores the rise in public programs established to protect cultural heritage is given in Benita J. Howell's edited volume, *Cultural Heritage Conservation in the American South*. These collected essays deal with tourism as a factor in the perpetuation and retention of southern folklore and culture.

The Seminole/Miccosukee involvement in tourism is well documented in several studies, and a few deserve mention here. Merwyn Garbarino's *Big Cypress: A Changing Seminole Community* is a thorough anthropological exploration of the impact of tourism and development upon the Native Americans of South Florida. David M. Blackard's *Patchwork and Palmettos: Seminole-Miccosukee Folk Art Since 1802* and Dorothy Downs' *Art of the Florida Indian: Nineteenth and Twentieth Century Seminole and Miccosukee Indian Art* give the best overview of the development of Seminole crafts as a tourist commodity. Historian Patsy West has written the most comprehensive and insightful analysis of the "Indian attractions" movement in "The Miami Indian Tourist Attractions: A History and Analysis of a Transitional Mikasuki Seminole Environment." Early impressions of the effects of tourism upon Seminole culture are found in

James L. Glenn's *My Life Among the Florida Seminoles* and Minnie Moore-Wilson's *Snap-Shots From the Everglades of Florida: Jungle Life of the Seminoles*. In addition, fieldwork conducted by Peggy A. Bulger for the Bureau of Florida Folklife Programs during her tenure there (1976–89) provided this chapter with contemporary examples of Seminole tourism and cultural transition. Interviews with Mary Billie, Ethel Santiago, and Jeanette Cypress were especially helpful.

The traditions of the Florida tourist began to be collected as early as the 1800s (Barbour, *Florida: For Tourists, Invalids and Settlers*) and continued into the WPA era, with Stetson Kennedy providing several items that have shaped tourist culture. Contemporary accounts of the Florida tourist are found in newspapers (Dave Barry), on the stage (Gamble Rogers), and in the Florida Folklife Archives.

Atlas of Florida. Edited by Edward A. Fernald. Tallahassee: Florida State University Foundation, 1981.

Ayo, Cristina and Jesus. Interview with Tina Bucuvalas. Miami, April 9, 1992.

Badone, Ellen. "Ethnicity, Folklore, and Local Identity in Rural Brittany." *Journal of American Folklore* 100: 161–90.

Balmaseda, Liz. "A Sacrifice of Secrecy." *Miami Herald.* April 21, 1989. Pp. 1E & 4E.

Bascom, William. "The Focus of Cuban Santería." *Southwestern Journal of Anthropology.* Vol. 6, No. 1 (1940): 64–68.

Bendix, Regina. "Tourism and Cultural Displays: Inventing Traditions for Whom?" *Journal of American Folklore* 102: 131–46.

Bert, Minnie. Interview with Tina Bucuvalas. Miami, February 24, 1988.

Bettelheim, Judith. "Jonkonnu and Other Christmas Masquerades." In *Caribbean Festival Arts: Each and Every Bit of Difference.* By John W. Nunley and Judith Bettelheim. Seattle: St. Louis Art Museum in association with University of Washington Press, 1988. Pp. 38–83.

———. "Carnaval and Festivals in Cuba." In *Caribbean Festival Arts: Each and Every Bit of Difference.* By John W. Nunley and Judith Bettelheim. Seattle: St. Louis Art Museum in association with University of Washington Press, 1988. Pp. 137–46.

Bettelheim, Judith and John Nunley. "The Hosay Festival." In *Caribbean Festival Arts: Each and Every Bit of Difference.* By John W. Nunley and Judith Bettelheim. Seattle: St. Louis Art Museum in association with University of Washington Press, 1988. Pp. 119–35.

Bettelheim, Judith, John Nunley, and Barbara Bridges. "Caribbean Festival Arts: An Introduction." In *Caribbean Festival Arts: Each and Every Bit of Difference.* By John W. Nunley and Judith Bettelheim. Seattle: St. Louis Art Museum in association with University of Washington Press, 1988. Pp. 31–37.

Billie, Mary. Interview with Peggy A. Bulger and Merri Belland. Big Cypress, Fla., 1979.

Biondi, Joann. "Miami Spice." *Caribbean Life and Travel* (March–April 1990): 70–79.

Blackard, David. *Patchwork & Palmettos: Seminole/Miccosukee Folk Art Since 1820*. Fort Lauderdale: Fort Lauderdale Historical Society, 1990.

Blanco, Isabelle. Interview with Tina Bucuvalas. Washington, D.C., May 28, 1992.

Borland, Katherine. "Final Report, Nicaraguan Traditions." Unpublished manuscript, Historical Museum of Southern Florida, 1991. 60 pp.

Boswell, Thomas D. and James R. Curtis. *The Cuban-American Experience: Culture, Images, and Perspectives*. Totowa, N.J.: Rowman & Allanheld, 1984.

Bretos, Miguel A. *Cuba & Florida: Exploration of an Historic Connection, 1539–1991*. Miami: Historical Association of Southern Florida, 1991.

Briggs, Betty. *Cracker in the Glades: A Family Portrait of Robert Storter, Fisherman, and His Family*. Naples, Fla.: Betty Briggs, 1980.

Bucuvalas, Tina. "Cuban Folk Arts in the Miami Area." *A Guide to the 34th Annual Florida Folk Festival, May 23–25, 1986*. White Springs: Bureau of Florida Folklife Programs, 1986. Pp. 4–7.

———. *Traditions: South Florida Folklife*. Miami: Historical Museum of Southern Florida, 1987.

Bulger, Peggy. "Steamboating on the Suwannee: Folk Culture at Work." In *The Steamboat Era in Florida*. Edited by Edward A. Mueller and Barbara Purdy. Gainesville: University of Florida, 1984.

Bullen, Adelaide K. "Florida Indians of Past and Present." In *Florida from Indian Trail to Space Age*. By Charlton Tebeau et al. Delray Beach, Fla.: Southern Publishing Co., 1965.

Burkart, A. J. and S. Medlik. *Tourism: Past, Present and Future*. London: Heinemann, 1974.

Burnett, Gene M. *Florida's Past: People and Events That Shaped the State*. Vol. 3. Sarasota: Pineapple Press, 1991.

Cantrell, Brent. "The Folklore of Little Haiti." In *Arts of the African Diaspora: African American and Haitian Miami*. Edited by Tina Bucuvalas and Brent Cantrell. Miami: Historical Museum of Southern Florida, 1990. Pp. 3–13.

———. "Key Largo to Marathon: A Report on the Folklife of the Upper Keys." *South Florida History Magazine* 3 (Summer 1990). Pp. 19–22.

Capron, Louis. "The Medicine Bundle of the Florida Seminole and the Green Corn Dance." In *A Seminole Sourcebook*. Edited by William C. Sturtevant. New York: Garland, 1987. Pp. 159–69.

Chillag, George. Interview with Brent Cantrell. Miami, July 7, 1992.

Cossio, Jane. *Cuban Home Cooking: Favorite Recipes from a Cuban Home Kitchen.* Surfside, Fla.: Surfside Publishing, Inc., 1989.

Cuba, A Country Study. Foreign Area Studies/American University. Edited by James D. Rudolph. Area Handbook Series. [Washington D.C.]: Secretary of the Army, U.S. Government, 1987, ©1985.

Cultural Heritage Conservation in the American South. Edited by Benita J. Howell. Athens: University of Georgia Press, 1990.

Curtis, James R. "Miami's Little Havana: Yardshrines, Cult Religion, and Landscape." In *Rituals and Ceremonies in Popular Culture.* Edited by Ray B. Browne. Bowling Green, Ohio: Bowling Green University Popular Press, 1980.

———. "*Santería:* Persistence and Change in Afro-Cuban Cult Religion." In *Objects of Special Devotion: Fetishism in Popular Culture.* Edited by Ray B. Browne. Bowling Green, Ohio: Bowling Green University Popular Press, 1981.

Dance, Daryl C. *Folklore From Contemporary Jamaicans.* Knoxville: University of Tennessee Press, 1985.

Densmore, Frances. *Seminole Music.* Smithsonian Institution, Bureau of American Ethnology, Bulletin 161. Washington, D.C.: 1956.

Dorschner, John. "A Whole New Ball Game." *Miami Herald.* Tropic Magazine. December 18, 1988. Pp. 8–17.

Douglas, Marjorie Stoneman. *The Everglades: River of Grass.* Reprint of 1947 ed. St. Simons Island, Ga.: Mockingbird Books, 1974.

———. *Florida: The Long Frontier.* New York: Harper & Brothers, 1967.

Douthit, Peter. Interview with Tina Bucuvalas. Big Pine Key, Fla., April 13, 1992.

Downs, Dorothy. *Art of the Florida Indian: Nineteenth and Twentieth Century Seminole and Miccosukee Indian Art.* Hollywood, Fla.: Seminole Art & Culture Center, 1989.

———. *Miccosukee Arts & Crafts.* Miami: Miccosukee Tribe of Indians of Florida, 1982.

Duany, Jorge. "Popular Music in Puerto Rico: Toward an Anthropology of *Salsa.*" *Latin American Music Review.* Vol. 5, No. 2 (Fall/Winter, 1984): 186–216.

Encyclopedia of Southern Culture. Edited by Charles Reagan Wilson and William Ferris. "Conch" by Guy Baily. Chapel Hill: University of North Carolina Press, 1989. P. 786.

Evans-Pritchard, Deirdre. "The Portal Case: Authenticity, Tourism, Traditions, and the Law." *Journal of American Folklore* 100: 287–96.

Flores, Esther. Interviews with Tina Bucuvalas. Miami, February 1, 1992, and April 11, 1992.

Florida. Department of Commerce. *1991 Florida Visitor Survey.* Tallahassee: 1992.

Florida. Department of State. Bureau of Florida Folklife Programs. *Florida Folk Artists and Apprenticeships 1987–1988.* Tallahassee: 1988.

———. "Four Corners of Earth." Seminole Video Project Rough Script, 5/22/84. White Springs: 1984.

———. "It's Our Way: Seminole Designs." Slide/Tape Program Teacher's Guide. Tallahassee: 1980.

———. "Palmetto and Sweetgrass: Seminole Basketry Traditions." Slide/Tape Program Teacher's Guide. Tallahassee: 1980.

———. "Seminole Palmetto Dolls: A Traditional Craft." Slide/Tape Program. Tallahassee: 1979.

———. *1985 Florida Folk Festival Program Book.* White Springs: 1985.

———. *1986 Florida Folk Festival Program Book.* White Springs: 1986.

———. *1987 Florida Folk Festival Program Book.* White Springs: 1987.

———. *1988 Florida Folk Festival Program Book.* White Springs: 1988.

———. *1989 Florida Folk Festival Program Book.* White Springs: 1989.

———. *1990 Florida Folk Festival Program Book.* White Springs: 1990.

———. *1991 Florida Folk Festival Program Book.* White Springs: 1991.

The Florida Almanac. Edited by Del Marth and Martha J. Marth. Gretna, Fla.: Pelican Publishing Co., 1985.

Florida Development Commission. *Tourism Report 1958–59.* Tallahassee: 1959.

———. *Florida Tourism Study 1965.* Tallahassee: 1965.

The Florida Handbook 1991–92. Compiled by Allen Morris. Tallahassee: The Peninsular Publishing Co., 1991.

Florida International University. Institutional Interior Design Team. *Little Havana Vernacular.* Miami: Florida International University, 1988.

Friedman, Robert A. "Making an Abstract World Concrete: Knowledge, Competence, and Structural Dimensions of Performance Among *Batá* Drummers in Santería." Ph.D. dissertation. Indiana University, 1982.

Garay, Olga. Interviews with Tina Bucuvalas. Washington, D.C., August 3, 1991, and Miami Beach, April 8, 1992.

Garbarino, Merwyn S. *Big Cypress: A Changing Seminole Community.* New York: Holt, Rinehart & Winston, 1972.

———. *The Seminole.* New York: Chelsea House Publishers, ©1989.

Glenn, James L. *My Work Among the Florida Seminoles.* Edited and introduction by Harry A. Kersey, Jr. Orlando: University of Central Florida Press, 1982.

Glubock, Shirley. *The Art of the Southeastern Indians.* New York: Macmillan, 1978.

Greenlee, Robert F. "Folktales of the Florida Seminole." *Journal of American Folklore* Vol. 58, No. 228 (April–June 1945). Pp. 138–44.

———. "Medicine and Curing Practices of the Modern Florida Seminoles." *American Anthropologist* Vol. 48, No. 3 (June–September, 1944): 317–28.

Greenwood, Davydd J. "Culture by the Pound: An Anthropological Perspective on Tourism as Cultural Commoditization." In *Hosts and Guests: The Anthropology of Tourism.* Edited by Valene L. Smith. Philadelphia: University of Pennsylvania Press, 1989.

Hancock, David. "A Moveable Feast." *Miami Herald.* September 10, 1990. Pp. 1B & 4B.

Handler, Richard and Jocelyn Linnekin. "Tradition, Genuine or Spurious?" *Journal of American Folklore* 97: 273–90.

Hanna, Alfred and Kathryn. *Lake Okeechobee: Wellspring of the Everglades.* New York: Bobbs-Merrill, 1948.

Historical Museum of Southern Florida. "Tropical Dreams: A People's History of South Florida." Exhibit. Miami: 1984.

Hosts and Guest: The Anthropology of Tourism. Edited by Valene L. Smith. Philadelphia: University of Pennsylvania Press, 1989.

Jackson, Joyce M. "African American and West Indian Folklife in South Florida." *South Florida History Magazine* 3 (Summer 1990). Pp. 11–18.

———. "African American Folk Culture in Miami." In *Arts of the African Diaspora: African American and Haitian Miami.* Ed. by Tina Bucuvalas and Brent Cantrell. Miami: Historical Museum of Southern Florida, 1990. Pp. 14–24.

Jahoda, Gloria. *Florida: A History.* New York: W. W. Norton & Co., 1976.

———. *The Other Florida.* New York: Charles Scribner's Sons, 1967.

Jackle, John A. *The Tourist: Travel in Twentieth Century North America.* Lincoln: University of Nebraska Press, 1985.

Jansonius, Remko. "Island Fantasies." *South Florida History Magazine* 1 (Winter 1991). Pp. 12–15, 28.

Jumper, David. Interviews with Tina Bucuvalas. Seminole Reservation, Hollywood, Fla., January 30, 1992, January 31, 1992, and April 9, 1992.

Juneja, Renu. "The Trinidad Carnival: Ritual, Performance, Spectacle, and Symbol." *Journal of Popular Culture.* Vol. 21, No. 4 (Spring 1988): 87–100.

Kennedy, Stetson. "Beaches & Lynchings." *Southern Changes* (Sept.–Oct., 1990). Pp. 21–22.

———. Interviews with Peggy A. Bulger. Jacksonville, Fla., 1981, 1984, 1988, 1990.

———. *Palmetto Country.* Tallahassee: Florida A & M University Press, 1989.

Kleinberg, Howard. "Among the Farmers." *Tequesta: The Journal of the Historical Association of Southern Florida.* No. L (1990): 53–71.

Klingener, Nancy. "The Old Man and the Key: Resort Cashes in on the Myth." *Atlanta Journal-Constitution.* July 26, 1992.

Lamme, Vernon. *Florida Lore Not Found in History Books.* Boynton Beach, Fla.: Star Publishing, 1973.

Llanes, José. *Cuban Americans: Masters of Survival.* Cambridge: ABT Books, 1982.

Loomis, Ormond. "Maritime Folklife: Fishing Gear." *A Guide to the 35th Annual Florida Folk Festival, May 22–24, 1987.* White Springs: Bureau of Florida Folklife Programs, Florida Department of State, 1987. Pp. 7–10.

———. "The Seminole Family Camp." *A Guide to the 33rd Annual Florida Folk Festival, May 24–26, 1985.* White Springs, Fla.: Bureau of Florida Folklife Programs, Florida Department of State, 1985. Pp. 17–20.

Lopez-Mata, Gisela. "From Riverside to Little Havana: The Transformation of a Neighborhood." *Cuban Heritage* Vol. 1, No. 2 (Fall 1987): 16–23.

Louis, Liliane Nerette. Interviews with Tina Bucuvalas. Miami, Fla., August 9, 1985, and January 30, 1992.

Lowenthal, David. *The Past is a Foreign County.* New York: Cambridge University Press, 1985.

MacCannell, Dean. *The Tourist: A New Theory of the Leisure Class.* New York: Schocken Books, 1989.

Manrara, Alberto and Maggie. Interviews with Tina Bucuvalas. Washington, D.C., February 15, 1992, and Miami, April 9, 1992.

Matthiessen, Peter. *Killing Mr. Watson.* New York: Vintage Books, 1991.

McIver, Stuart. *True Tales of the Everglades.* Miami: Florida Fair Books, 1989.

McLelland, Perry. Interview with Jan Rosenberg. Lake Worth, Fla., August 15, 1987.

McWhinney, Grady. *Cracker Culture: Celtic Ways in the Old South.* Tuscaloosa, Ala.: University of Alabama Press, 1988.

Meadows, Gail. "A Walk In Baby Heaven." *Miami Herald.* 9/87? Pp. 1–2B.

Metropolitan Dade County, Office of Community and Economic Development, Historic Preservation Division. *From Wilderness to Metropolis: The History and Architecture of Dade County (1825–1940).* Miami: 1982.

Mohl, Raymond A. "Black Immigrants: Bahamians in Early Twentieth Century Miami." *The Florida Historical Quarterly.* Vol. LXV, No. 3 (January 1987): 271–97.

Moore-Wilson, Minnie. *Snap-Shots from the Everglades of Florida: Jungle Life of the Seminoles.* Tampa: Tampa Tribune Publishing Co., 1917.

Mormino, Gary R. "Roadsides and Broadsides: A History of Florida Tourism." In *Florida Endowment for the Humanities Magazine.* (1988?): 14–19.

Neill, Wilfred. *Florida's Seminole Indians.* St. Petersburg, Fla.: Great Outdoors Publishing Co., 1956.

Newman, Joe. "Plan for a Hurricane: Keep Tourists Coming." *Atlanta Constitution-Journal.* August 7, 1992.

Nunley, John. "Masquerade Mix-up in Trinidad Carnival: Live Once, Die Forever." In *Caribbean Festival Arts: Each and Every Bit of Difference.* By John W. Nunley and Judith Bettelheim. Seattle: St. Louis Art Museum in association with University of Washington Press, 1988. Pp. 84–117.

Nusz, Nancy. "South Dade County Folklife." *A Guide to the 34th Annual Florida Folk Festival, May 23–25, 1986.* White Springs: Bureau of Florida Folklife Programs, 1986. Pp 8–12.

O'Connor, Inez Armengol. Interview with Tina Bucuvalas. Miami, April 12, 1992.

Ojito, Mirta. "Keeping the Memories Alive." *Miami Herald.* April 26, 1992. Pp. 1J & 3J.

Olsen, Dale A. "Latin American and Caribbean Music in South Florida." In *Traditions: A Celebration of Latin & Caribbean Music.* Pp. 3–8.

Osceola, Gloria Cypress. Interview with Tina Bucuvalas. Miccosukee Indian Village, Miami, February 26, 1988.

Otto, John S. "Open-Range Cattle-Herding in Southern Florida." *Florida Historical Quarterly* Vol. LXV, No. 3 (January 1987): 317–34.

Owen, Blanton. "Traditional Florida Ranching." *Florida Folk Festival, May 25–27, 1984.* White Springs: Bureau of Florida Folklife Programs, Florida Department of State, 1984. Pp. 2–16.

Padgett, Norman. Interview with Jan Rosenberg. West Palm Beach, Fla., October 13, 1986.

Paireault, J. P. and Jeremy Thomas. *The Everglades: A Timeless Wilderness.* New York: Crescent Books, 1985.

Parks, Arva Moore. *Miami: The Magic City.* Tulsa, Okla.: The Continental Heritage Press, 1981.

Peithman, Irving. *The Unconquered Seminole Indians: Pictorial History of the Seminole Indians.* St. Petersburg: Great Outdoors Association, 1957.

Perry, Richard J. "Why Do Multiculturalists Ignore Anthropologists?" *The Chronicle of Higher Education.* March 4, 1992.

Pierce, Charles W. *Pioneer Life in Southeast Florida*. Edited by Donald W. Curl. Coral Gables, Fla.: University of Miami Press, 1970.

Pratt, Theodore. *The Barefoot Mailman*. Reprint of 1943 edition. St. Simons Island, Ga.: Mockingbird Books, 1989.

Proby, Kathryn Hall. *Mario Sanchez: Painter of Key West Memories*. Key West, Fla.: Southernmost Press, Inc., 1981.

Pulliam, Nisha. "Crack Whip Maker Gets Attention." *Palm Beach Post*. July 14, 1990. P. 3D.

Rawlings, Marjorie Kinnan. "Cracker Chidlings—Real Tales From the Florida Interior." *Scribner's*. February, 1931: 127–31.

———. *Cross Creek*. New York: Duell, Sloan and Pearce, 1942.

Reed, Randy. Interview with Tina Bucuvalas. Miami, Fla., July 1, 1992.

Roberts, John Storm. *The Latin Tinge: The Impact of Latin American Music on the United States*. Tivoli, N.Y.: Original Music, 1985.

Rose, Bill. "The Wild, Wild East." *Miami Herald*. February 10, 1991. Tropic Magazine Section. Pp. 6–13.

Rosenberg, Jan. "Robert James Rudd: Cypress Furniture Maker." *South Florida History Magazine*. Vol. 2 (Spring 1989): 10–15.

Rotenstein, David S. "The Helena Blues: Cultural Tourism and African-American Music." *Southern Folklore* 49 (1992): 133–46.

Schaefer, Bill. Interview with Tina Bucuvalas. Homestead, Fla., July 2, 1992.

Shoumatoff, Alex. *Florida Ramble*. New York: Harper and Row, 1974.

Shroder, Tom. "Florida's Indians: A Question of Survival." *Fort Myers News-Press*. Special Report. Sunday, May 31, 1981.

Shubow, David. "Sponge Fishing on Florida's East Coast." *Tequesta: The Journal of the Historical Association of Southern Florida*. 29 (1969): 3–15.

Smith, E. A. "Frog." Interviews with Peggy A. Bulger. White Springs and Naples, Fla., 1978, 1980, 1983.

Smith, Mike. *South Florida Frontiers*. Miami: Florida Power & Light Co., 1957.

Smith, Wayne S. *Portrait of Cuba*. Atlanta: Turner Publishing, Inc., 1991.

Sommers, Laurie K. "Caribbean Music in Miami." *A Guide to the 34th Annual Florida Folk Festival, May 23–25, 1986*. White Springs: Bureau of Florida Folklife Programs, 1986. Pp. 13–16.

———. "Caribbean Music in South Florida." *South Florida History Magazine* 3 (Summer 1990). Pp. 5–10.

———. "Final Report, Nicaraguan Traditions." Unpublished manuscript, Historical Museum of Southern Florida Folklife Archives, 1991.

———. "Musical Traditions in Miami's New Managua." Unpublished manuscript, Historical Museum of Southern Florida Folklife Archives, 1991.

The Steamboat Era in Florida. Edited by Edward A. Mueller and Barbara Purdy. Gainesville: University of Florida Press, 1984.

Steinback, Robert L. "Builders Make Dream Boats Come True." *Miami Herald.* July 19, 1987. P. 7B.

Stone, Robert. "Final Report for Keys Folklife Project." Unpublished manuscript, Historical Museum of Southern Florida Folklife Archives, 1989.

Sturtevant, William C. "Creek into Seminole." In *North American Indians in Historical Perspective.* Edited by Eleanor Burke Leacock and Nancy Oestreich Lurie. New York: Random House, 1971. Pp. 92–128.

———. "The Medicine Bundles and Busks of the Florida Seminole." *Florida Anthropologist* 7 (1954): 31–70.

Swait, Jimmy. Interview with Tina Bucuvalas. Medley, Fla., December 5, 1986.

Thybony, Scott. "The Black Seminole: A Tradition of Courage." *Smithsonian* Vol. 22, No. 5 (August 1991): 90–101.

Tasker, Fred. "Native Americans: Tragedy and Renewal." *Miami Herald.* January 9, 1992. Pp. 1-2F.

Tebeau, Charlton. *A History of Florida.* Coral Gables, Fla.: University of Miami Press, 1971.

———. *Man in the Everglades: 2000 Years of Human History in the Everglades National Park.* Coral Gables, Fla.: University of Miami Press, 1968.

———. *The Story of the Chokoloskee Bay Country.* Reprint of 1955 edition. Miami: Florida Flair Books, 1991.

Teems, David. Interview with Tina Bucuvalas. Miami, April 12, 1992.

Thompson, Robert Farris. *Flash of the Spirit: African & Afro-American Art & Philosophy.* New York: Vintage Books, 1984, ©1983.

Tiger, Lee. Interview with Tina Bucuvalas. Miami, April 11, 1992.

Veciana-Suarez, Ana. "Dominoes—They're More a Way of Life Than a Game." *Miami Herald.* April 21, 1988. Pp. 1B & 6B.

———. "The Hard Grind of Sugar: Florida's Mills are a 'Little Piece of Cuba.'" *Miami Herald.* February 14, 1988. Pp. 1 & 8G.

Velardi, Carlos. Interview with Tina Bucuvalas. Miami. July 24, 1992.

Vlach, John Michael. *The Afro-American Tradition in Decorative Arts.* Cleveland: Cleveland Museum of Art, 1978.

Waterman, Pat. "Cuban Coffee." In *Ybor City Folk Festival 1987.* Ybor City, Fla.: Ybor City Museum Society, 1987. Pp. 10–11.

Watson-Espener, Maida. "Ethnicity and the Hispanic State: The Cuban Experience." In *Hispanic Theatre in the United States*. Edited by Nicholas Kanellos. Houston: Arte Publico Press, 1984.

Weisman, Brent Richards. *Like Beads on a String: A Culture History of the Seminole Indians in Northern Peninsular Florida*. Tuscaloosa: University of Alabama Press, ©1989.

Wells, Sharon. *Forgotten Legacy: Blacks in Nineteenth Century Key West*. Key West: Key West Historic Preservation Board, 1982.

Werne, Jo. "Oh, Baby! How Your Furniture Store Has Grown From Its Humble Start." *Miami Herald*. July 22, 1990. Pp. 1 & 11J.

West, Patricia. "Glade Cross Mission: An Influence on Florida Seminole Arts and Crafts." *American Indian Art Magazine* (Autumn 1984): 58–67.

———. "The Miami Indian Tourist Attractions: A History and Analysis of a Transitional Mikasuki Seminole Environment." *The Florida Anthropologist* 34 (1981): 200–24.

Works Projects Administration for the State of Florida. Federal Writers' Project. *Florida: Guide to the Southernmost State*. American Guide Series. New York: Oxford University Press, 1967, ©1939.

———. *The Seminole Indians in Florida*. Gainesville, Fla.: University of Florida, 1939.

Yonker, Dolores. "Rara in Haiti." In *Caribbean Festival Arts: Each and Every Bit of Difference*. By John W. Nunley and Judith Bettelheim. Seattle: St. Louis Art Museum in association with University of Washington Press, 1988. Pp. 147–55.